MECHANICS-
MERCANTILE
LIBRARY.

Arthur F Mathews '06

LEGENDARY BRANDS

LEGENDARY BRANDS

LAURENCE VINCENT

UNLEASHING THE POWER OF STORYTELLING
TO CREATE A WINNING MARKETING STRATEGY

Dearborn™
Trade Publishing
A **Kaplan Professional** Company

This publication is designed to provide accurate and authoritative information in regard to the subject matter covered. It is sold with the understanding that the publisher is not engaged in rendering legal, accounting, or other professional service. If legal advice or other expert assistance is required, the services of a competent professional should be sought.

Vice President and Publisher: Cynthia A. Zigmund
Editorial Director: Donald J. Hull
Acquisitions Editor: Mary B. Good
Senior Project Editor: Trey Thoelcke
Interior Design: Lucy Jenkins
Cover Design: Design Solutions
Typesetting: the dotted i

Published by Dearborn Trade Publishing, a Kaplan Professional Company

Printed in the United States of America

02   03   04   10   9   8   7   6   5   4   3   2   1

Library of Congress Cataloging-in-Publication Data

Vincent, Laurence.
    Legendary brands : unleashing the power of storytelling to create a winning marketing strategy / Laurence Vincent.
      p.   cm.
    Includes index.
    ISBN 0-7931-5560-6
    1. Brand name products.   2. Brand name products—Marketing.
   3. Customer relations.   I. Title.
    HD69.B7 V563 2002
    658.8′27—dc21

                                                 2002012222

Dedication

for Jeanette, *semper amemus*

CONTENTS

ACKNOWLEDGMENTS   ix

PART I
1. All Brands Are Not Created Equal   3
2. Brand Mythology   19
3. Myth and the Narrative of Legendary Brands   51
4. Legendary Brands and Personal Narrative   77

PART II
5. Investigating Brand Narrative   101
6. Crafting Brand Narrative   121
7. Communicating Brand Narrative   165
8. Brand Culture   187

PART III
9. Cobranding, Sponsorship, and Partnership Marketing   215
10. Brand Agents   233
11. Nonlinear Branding   255
12. Rescuing the Troubled Brand   267
13. Brand Narrative and the Body Politic   279
14. The Dark Side of Brand Mythology   293

END NOTES   309
INDEX   313

ACKNOWLEDGMENTS

I **am sincerely** grateful to the legendary storytellers and marketers who took time out of their busy schedules to meet with me: Lawrence Flanagan, Carl Gustin, Michael Kaye, Joyce King-Thomas, Norman Lear, Steve Le Neveu, Lin MacMaster, Ty Montague, Gerard Muenchen, Dennis Rook, and Elisa Romm. It was a great privilege to gain the insights of these shapers of popular culture. This book is a tribute to their accomplishments and generosity.

Thanks to the entire crew at Cabana Group. Special honors to Catherine Davie for supporting me without complaint through each new draft of this material. Thanks also to Jim Sheehy for being a constant sounding board and occasional devil's advocate.

Many thanks to the entire staff at Dearborn Trade Publishing, but especially to my editor, Mary Good. She was everything a great editor should be: coach, counselor, and collaborator.

Thanks also to my agent, Kathleen A. Welton, whose confidence and enthusiasm for this project brought it to fruition.

The impetus for this book began while I was working for the late theatrical impresario, James A. Doolittle. He was a Legendary Brand all by himself. His influence on my career and my thinking gave me the confidence to try writing a book. I will be forever grateful to him.

I have often been accused of insanity because I decided to pen a book while simultaneously starting a new business and raising a young family. I think I'm pretty sane, but if I am, it is only because so many people supported me along the way and contributed generously to this project. For starters, thanks to my business partners at Cabana Group—Hap Deneen, Mitch La Grow, and Neil Patel—who gave their full support to the project, cheered me on during some very frustrating times, and kept me laughing. Thanks to the mentors who have coached and believed in me: Ellen Ketchum, Sallie Merritt Green, Hilary Meserole, Pamela Richardson, Serena Tripi, and Michael Widman.

Thanks to my grandmother, June Callihan—the greatest role model of perseverance and dedication I have ever known. My love and thanks to my mother, Kathleen, who sacrificed nearly everything to help me succeed and instilled within me the inspiration to pursue the writer's path. Thanks also to my sisters, Kelly and Lisa, for not allowing me to take myself too seriously (yes, I'm doing it now). I owe a debt of gratitude to my children, Lucas and Jordan, because they made life fun during the un-fun writing process. But most of all, thanks to Jeanette, my wife. Without her I could not sign my name, let alone write a book. She is the best friend I've ever had, the most loving person I've ever known, and still the most beautiful woman I've ever seen. Though she would never accept any credit for this book, if not for her affection, patience, and steadfast belief in me, I might never have finished it. For this and so many other reasons, I dedicated it entirely to her.

PART ONE

In the next few chapters we will examine brand narrative, which separates Legendary Brands from all the rest. This section of the book is more theoretical than it is application oriented. If you already believe that Legendary Brands gain their staying power because they are storytellers, then skip ahead to Part II, which provides tools and techniques for developing brand narrative. I might suggest that you skim Chapter 2, which outlines a process called the Brand Mythology Cycle.

For those who are not yet convinced that Legendary Brands succeed because they craft excellent and engaging stories, read on.

The job of any marketer is to sell. That task may be achieved by overtly direct communications with the consumer, as in the barrage of dealer-driven automobile advertisements that shout low APRs and cash back incentives. It can also be achieved indirectly, by investing in brand advertising that seeks to influence consumer purchase decisions over time by psychological influence and positioning.

For the most part, this book is concerned with the latter method. Though they may frequently utilize the direct "call to action" advertising of the former, Legendary Brands become legendary by their dynamic brand communications. This form of marketing is not ideally suited to the "share shift" and "return on investment" focus of accountants and financiers. Yet, over time, these brand development efforts achieve both goals.

In the chapters that follow, you will learn how story enables Legendary Brands to achieve these goals. Throughout the ages, great storytellers have influenced the actions of men. Today, Legendary Brands continue this tradition, often in strange and unusual ways. The transformation of this tradition is the subject we consider next.

ALL BRANDS ARE NOT

CREATED EQUAL

In April, 2001, the cover of *Forbes* magazine brandished a picture of Apple Computer CEO Steve Jobs peering through the window of an iBook with a bumptious smile. The headline: Cult Brands. The feature article profiled a growing number of brands that generate phenomenal consumer enthusiasm—extending beyond mere purchase loyalty. The article described fanatical consumers who "marry" their Mazda Miatas (literally), camp out overnight at the opening of a new Krispy Kreme doughnut store, and pay thousands of dollars for a bottle of Screaming Eagle Cabernet Sauvignon.

A fault line divides the marketing topography into two tectonic plates that occasionally touch and rub against one another, but occupy distinct regions in the mind of the consumer. One of the plates is immense and inhabited by the majority of consumer brands. Some of the brands in this region are marketing stalwarts, like Tide, Folgers, and Buick. These brands are well known and highly profitable, but consumer loyalty stems from their quality, price, or functional or epistemic value. Some of these brands are legacy brands. For instance, the consumers may remain loyal to them because their parents were loyal to them. But the attachment between the consumer and the brand does not extend far beyond this nostalgic or diligent rationale.

The other plate, though much smaller, is the terrain of a different set of brands. These are to consumers what prophets are to the faithful. When these brands speak, consumers listen intently. When these brands act, consumers follow. When consumers describe these brands, their descriptions are filled with emotion, exuberance, and a vocabulary that treats the brand like a beloved friend. These brands are not just marketing constructs; they are figures in the consumer's life.

These two segments are vastly different in the mind of the consumer, yet demarcating the fault line is tricky. Instinctively, most marketers and consumers can sense a difference between the two, but identifying the difference is problematic and frustrating. To complicate the assignment, many of the conventional methods we rely upon in business do not adequately solve the problem.

SIZE DOESN'T MATTER

Our first instinct is to measure and compare the size of the two groups of brands. The brands that sell more, charge higher prices, or spend more to promote themselves might be the cult brands. It does not take very long to realize that this methodology does not work.

General Motors spends more than any other advertiser in the automobile industry to promote its brands. It outranks the others in terms of sales, too. Yet, unlike the fanatical throngs of Miata owners, there are no reports of consumers congregating with their friends and family to legally wed their Cadillac, Buick, or Pontiac vehicle. Wellsprings of loyal drivers exist throughout the world—some of them only buy GM vehicles—but their devotion does not compare to the inspired actions of the driver of a Miata, a VW Beetle, or Porsche Boxter.

Market capitalization does not work either. Apple Computer trades much lower than HP, Compaq, or Dell. Yet as a brand, it attracts the most zealous aggregation of disciples in the computer industry. When *Fortune* columnist Stewart Alsop chastised Apple in 1997 for sluggish performance and management gaffes, he received such an overwhelming deluge of letters from Apple customers that his next column detailed the agony of speaking out against the brand's management missteps. Alsop claimed that some of the responses included threats against him. Recently, when Apple opened its first retail store in the Glendale Galleria in Los Angeles, so many consumers wanted in that the line extended outside the mall and far down the adjacent street (ironically, a street named Brand Boulevard). There are few Dell or Compaq customers that would go to such extremes.

TENURE DOESN'T MATTER

Starbucks recently celebrated its 25th anniversary. In its short life span, it has inspired tremendous brand enthusiasm—more so than any other coffee brand, including venerable players such as Nescafe, Maxwell House, Folgers, and Yuban. True, its competitors do not operate coffeehouses throughout the world, but they also cannot command the price that Starbucks does in the grocery aisle. Each of these competitors would have a hard time expanding their brand into complementary food products, appliances, and other goods, which Starbucks has done rapidly and with significant consumer interest. Starbucks appears to mean more to its consumers than a good cup of coffee, and its relative youth does not seem to affect its stature.

QUALITY DOESN'T MATTER

I suppose this is the most unflattering dimension to the cult brands, but the quality of the product does not seem to be the differentiating factor. Many of the products and services produced by ordinary brands are as good, if not better, in total quality than the products and services of the cult brands. Many amateur basketball players prefer Converse shoes to Nike in terms of quality, yet Nike ranks higher on their scale of greatness.

GEOGRAPHY AND REACH
DON'T MATTER

Kistler Vineyards is a small wine producer in the Sonoma Valley of California. Most American consumers have never heard of Kistler, yet its biannual release of Chardonnay is one of the most sought after by wine enthusiasts. These consumers are so attached to the Kistler brand that they find themselves ordering far more wine then they need out of fear that they may be dropped from the Kistler mailing list, or that their allocation will be reduced. On the other hand, Gallo is the 800-pound gorilla of wine and is sold throughout the world. It is best known for its "jug" wines, but even its high-end, highly rated, award-winning varieties do not fetch the price or enthusiasm certain wine aficionados attach to Kistler.

ADVERTISING AND DESIGN
DON'T MATTER

During the Internet boom, the world's leading advertising agencies and design companies enjoyed a windfall of new business. Some of the best creative personnel in the business worked on nascent technology brands. They produced high-quality advertising, clean and innovative identity and package designs, and beautiful product styling. Few of the brands lived to tell the tale, largely because the business concept evaporated. Yet, thinking back just a year or so, most consumers cannot recall the great advertising—and during the heyday, the advertising did not seem to generate consumer euphoria.

Proctor & Gamble hires great advertising agencies to promote its vast portfolio of products. Yet despite this investment, few of them achieve cult status. Within the ranks of the creative agencies like TBWA\Chiat\Day, Goodby Silverstein & Partners, and Wieden + Kennedy, only a fraction, if any, rank in the cult brand category. Clearly, good advertising and innovative design are not the distinguishing factors.

LEGENDARY BRANDS

We need a working definition to differentiate the brands that generate such fascinating consumer behavior. I call them *Legendary Brands*.

Legends Are Entities That Attract Much Attention

Legends, in the popular vernacular, are notable people who attract a lot of attention. Elvis Presley was a legend in his own time, and continues to be a legend for all time. So are Marilyn Monroe, John Lennon, Andy Warhol, and Mahatma Gandhi.

A Legendary Brand is different from other brands because it projects a sense of celebrity within its consumer base. It takes on a human persona, and attracts a following in much the same way that human celebrities do.

Legends Are Keys

The word *legend* is often used to describe a key, particularly an inscription used to interpret something. Thus, the legend on a map helps the reader to understand the various symbols used.

Legendary Brands are also keys. They stand for concepts, values, and objects that consumers use to interpret meaning in their own lives. Consumer perceptions of Legendary Brands go beyond rational understanding of quality, function, and monetary value. The brands are often described as representing the personality of the consumer. The oft-heard response is that the Legendary Brand is "a lot like me" or "a lot like people I admire."

Just as religious symbols and artifacts are often used to navigate one's sacred ideology, a Legendary Brand allows consumers to order themselves in social, cultural, and personal space. More and more consumers appear to define a part of their identity by their brand usage. The brands that dominate this demarcation of identity are always Legendary Brands.

Conversely, Legendary Brands are also a key for the marketer. They are a key to understanding the consumer. As you will see in the pages that follow, Legendary Brands imbue social, cultural, and existential values that form the basis for the consumer bond. When we understand what brands mean to consumers, we gain valuable insight into consumer behavior, motivation, and identity.

Legends Are Stories

Finally, a *legend* is a "story handed down for generations among a people and popularly believed to have a historical basis, although not verifiable."[1] This definition uncovers the central premise of the theory of Legendary Brands: Legendary Brands are based on narrative construction, and the narrative they tell is the basis of their emphatic consumer affinity.

THE EMERGENCE OF LEGENDARY BRANDS

While strong consumer brands have been around for generations, Legendary Brands are a particularly new phenomenon. There are four factors that relate to their emergence.

People with Flexible Identities

Author Neal Gabler best sums up our present cultural order when he refers to each of us as an actor in a life movie, or "lifie." He further argues that we switch between movies on a frequent basis throughout our day. In one moment, we may play the role of a daring hero, in the next the role of a tortured slave. Like great method actors, we are able to reconstruct a character profile for ourselves based on the situation at hand, and act accordingly. His summation of the way in which we presently view ourselves confirms what sociologists and cultural anthropologists have espoused for decades: the theory of post-modernism. Postmodernism asserts a new social order governed by democracy and populated by people who continuously adapt their behavior and their identity to life's rapidly and ever-changing circumstances. One individual may have four or five identities, each suited to a different purpose. Postmodernism further argues that our social order is influenced and often governed by popular culture and mass media. Whereas these entities once "held a mirror" to our society, they now define it.[2]

Postmodernism is important to the study of Legendary Brands because it destructs the bonds between age-old social orders, omnipotent marketing practices, and cultural orientation. In the postmodern world, people have multiple identities. Their identity is subject to modification as cultural tastes change. Most important, consumers living in the postmodern world seek a narrative (or narratives) upon which to base their identity.

The Death of Dogma

In the past, our lives were dominated by overarching storylines, or metanarratives, that helped us order our world, guide our behavior, and orient ourselves within our culture. Catholics governed their lives by a strict dogma, and they knew the consequences of straying from narrative guidelines. The Catholic faith's interpretation of the Christian narrative provided a clear mental model for its followers.

In Paris, in the late nineteenth century, the Impressionists developed their own metanarrative, which governed their actions. This narrative was not constructed around religion, but around art and what it must represent to the human soul. All of the great impressionist painters subscribed to this metanarrative, and through their actions it distilled down to nonartists and French culture.

In America, the death of metanarrative is clearly seen in the three dominant adult populations. The generation that served our country in World War II is generally delineated by the metanarrative of that era. Patriotism, service to country, and hard work are all common themes in this narrative. It is a generation so remarkable and distinct that many authors, including television newsman Tom Brokaw, find it important to chronicle the lives and the experiences of this important generational movement that literally built the American economic foundation from which we all profit.

Following the World War II generation, the next great generation movement was the baby boom, or "boomers." Again, certain meta-narratives persist within this generation. This was the generation forced to deal with troubling social issues, such as civil rights, American intervention in world conflicts, and the relationship between government and civil liberties. The metanarrative of the boomers linked fast to activism. As they now move into retirement, we can expect this narrative to manifest in new ways, but its foundation is unlikely to change.

Contrast these two generations with Generation X. While many Gen-Xers take offense to the notion that their generation stands for nothing, there is a strong case to be made that it is a generation without a metanarrative. Generation X and the ridiculously labeled "Generation Y" are perhaps the most eclectic subcultures to emerge in the modern world. Despite fleeting attempts to the contrary, it is difficult to pinpoint a single theme that defines these demographic segments; evidence that postmodernism is more than a theory.

Chalk it up to the jading of consumer culture, the advance of scientific discovery, or the dispersion of communities; the reality is that most of us do not subscribe to one overarching narrative anymore. Our culture is shifting to a culture of people that may govern their lives by several narratives, each suited to a particular situation or time in their life.

Dominic Strinati argues that our culture has become "atomized." Atomization means that "a mass society consists of people who can only relate to each other like atoms in a physical or chemical compound . . . who lack any meaningful or morally coherent relationships with each other."[3] Occasionally, a galvanizing event like the tragedy of September 11, 2001, offers coherence, and we act as one. Otherwise, however, we bounce off one another taking meaning from the source ideal for the moment.

If this sounds like a jaded view of the world, it need not be. The death of metanarrative gives birth to individualism. Unfortunately, it is our nature to grab hold of an identity-defining metanarrative. We've been doing so for thousands of years. When society cannot offer the narrative, we search for something to provide an outline. Legendary Brands rise to this task.

The Advent of Consumerism

Make no doubt about it, we live in a society much more focused on the consumption of goods and services than their production. Consumption is king. We define ourselves, our lives, and our well being by what we consume. Our consumption habits are now a form of social currency. The man who uses Callaway golf clubs, drives a Jaguar, and wears Ralph Lauren apparel makes a statement about his identity. He is a man separate and apart from the man who uses a Penn fishing reel, drives a Dodge Durango, and wears Levi's.

The new consumer culture creates high demand for goods and services that serve to differentiate us. Faced with so many choices, only a few über-brands can do the job—hence the development of Legendary Brands.

The role of Legendary Brands in this context is both alarming and comforting. Brands are fast becoming the arbiters of social stratification. It is not hard to take this thought to an extreme and imagine Orwellian scenarios where a few marketing gurus determine the advancement of civilization. On the other hand, and as we shall see in this book, Legendary Brands are not really owned by marketers. There was a time, shortly after World War II, when they flirted with authoritarian control. Today, however, if they succeed in playing a role in the new consumer culture, their ownership quickly transfers to the consumers that elevate them. Marketers may deceive these fanatical consumers, but in the end, if the marketer does not serve them well, or if the sheen wears off to reveal subterfuge, the consumers revolt. Legendary Brands can only exert their influence while consumers elevate them to Legendary status.

Consumerism and the emergence of Legendary Brands is distasteful to many, even inspiring militant reactions from social critics. They see any material on the subject of building brands that supply existential, metaphysical, or personal value to consumers as adding to a social problem. If it were possible, however, to unjustly control consumers through marketing and branding tactics, it would surely be transparent. With the advent of consumerism comes a very savvy consumer audience. Today's consumers are skeptical and they are very aware of the marketing messages that surround them. Consumers judge brands with a notion that they are guilty until proven innocent.

It is a great myth in itself to believe that marketing executives have the time or the insight to devise plans that control consumer "lemmings." Anyone who has worked for a Legendary Brand, whether on the inside or as part of an agency, knows that the time constraints and demands of the job are too great to allow time to scheme world domination. Advertising agencies scamper to deliver the next commercial, while brand managers scrutinize z-scores, share shift, and promotional plans. Most of these executives are consumers themselves, and very cynical of other marketers' motives.

Consumerism is a trend created more by consumers than by marketers. Many are quick to assume that marketers created the trend, but it is just as easy to assume that marketers merely responded to consumer demand. Strong evidence exists to demonstrate that consumers control the fate of brands, rather than the reverse. When brands go too far to exploit the affinities of consumers, they fall and fall hard. Consumers see through it and punish the marketer. Take Nike, for example. When it was revealed that Nike shoes and apparel were being manufactured through the exploitation of child labor, the consumer response was so great that Nike suffered its first, true threat to its unscathed balance sheet. It reemerged as a favorite of consumers only after changing its practices.

If anything, marketers are not doing enough to satisfy the needs of the new consumer culture. Consumers crave brands that *do* stand for something, brands that help provide meaning and order in their lives. We can sit back and view this phenomenon as the decline of civilized man, or we can find a way to elevate brand responsibility.

Media Saturation and Story-Driven Advertising

In light of the preceding trends and evolutionary factors, the trend towards more media and story-driven advertising should not seem unnatural. We live in the most media saturated time in history. With so many consumers looking to buy, advertisers want every opportunity to sell.

Watching television "is now the dominant leisure activity of Americans, consuming 40 percent of the average person's free time as a primary activity."[4] So says Todd Gitlin in his book *Media Unlimited*. He goes on to point out the massive penetration and use of other forms of media, from newspapers to compact disc players. Not only are consumers being exposed to more and more media, this media contains more and more marketing messages. The scope and the speed of advertising has accelerated at an unprecedented pace.

In the age of postmodernism and its offspring, consumerism, we have become quite good at filtering through the abundance and rapidity of marketing messages. We are not alone in these endeavors. Technology is also helping. Devices like TiVo help consumers weed out unwanted messages and manage their media content.

Faced with this environment, advertising is changing. During the last quarter of a century the advertising world evolved into a sophisticated industry that excels at the manufacture of 30-second movies. Today it is difficult to determine which has greater influence over the other, the modern motion picture industry or advertising. Broadcast advertising borrowed heavily from motion picture production techniques, on and off screen talent, and the narrative structure of film. On the other hand, today's motion pictures must now tell stories faster, with less exposition and more visual communication than ever before. The reason they must is because consumers have grown accustomed to the kind of storytelling that is delivered to them at each commercial break.

The story-driven ad appears to work because people would much rather be told a story than preached to buy. The old technique of shouting "buy" repeatedly at consumers is over. Ty Montague of the Wieden + Kennedy advertising agency in New York City refers to this technique as *monologue*. Effective advertisers learned to build a dialogue with consumers by drawing them in with story. The technique works so well that some of these advertisements now attract audience attention on their own, appearing in television shows dedicated to innovative advertising, winning awards, and popping up on Web sites for consumers to download and enjoy.

The latest trend is toward a greater integration between advertising and content. Talent agencies, production companies, and media networks are shaking hands with advertisers, their agencies, and brand managers. The goal is to create content that does not require commercial breaks because the story of the programming will support the brand. Extroverted product placement deals occupy the lowest level of such ventures. The future, however, is likely to go beyond product placement. Brand narratives brought to life in 30-second advertisements, such as Apple's famous "1984" commercial, are likely to find longer viewing times. That commercial, which aired during the 1984 Super Bowl broadcast, featured a riveting sequence of images and story that dramatized Macintosh's core selling proposition: freedom to be productive through radical ease of use. This proposition was asserted without showing the product or cluttering the story with logos. In future mergers between content and marketing, neither the product or the brand may appear in the entertainment content, but the marketer will find a way to match their brand narrative to the story in such a way that the two are inseparable in the mind of the consumer.

It is in this environment that Legendary Brands are poised to continue their era of dominance. Legendary Brands are built on narrative— a metanarrative that affords them consumer loyalty. They are the brands best suited to story-driven advertising and they will be the brands most likely to leverage the coming change in advertiser-supported content.

THE PURPOSE OF THIS BOOK

The inspiration to pen this book began with a very simple premise—that the truly great consumer brands tell a story. Understanding, developing, and managing brand equity over time requires mastery of the story. In my career I have had the privilege of working in both the realm of the marketer and the realm of the storyteller. In studying Legendary Brands, I was struck by the common ground shared by storytellers and brand managers. Though their lingo, methods, and approach differ, the end product is essentially the same—a compelling narrative that attracts a valuable audience.

Thinking of brands in terms of narrative dates back to the 1950s and the pioneering work of great advertising agencies and influential researchers. Strangely, much of this great work rests in libraries instead of in marketing practice. It's a shame, because the need for a narrative view of brand marketing has never been greater.

To write this book, I talked with many in the marketing trade. I approached it not as an expert, but as a student. I met with leaders in legendary advertising agencies and creative houses. I met with the senior marketers of some of the greatest brands in the world. I also met with casual observers of the marketing trade. Again and again, I heard these people refer to the story, the theme, or the spine of the campaign. Drilling beneath the surface, I discovered that they all meant the same thing—the narrative of the brand.

I believe the managers of Legendary Brands must think with a new vocabulary. They must think in the language of the storyteller. Instead of strategic plans, they need to think of their brand myth or narrative. Instead of campaigns, they need to think of story arcs. Instead of consumers, they need to think of audiences. Instead of spokespeople, sponsorships, and products, they need to think of characters in a larger story. Instead of retail environments, they need to think of narrative settings.

Legendary Brands are their strongest when they serve up the story their consumer audience expects. They delight beyond belief when that story delivers a new twist, a touch of the familiar with a pinch of novelty. Every great story takes the characters, and the audience, on a journey. Legendary Brands sustain consumer enthusiasm over long periods by doing the same. The difference between an ordinary brand and a Legendary Brand is that the Legendary Brand activates a brand narrative.

This book will serve to help marketers think like storytellers. It provides a look at the narrative cycle that binds consumers to the brand. It liberates storytelling and promotes it to a strategic device, rather than the function of copywriters.

STRUCTURE OF THE BOOK

I have divided the material into three parts. Part I digs into the theory behind Legendary Brands. It explores the Brand Mythology cycle, which explains the circular relationship between beliefs, brands, narrative, and consumers. Part I also delves further into the role of narrative in our lives, first by exploring the power and predominance of myth in all cultures of the world, and then by examining personal myth—a thoroughly postmodern approach to identity formation.

Part II focuses on application. If narrative is the key to Legendary Brands, then Part II provides tools and techniques for crafting and managing narrative. Notice that I use the term *craft*. This is not a semantic flourish, but an important distinction. Brand narratives are crafted. Crafts can be learned. Many people are put off and frightened by the craft of storytelling. It has a mystical quality that some believe is more connected to artistry and talent than hard work. Truth be told, storytelling is a craft. Talent and artistry enhance the end product, but great stories emerge from diligent craftsmanship—so do great brands.

Part II examines four important applications for the brand manager. We first look at the role of consumer research. Research provides Legendary Brands one way to gain audience feedback. From it, the brand manager can make modifications to the brand narrative. We next turn our attention to strategy, and discuss the development of a brand bible, the strategic instrument that enables brand managers to manage their brands over time. Following this material, we explore the role of communications, and consider all of the ways that a brand can touch a consumer with its narrative. We especially look at narrative touch points that extend beyond the television or print advertisement, and consider those touch points that deliver sensory or experiential elements. Finally, we examine brand cultures—a distinct element unique to Legendary Brands. Brand cultures do not exist in a vacuum. They have an impact on the brand over time. If it is indeed possible, we explore the methods for managing a brand culture.

In Part III, we journey through specific instances and applications of brand narrative. Part III is a field guide. It is a reference point to study cases where brand narrative played a crucial role. We also look beyond the realm of traditional consumer brands. It is not just soft drinks and automobiles that occupy the Legendary Brand domain. We explore political campaigns, nonlinear environments, and marketing partnerships as an extension of Legendary Brand theory.

FINAL THOUGHT: It's Not for Everyone

Not every brand must become a Legendary Brand. Proctor & Gamble is one of the world's greatest success stories. Its brand portfolio is a power house of consumer packaged goods. I would argue that hardly any brand in that portfolio qualifies as a Legendary Brand. I would also argue that most of them shouldn't try to be Legendary Brands.

If every brand becomes a Legendary Brand, then Legendary Brands lose their value. At the end of the day, consumers do not seek meaning in everything they buy. In fact, many marketers make a mistake when they make the assumption that consumers put a lot of thought into their purchasing behavior. Consumers buy on impulse. They buy from habit. They buy for expediency. They buy sometimes because they want a change. There are myriad reasons that govern consumption behavior. Your brand can be very successful and even gain great consumer loyalty without becoming a Legendary Brand.

This book is not intended to provide a framework applicable to all brands. Many great books on branding have already defined a framework that suits the needs of general-purpose brands. This book focuses on one specific brand type—the Legendary Brand. It is a unique animal, and it requires a unique management technique.

CHAPTER 2

BRAND MYTHOLOGY

In the last chapter we found that there are two kinds of consumer brands: ordinary product brands and Legendary Brands. Explaining why Legendary Brands are different from ordinary product brands is difficult, even for seasoned marketers and advertising professionals. Very often the diagnostic criteria provided sound a lot like former Supreme Court Justice Potter Stewart's prescription for distinguishing pornography from other sexually provocative material: "I know it when I see it."

There is a fundamental distinction between Legendary Brands and all other product brands. Legendary Brands subscribe to a brand mythology. Ordinary product brands do not. Brand mythology uses narrative to convey a worldview, a set of sacred beliefs that transcend functional and epistemic product attributes. This narrative, which connects the consumer and the brand in a kind of existential bond, is the foundation of the brand's strength. Brand mythology operates in a self-fulfilling cycle that engages consumer participation. In this chapter you will learn the dynamics of this cycle and the way in which it operates. Specifically, you will realize that:

- Brand mythology acts upon the cognitive orientation centers of the brain in much the same way that religion and other deeply held philosophical beliefs do.
- Legendary Brands, like most religions, gain their strength through narrative.
- From an anthropological perspective, sacred beliefs, narrative, and the communities that subscribe to them form a cyclical system that provides the unusual phenomena of Legendary Brands.

SACRED BELIEFS: The Secret Weapon of Legendary Brands

Legendary Brands bond with consumers through sacred beliefs, a special set of mental constructs that allows us to existentially orient ourselves, whereas ordinary product brands usually form a bond with the consumer from purely functional attributes. For example, most consumers who claim loyalty to a laundry detergent say that it is the consistent and quality results of the product that affect their purchase decision. Legendary Brands, on the other hand, bond with the consumer by asserting or affirming fundamental beliefs that consumers use to explain the meaning of their lives.

Famed mythologist Mircea Eliade asserts that man can live only in a sacred world, "because it is only in such a world that he participates in being, that he has a real existence."[1] Our sacred beliefs define who we are, what we value, and which lifestyle we choose. Put simply, they define our very being. They can range from heady questions such as, "Is there a God?" to personal perspectives such as, "What is more important to me, money or family?"

Every human, religious or not, maintains a set of sacred beliefs. It is biological, and a strange consequence of our natural selection strategy. Humans evolved into abstract thinkers. Unlike other animals, we can consider life-or-death situations before they occur and we can formulate various survival strategies. Abstract thinking is thus fundamental to our evolutionary fitness because, compared to the rest of the animals that populate our planet, we are relatively defenseless and vulnerable to predators. We have no fangs, claws, deadly venom, or brute strength. We cannot exceed speeds of fifty miles per hour or take to the skies without significant technological assistance. We are primitive climbers, swimmers, and jumpers. And, by and large, our sensory organs (smell, taste, touch, etc.) are not nearly as perceptive as those of other animals. Abstract thinking, however, gives us the power to contemplate a counter-response to each of these potentially dangerous disadvantages and outwit competitive species. This ability to problem-solve made it possible for us to coexist with potential predators, reproduce in hostile environments, and, in many cases, shift from the hunted to the hunter.

Because abstract thinking and our ability to problem solve is crucial to our survival, it is more than a feature enhancement. It is a compulsive adaptation that is forced by the limbic system. It is a survival mechanism, which is why humans demonstrate great anxiety and metabolic stress when an observable phenomenon cannot be explained. We are biologically driven to make sense of all that is around us. This compulsive problem-solving imperative in our brains also causes us to consider, in the words of cognitive psychologist Steven Pinker, "fascinating but biologically functionless activities."[2] This byproduct of our cognitive wiring is the basis for our sacred belief systems. In a sense, "religion and philosophy are in part the application of mental tools to problems they were not designed to solve."[3]

It is, therefore, part of the biology of human beings to contemplate existential and philosophical questions and to develop a set of beliefs, or explanatory logic, to answer them. That Legendary Brands act upon these sacred beliefs is fundamental to what separates them from other brands and bonds them so strongly with consumers.

BRAND MYTHOLOGY: A System That Validates Sacred Beliefs

For at least as many years as we have recorded history, we know that human beings consistently sought to define meaning in life through a set of sacred beliefs. Early humans eventually bonded with others who shared similar beliefs. Band communities were born in which men and women gathered and lived together under a common set of values and principles. The sacred beliefs held by these band communities were usually attached to some physical entity, which provided concrete evidence that the beliefs were valid. It also enabled the belief system to:

- be passed down to future generations,
- justify the laws created by the community, and
- invalidate the competing sacred beliefs of rival communities that threatened their culture.

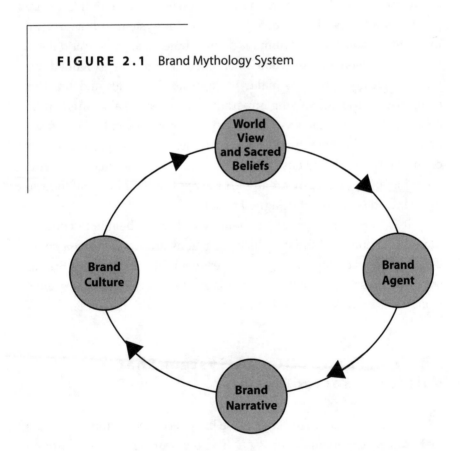

FIGURE 2.1   Brand Mythology System

The way in which the communities connected the beliefs with the physical entity was through the device of narrative. To keep the narrative alive, they performed rituals and they created symbols that signified critical components of the narrative. In turn, these rituals and symbols strengthened and occasionally altered the underlying set of sacred beliefs. This cycle is the basis for most cultures. It is also the workings of brand mythology.

Just as a hurricane gains its awesome strength from the reciprocal system that fuels it, Legendary Brands generate power through the Brand Mythology System (see Figure 2.1). This system contains four components: a worldview comprised of a set of sacred beliefs, a brand agent, brand narrative, and consumer participation through a special set of consumer feedback activities.

SACRED BELIEFS AND
THE STRANGE CASE OF ATHEISTS

Dan Baker has only been inside a church once, to attend the funeral of a close friend. He was raised the son of a chemical engineer in a house absent of religion. His father was raised in an Episcopalian family, but separated from the church when he saw "hypocrisy and scientific implausibility." Dan grew up believing that a scientific reason could be found for any inexplicable phenomenon. It is ingrained in him that we are born and die because of purely biological cause and effect relationships. He firmly believes that once we die, we cease to exist and nothing more.

Atheists are often cited as proof that not everyone holds sacred beliefs. Because Dan does not appear to ponder upon the metaphysical origins of his existence or the afterlife, it is argued that he holds no sacred beliefs. However, sacred beliefs extend beyond the question of "Is there a God?"

Dan served in Vietnam and earned a Purple Heart for rushing back into a battery of bullets to rescue a fellow soldier. Why would any sane human being put himself into mortal danger to save the life of another human being? Apparently, Dan believes it is sometimes right to subordinate self-interests to save the lives of others. This is a sacred belief.

When Dan returned from Vietnam, he went to college and earned a law degree at the top of his class. He is now a partner in a respected New York law firm. He bills more than 2,300 hours each year, which makes him one of the top earners for his firm. Dan is financially secure, so why does he feel the need to work so many hours instead of engaging in more relaxing or sedentary activities? It appears Dan may believe that it is important to be well respected by his peers, or he may believe that hard work is an important personal standard. Both of these are sacred beliefs.

Finally, Dan is married. He met his wife in law school and they were married (by a justice of the peace) shortly after he graduated. They have two children. Why would a guy like Dan get married or have children? Perhaps he believes that life should be shared, or he enjoys the friendship and affection of his mate. He obviously believed it was so important that he went through a very formalized ritual to pair with another in the eyes of the law when, in today's society, it is acceptable to live with another and mate without a contractual bond. Even if his children are merely the result of a biological process designed to ensure the longevity of Dan's genes, it is doubtful that Dan thinks of them in this way. He is likely to feel so strongly about his children that he will put their lives before his own and be willing to invest money in their futures beyond what is necessary for their survival. These, too, are sacred beliefs.

Sacred beliefs exist in many forms. Religion may be one of them, but there are many others. All of us, even atheists, hold some things in life to be sacred. If we didn't, we would be no different than machines.

Myth is a "traditional story of ostensibly historic events that serves to unfold part of the worldview of a people or explain a practice, belief, or natural phenomena," according to Webster. The occidental mythology of ancient civilizations served to explain the mysterious workings of the natural world through stories about the struggles and conquests of Gods and Heroes. Today, brand mythology serves a similar purpose. Scientific discovery answered many of the mysteries of the natural world, but it has not satisfactorily resolved the complex questions we have about our social existence, our sense of self, and our relationship to the world at large. Brand mythology has curiously interceded. Like ancient mythology, it works through narrative devices.

BELIEFS AND AGENTS:
A Symbiotic Relationship

By themselves, sacred beliefs may be self-evident, but they alone cannot serve as a cultural faith. For one thing, it is difficult to prove or disprove the validity of any single belief on its own merit. Because they are abstract hypotheses, they require some kind of physical proof before our minds allow them to rule our behavior.

Consider the following example: You are a black man who lives in rural Alabama. The year is 1963. Throughout your entire life, you have only known a segregated world. Your rights have been denied. People with your skin color have been abused and oppressed. Nevertheless, you have learned how to live under these conditions. You come across a simple sentence that reads, "We hold these truths to be self-evident, that all men are created equal." No evidence is presented to support this argument. All you have to evaluate this statement is the statement itself.

Chances are you will be unlikely to accept this belief as truth. You have no proof that this is factual, and the circumstances of your life seem to argue the contrary.

Now, imagine the same circumstance with one difference. You hear those same words from a charismatic preacher by the name of Dr. Martin Luther King, Jr. He comes from a similar upbringing as yourself and he speaks with the authority of life experience. You know that this man has gone to jail because he refused to yield and yet today he is free. He has continued to stand up for that simple sentence no matter what adversity came into his path. Despite a multitude of setbacks, he has been recognized by such influential people as the new President of the United States. You now have physical evidence that the postulate is true. You are more likely to adhere to this belief as a result.

It is our nature to seek proof for our beliefs. We usually find it in the form of an agent. An agent is physical evidence that our worldview is valid. Agents are not always people, although people are the most powerful agents. The only prerequisite for an agent is that it must satisfy the test of tangibility. We must be able to attach our worldview to a person, place, or thing.

The worldview espoused by Legendary Brands is always connected to a physical agent. For example, Martha Stewart is the agent for the products that carry her name. Functionally and qualitatively, these products are arguably no different from competitive offerings. However, Martha Stewart, the person, embodies a worldview that resonates with millions of people. Her existence gives validity to the sacred beliefs these people hold dear. That's why they buy her products.

THE CLOTH OF VALIDATION

In the northwestern region of Italy, along the shores of the Po River, rests the medieval city of Turin. It is a place of rich history and culture, but it is best known throughout the world for the cloth—14 foot, three inches in length—that it houses within its stately cathedral. The Shroud of Turin is believed by many to be the sacred burial cloth of Jesus Christ. Despite the fact that recent scientific and historical evidence casts doubt and controversy about its authenticity, this eerie relic inspires pilgrimages and awe by millions who view it as proof positive that Christ lived. Jesus Christ is the agent of the Christian faith and the Shroud is one of many pieces of tangible "evidence" to Christians that he existed. The Shroud is a form of validation to many people that what they believe is accurate. It satisfies any doubt they may have had about Christ's existence and the validity of the set of beliefs he embodied.

Alternately, the worldview associated with the Harley-Davidson brand is agented by the product itself. The raw and noisy muscle of a Harley-Davidson motorcycle is physical evidence in favor of the libertarian philosophy of its customer base (i.e., obtaining power by going against the grain, achieving identity by refusing to conform, and pursuing personal liberty to the verge of lawlessness). Consider the public outcry when Harley was acquired in 1981 and its new owners tried to quiet the engineering and styling of the product. They tried to make Harley conform. Doing so invalidated the sacred beliefs of the brand.

Agents and their corresponding worldview are essential elements of brand mythology. They are symbiotic entities that require one another like a chicken and egg, a fitting analogy because it is often difficult to determine which came first. Some brands gain their worldview by adopting the sacred beliefs associated with an agent. Others find an agent that matches their worldview. For example, would Nike have become a Legendary Brand without having adopted the worldview of brand agents Steve Prefontaine or Michael Jordan? In its statement of philosophy, Nike credits Prefontaine for defining "the soul of the Nike brand" in his oft-repeated advice to young runners, "to give anything less than your best is to sacrifice the gift." Prefontaine may have defined Nike's worldview but, for most disciples of Nike, Michael Jordan proved it true. He proved that you are, indeed, your greatest opponent each time millions of fans watched him beat his own record, often through heroic athletic efforts that seemed to defy the laws of physics.

In contrast, would Harvard University be as influential today if not for the sacred beliefs that govern it? The campus, its famous shield, and its roster of influential alumni are powerful brand agents, but it is Harvard's sacred philosophy, "Veritas," known throughout the world that probably came first in its brand mythology.

NARRATIVE: The Tie That Binds

While agents are an indispensable focal point for a set of sacred beliefs, they really do not have much of a connection without narrative. Narrative is the most critical component of brand mythology. Robert McKee, one of Hollywood's venerable story sages, eloquently described the connection between narrative and belief systems in his book, *Story: Substance, Structure, Style, and The Principles of Screenwriting*. In his words, "storytelling is the creative demonstration of truth. A story is the living proof of an idea, the conversion of idea to action. A story's event structure is the means by which you first express, then prove your idea. . ."[4]

There are three main reasons that narrative is essential to a sacred belief system. First, it binds the belief system with an agent, thus giving people a material rationale for believing as they do. Second, the narrative stimulates emotions that distort the logical thought process in favor of the sacred beliefs concerned. Finally, narrative prescribes the behavior that is required to live the belief system and conform to its brand culture.

The principles of the Buddhist faith resonate as universal truths for many peoples of the world. These principles, however, coalesce through the proofs demonstrated by Buddhist scripture. It is the story of Buddha's transformation from an unenlightened prince to the blessed earthly ambassador of the heavens, his words and deeds along the journey, and the substance of his character revealed through the narrative that binds him inextricably with the sacred beliefs of the Buddhist faith. Without this story, he would be no different from any other ancient man of the East.

Narrative is a powerful device for binding an argument with an entity. Gerry Spence, the charismatic lawyer from Montana who achieved fame for his masterful legal strategy in the Karen Silkwood and Randy Weaver trials, attributes his many successes to storytelling. In the Silkwood trial, Spence used a simple story to convince a jury that the defendant, Kerr-McGee, was responsible for the harmful exposure to nuclear radiation that Ms. Silkwood experienced. "I told the jury the story of a case in old England in which a citizen brought a lion onto his property, and though he had taken precautions to keep it caged, it somehow escaped and mauled his neighbor. The old common-law court held that the lion's owner was liable, for the beast was inherently dangerous as the owner well knew, and the owner, not the innocent neighbor, should therefore bear the risk of injury from the escaping lion."[5] Spence produced plenty of physical evidence to back his claim, but he attributes his successful jury persuasion to the connection made by narrative devices.

Legendary Brands, too, use narrative to link a worldview to a physical agent. Consider Ralph Lauren and the Polo brand of fragrances and apparel. Through the narrative of its advertising, fashion shows, and product design, the brand links a desirable social culture to the sacred belief that fashion and style must be simultaneously active and refined. The brand communicates this through two separate storylines. One is the semireal story of Ralph Lauren, the man, who is frequently photographed at culturally significant events, socializing with famous people, and influencing the fashion decisions of trendsetters. The story implies that any party or social affair that this glamorous and exciting social group organizes is incomplete without the presence of Ralph Lauren. Though Lauren is rarely the protagonist of this brand story, he is a recognizable character and his presence in the story binds his brand with fashion-oriented sacred beliefs.

The second brand story also connects a social culture with the brand's sacred beliefs. The brand agent in this story is not a single person, but rather an anonymous culture of affluent people. They appear within an active and comfortable lifestyle. Each time the story is told, these people are enjoying life in a manner consistent with Ralph Lauren's worldview. For example, recent Ralph Lauren television advertisements show attractive, youthful people racing yachts, visiting exotic places, and, of course, playing the very demanding but refined sport of Polo. Therefore, the proof is made that the Polo brand is an agent of the refined elite. Interestingly enough, the largest group of consumers that purchase Polo products are not the cultural elite, but rather the middle class or those aspiring to enter this enlightened cultural set. For this group of people, Ralph Lauren and Polo reinforce their worldview even though the goal to be obtained from this worldview is not yet manifest.

One way narrative makes such an effective connection between sacred beliefs and brand agents is through the provocation of a powerful emotional response. When presented with more than one logical conclusion to a cognitive problem, our minds tend to choose the option charged with the greatest emotional weighting (as the example in the following sidebar demonstrates). By coloring our logic with emotion, stories weight our analysis in favor of the argument tied to the emotional response.

BIOLOGY GIVES US "THE WILLIES"

The link between logical thought processing and emotional response centers in the brain is biological and the result of a superior adaptation in the human animal. Neuroscientists Andrew Newberg and Eugene D'Aquili illustrate how this adaptation works and why it benefits us by considering a hypothetical primitive hunter-gatherer.

The man enters the forest to hunt for game, but he is no sooner in the thick of the trees than he hears a noise in the bushes. His mind immediately responds by presenting two options: a leopard or game.

The hunter realizes that he is in leopard country and he recalls seeing leopard tracks along the path. It is therefore logical to assume that the noise might be caused by a leopard. On the other hand, he knows from experience that leopards do not hunt during this time of day and he recalls that the tracks he saw looked as though they were a few days old. This leads him to conclude that the noise came from some other animal. The hunter is faced with two choices: to flee may cost him dinner, but to stay might cost him his life.

In their example, Newberg and D'Aquili consider what might be going on in the emotional center of the man's brain. On the one hand, he might feel sporting and positive emotions associated with the hunt. On the other hand, he visualizes the agony and terror of being attacked by a leopard. He may compound this by recalling memories of a time in the past when he was chased by a big cat, in circumstances very similar to the present situation. The negative emotions outweigh the positive and the man flees.

The man never knew conclusively whether the sound came from a leopard. Both of his conclusions were equally valid based on the evidence provided, but the emotions associated with the potentially life-threatening attack colored one of the conclusions and determined his behavior.[6]

Stories can make us laugh, cry, and tense up in fear. During a storytelling experience, we project ourselves into the narrative and trick our minds into believing that we are experiencing what the characters experience. It is a strange cognitive response in consideration of the demonstrable anxiety we provoke by willfully expending emotional energy towards a circumstance that is utterly contrived. Why would we elect to experience uncomfortable emotional states such as grief, terror, and rage? Ironically, the stories that stand the test of time and gain the greatest public sentiment are consistently the stories that provoke negative emotional response. Consider the staying power of popular films, books, and theatrical productions such as *Casablanca*, *War and Peace*, *Psycho*, *Death of a Salesman*, *Hamlet*, *Les Miserables*, and *Terms of Endearment*.

It is the same force that causes us to cry while watching *Bambi* that strengthens our bond with Legendary Brands. If the brand is charged with enough emotion, we may willingly dismiss the well-reasoned counterarguments offered up by the methodical logic centers of our brain. It is this kind of weighted logic that makes us favor a Legendary Brand over an equal or better-quality ordinary brand. Storytellers call this the willing suspension of disbelief. Salesmen call it marketing.

Any good political consultant knows that the difference between the client and the opposition is often miniscule. It is no surprise that the first angle of attack in a political campaign is to build a story around the candidate that provokes emotion from the constituency. Americans have come to dread election season because it invariably arrives with a slew of political attack ads. The purpose of these ads is to create strong negative emotions towards the opponent and positive emotions toward the candidate. Though people profess to hate such tactics, they survive because they work, even when significant factual data to the contrary is abundant.

Consider the famous Johnson/Goldwater race of 1964. Despite the fact that during his congressional career, Lyndon Johnson supported legislation that contributed to a significant buildup of nuclear weapons, and even though he played a visible role in the escalation of the conflict in Vietnam, his campaign masterfully eliminated Barry

Goldwater's claim to the White House. It did so by running one simple television advertisement that emotionally tied Goldwater with nuclear holocaust. In the advertisement, an adorable, innocent child sits in a field picking petals off of a flower. With each petal, she counts down. Interspersed with her counting, images appear of a nuclear missile about to launch accompanied by the ominous countdown of a mission control facility. As both child and missile reach zero, a mushroom cloud appears with text urging Americans to prevent World War III by reelecting Johnson. The spot terrified most Americans, playing into their fears that nuclear war was imminent. It secured Johnson's re-election.

Emotional provocation through narrative is the winning backhand of most Legendary Brands. Technical data suggests that Kodak film is indeed superior compared to some competitive products offered by Fuji or Agfa. But most consumers honestly cannot tell the difference. Nevertheless, these same consumers often prefer the Kodak brand. Their preference has less to do with technical superiority and more to do with the legacy of emotional advertising Kodak produced to build the brand. The "Kodak Moment" and "True Colors" campaigns offered touching episodes from a sentimental scrapbook of American family life. Millions of consumers came to favor Kodak because the emotional Kodak narrative led them to believe it was a trusted part of their family, in spite of the fact that competitive products were often less expensive and produced quality photographs that only professionals could differentiate from Kodak. These people just felt they could trust Kodak, and only Kodak, with their most precious life memories.

In recent years, Kodak's market value declined. Fuji, its fiercest competitor, established manufacturing facilities in the US and generated significant share shift from a grueling price war. On top of this, digital imaging and the increasing penetration of computers in the household is eating into film and photographic paper consumption. These factors have hurt Kodak's business. But one also has to wonder if part of the loss in market value occurred because of Kodak's simultaneous decision to retire the emotional brand campaigns of the past. Where once Kodak focused on the emotional rewards of capturing life's most important experiences to relish the memories later, Kodak distanced itself from the concept of a "Kodak moment." Instead, Kodak introduced a new concept to consumers: "Take Pictures. Further."

The strategic rationale for this campaign made perfect sense. It focused upon emerging technologies in imaging, such as digital cameras, photographic manipulation software, and digital transmission of photographic images. Yet it lacked the emotional depth of Kodak's brand narrative. The campaign was also hard for many Kodak consumers to understand. The advertising associated with "Take Pictures. Further." focused on functional applications enabled by Kodak technologies. It was product-focused advertising at its best, but despite admirable creative and significant media exposure, when asked what consumers recalled most about Kodak advertising, most consumers recalled the "Kodak Moment" concept rather than "Take Pictures. Further."

The essence of Kodak's brand narrative is its tie to memories, nostalgia, and reverence for past events. It is no surprise that Kodak recently abandoned "Take Pictures. Further." and introduced its new campaign, "Share Moments. Share Life." This new marketing effort, imbued with heartfelt imagery and emotional episodes from American life, rekindles the spirit of the Kodak brand narrative and demonstrates the power of the brand promise. It reminds consumers how precious their memories are, and encourages them to take more pictures in order to share those memories.

Narrative prescribes the customs and behavior that are necessary for the individual to benefit from the belief system. It tells people how to behave implicitly and explicitly. Let us return to religion to understand the mechanics of this process.

In each of the four holy gospels of the Christian faith, Christ demonstrates how the people of the faith must behave to subscribe to the sacred beliefs. The narrative shows him doing this in two ways. In the first, he gives explicit direction about what is right and what is wrong. This is precisely the purpose of the Sermon on the Mount, in which Christ literally tells those who follow him how to behave. He even goes so far as to teach them how to pray. This is an example of narrative providing explicit behavioral instruction.

Christ also demonstrates the target behavior by example. Christ's actions within the narrative provide a behavioral model for those who follow him. When he denies himself earthly pleasures, it is inferred that those who wish to benefit from the Christian ideal of heaven must live a life of modesty. When he forgives a man who has done terrible things, his followers learn that they too must forgive those who have "transgressed against them."

The Christian faith's use of narrative to prescribe behavior is not unique. In fact, in nearly every organized religion, a narrative exists that dictates the behavior required to participate in the faith. Many great Legendary Brands also use narrative to influence consumer behavior.

Hallmark is arguably a Legendary Brand. While it is a brand that has not fully exploited its brand value, Hallmark is associated with life's great moments and it has masterfully used narrative to explicitly prescribe consumer behavior. It is often said that Mother's Day is the greatest holiday Hallmark ever invented. While perhaps a trite statement, consumers observe this unsanctioned holiday largely because of narrative provided by greeting card companies, such as Hallmark. Artfully produced television and print advertisements rekindle the personal narrative each of us has with our mother, and urges us to show our respect and gratitude by sending her a greeting card that uniquely expresses our true feelings.

In fairness, it is, after all, the purpose of advertising to influence consumer behavior. The objective of every advertiser is to implicitly prescribe acts of consumer behavior (e.g., "Buy the product!"). Legendary Brands, however, dole out the prescription through story. These brands do not yell at the consumer to buy, buy, buy. They instead engage them in a narrative that makes the consumer want to buy because they identify with narrative components. Nike's brand narrative prescribes the consumer to get out and exercise, "Just Do It." Buying Nike product is almost an afterthought. Hallmark tells the consumer to take the effort and connect with someone they love. MasterCard, in its new "Priceless" campaign, encourages consumers to focus on the events in life that no amount of money could ever buy (e.g., the joy you experience watching your toddler spend all day playing with the box that contained the gift you bought him, or laughing with your grandmother during the time she teaches you to make her legendary stew). Each of these brands prescribes behavioral activities that connect to sacred beliefs. This behavior makes life better for the consumers that subscribe to this worldview. It also sells more of the brand's product.

Narrative is a remarkably influential device. In Chapters 3 and 4 we will explore it in greater detail. For the moment, we must complete the brand mythology cycle, which calls for a study of brand culture.

BEHAVIORAL ACTIVITIES: Adding Humans to the System

Legendary Brands could not generate their tremendous value without being purely human in character. To be human means that these brands live and die in the hearts of consumers. The consumers feel ownership of the brand and it becomes a part of their cultural existence. This brand culture develops from some very special behavioral activities.

- The formation of social or band communities
- The practice of rituals
- The use of symbols

We shall examine each of these independently, although they exert their greatest strength in conjunction with one another.

Legendary Brands gain strength by the formation of brand tribes that share an affiliation with the sacred beliefs of the brand. These tribes may congregate formally or in a very discreet way. Functionally, consumers who participate in these tribes do so as further validation for their beliefs. Writing off brand tribes as one more brand agent for the worldview would be a mistake. A deeper issue is at play. The tribe's social construction helps to define the polarities of sacred space. For example, those who belong to the Krispy Kreme brand tribe often view all other doughnuts as inferior. It's an "us versus them" view of the world. Krispy Kreme loyalists will drive miles out of their way to get a dozen "sacred" pastries rather than visit their corner doughnut shop that serves ordinary or "profane" products.

On the surface, Krispy Kreme tribal polarities may seem superficial. After all, few people define their lives based on the sacred qualities of a sugared pastry. It is not the product that gives tribes power. It is what the product stands for. People who go to the trouble of buying Krispy Kreme doughnuts may connect with one another based on sacred beliefs of authenticity and Puritan values. They believe that it is better to go for quality and simplicity over mass-produced homogeneity. When they meet others who share the same passion for Krispy Kreme, a bond is formed that creates social understanding.

Starbucks is an über-Legendary Brand. It has a brand tribe that is rapidly multiplying, with meeting houses almost everywhere. Rare is the occasion when a loyal Folgers Coffee drinker will wait in line to buy a can from their favorite supermarket. Starbucks loyalists not only wait in line, they often make a visit to their favorite Starbucks location a mandatory part of their daily routine. Step inside a local Starbucks and you are likely to find a group of people that are on a first-name basis. They comfortably recline on sofas and plush chairs while reading the paper. They would rather sip coffee in their local Starbucks than in any place else in the world. When they travel, they seek out a Starbucks in much the same way that Christian crusaders sought local cathedrals for refuge and nourishment.

The Starbucks brand tribe doesn't just believe the Starbucks worldview: they live it. They internalize it, make it a part of their daily lives, and share it with one another. When two perfect strangers meet, each with a Starbucks coffee in hand, an instant social bond is established. If both of the strangers are brand loyalists to Starbucks (as opposed to having chanced upon a Starbucks product), it is likely that each of them will use the Starbucks worldview, along with other data, to develop a cognitive sketch of what the person on the other end of the handshake is all about. "Biographies of things can make salient what might otherwise remain obscure. For example, in situations of culture contact, they can show what anthropologists have so often stressed: that what is significant about the adoption of alien objects—as of alien ideas—is not the fact that they are adopted, but the way they are culturally redefined and put to use."[7]

Loyalists to the Linux operating system exhibit similar tribal behavior. Not only do these people connect socially based on affiliation to Linux, but because they can shape the physical make-up of the product, and they create social meaning through product use. Linux is an open-source operating system, meaning that anyone can alter the digital code. Linux users interact on a frequent basis and form communities that make it their mission to improve and promote the Linux operating system. In the process, they form friendships with one another and cluster into groups that share similar values.

Ordinary product brands, such as Folgers Coffee or the Unix operating system, have loyal users. The difference between these brands and Legendary Brands is that the users don't use the brand to form their view of the world and the social order that it holds. The products of ordinary brands are rarely a form of social currency. Legendary Brands, on the other hand, have products that come to life and gain meaning through their use in consumer ritual. In religion, a ritual is a re-enactment of a part of the brand narrative. For example, in the aboriginal Aranda tribe of Central Australia, young boys between the ages of ten and fourteen participate in a ritual within which they are tossed into the air several times by the men, while the women chant and dance.[8]

Victor Turner, a leading anthropologist and expert on the ritual process, found that such rituals induce a feeling of oneness with sacred space by a quality he called *liminality*, or *thresholdness*. Liminality is said to reduce participants to their lowest common denominator, voiding them of any previous sense of identity. The Aranda boys, therefore, begin the ritual as children, but are transformed in the rite, to emerge changed as the men of the tribe.

Patterns of such behavior can be seen in Legendary Brands. Whenever a customer buys a new Saturn, the dealership initiates the customer into the Saturn family with a simple ritual. The entire dealer team assembles around the customer, standing next to the new Saturn. The dealer team chants a welcome statement and then applauds and cheers on the new member of the "Saturn family." To commemorate the experience, a photograph is taken and placed into a personalized calendar that is sent to the initiate. Thus, the Saturn customer goes from an ordinary person, into the purchase process, a state of liminality, and emerges a Saturn owner.

Rituals can have a physiological effect on the individual that creates a powerful emotional response. The intense concentration of the brain that occurs in ritual practice, coupled with rhythmic patterns that often accompany ritual acts (music, dance, chanting, etc.), force the hippocampus, a regulatory center of the brain, to inhibit neural flow. In essence, your brain turns down the volume. Scientists believe that one of the affected areas, as a result of this inhibiting action, is the orientation center of the brain. The result is that we feel apart from ourselves. We may feel like we are in a trance or we may experience a very calming but disorienting sensation. Generally, we feel very good and our perception of the sacred beliefs and their associated agent(s) are heightened.

"When religious ritual is effective, and it is not always effective, it inclines the brain to adjust to cognitive and emotional perceptions of the self in a way that religiously minded persons interpret as a closing of the distance between the self and God."[9] For a period, however brief, the individual and the set of sacred beliefs become one.

It is this "godly" state that gives the ritual of Legendary Brands such power. Once a month, several hundred Vespa owners gather together to do a group ride through the streets of Manhattan. The Vespa, a stylish Italian motor scooter, is closely associated with a romantic ideal of freedom. People who love their Vespa often describe it with the imagery of a Roman holiday. The ceremonial group ride is a ritual that rekindles that romanticism and transforms the rider for a brief time, reinforcing brand loyalty.

Another group of riders gathers once a year in Barstow, California. There are not many Vespas in this ride, however. It is the Guggenheim Museum's annual motorcycle trek from Barstow to Las Vegas. The first of these rides was designed to promote the Guggenheim's exhibition, "The Art of the Motorcycle." The ride is now a ritual act in support of art itself. Led by the museum's unconventional President, Thomas Krens, and his close group of celebrity friends (which includes model Lauren Hutton, and actors Dennis Hopper, Jeremy Irons, and Lawrence Fishburn), the ride is a symbolic rite that ties to the Guggenheim's sacred belief of advancing art to advance culture. The people who participate do it for fun, but they also describe it as a spiritual experience.

Of course, one of the great byproducts of rituals and brand culture is a library of symbols. Just as the gangs of today use symbols to note their affiliations, the tribes of brand cultures use symbols to connect with the brand. Symbols are often the badges of tribal membership. Symbols appeal to our visually oriented mind. The phrase that a picture is worth a thousand words is more true than most people realize. One simple image can trigger an emotional response much faster than a sentence in a book. Glancing on a picture of a deceased loved one is more likely to conjure instant sadness and even a physical response of tears, more so than reading about them or talking about them with others. This is the root of symbolic power. Symbols provide instant visual representation of a meaningful construct. Put simply, they trigger a logical belief that is linked to emotions.

Legendary Brands use symbols in a special way. Symbols most always remind the individual of a brand narrative. For example, loyal American Express card members subscribe to a brand narrative that connects the sacred belief of smart financial management with a culture of upwardly mobile people that are financially successful. The American Express card is a badge of honor. To carry a card, the card member must make some sacrifices. For example, the card member usually pays an annual fee to have an American Express card, and this fee is greater than the annual fees charged by competitive bank cards. Also, the typical American Express card is a charge card, not a credit card. That means that the card member must pay the entire balance upon delivery of a statement, unlike credit cards in which the balance can be revolved. Visa and MasterCard members can elect to pay only a portion of their bill when it arrives.

Why would someone who values money and financial management show pride in producing a card that costs more and is less flexible? American Express card members delight in producing their cards at point of purchase. The card is a symbol of their financial status and their participation in the American Express brand narrative. The annual fee is a meaningful symbol of membership for card members, a kind of ritual initiation. The fact that they must resolve their balance each month reasserts their sacred belief of smart money management. It tells others one of two things: the card member never spends more than he or she can afford (i.e., the member is a disciplined consumer), or resolving a monthly card balance is not an issue for this card member (i.e., the member is loaded with cash). The American Express card is thus a powerful brand symbol that reinforces a narrative that differentiates an American Express card member from other credit card holders.

Automobiles and fashion are the ultimate symbols of consumer brand narratives. Women who carry Kate Spade handbags are actually carrying a symbol of a metropolitan fashion narrative. It is also a narrative of authenticity and individual expression (despite the possibility that Kate Spade handbags have become so predominant in Los Angeles and New York that they actually say more about homogeneity than they do about uniqueness).

An automobile is nothing more than a locomotive symbol. A humorous Internet posting even went so far as to categorize individuals by the cars they drive (see the sidebar). Humor aside, automobiles are largely the value of their brands. The people who drive them also see them as symbols of a brand narrative they wish to communicate about themselves. Many people who drive a Mercedes Benz wish to let others know that they are part of the upper class. Saturn owners wish to communicate practical American values. People who drive the Nissan Xterra want others to know that they live life to the extreme and enjoy adventure.

YOU ARE WHAT YOU DRIVE

Automobiles are very visible symbols of a consumer's personality. A humorous Internet chain mail attempted to decipher the meaning of some of these brand symbolic affiliations.

- *Acura Integra:* I have always wanted to own the Buick of sports cars.
- *Buick Park Avenue:* I am older than 34 of the 50 states.
- *Cadillac Eldorado:* I am a very good Mary Kay salesman.
- *Cadillac Seville:* I am a pimp.
- *Chevrolet Corvette:* I'm in a mid-life crisis and I wear a toupee.
- *Chevrolet El Camino:* I am leading a militia to overthrow the government.
- *Datsun 280Z:* I have a kilo of cocaine in my wheel well.
- *Dodge Daytona:* I delivered pizza for four years to get this car.
- *Ford Mustang:* I slow down to 85 in school zones.
- *Ford Crown Victoria:* I enjoy having people slow to 55 MPH and change lanes when I pull up behind them.
- *Geo Storm:* I will start the 11th grade in the fall.
- *Honda Civic:* I have just graduated and have no credit.
- *Honda Accord:* I lack any originality and am basically a lemming.
- *Infiniti Q45:* I am a physician with 17 malpractice suits pending.
- *Jaguar XJ6:* I am so rich I will pay 80K for a car that is in the shop 280 days per year.
- *Lincoln Town Car:* I live for bingo and covered dish suppers.
- *Mercedes 500SL:* I will beat you up if you ask me for an autograph.
- *Mercedes 560SEL:* I have a daughter named Bitsy and a son named Cole.
- *Mazda Miata:* I do not fear being decapitated by an eighteen-wheeler.

- *MGB:* I am dating a mechanic.
- *Nissan 300ZX:* I have yet to complete my divorce proceedings.
- *Nissan Exterra:* I snowboard naked while playing with scissors.
- *Oldsmobile Cutlass:* I just stole this car and I'm going to make a fortune off the parts.
- *Peugeot 505 Diesel:* I am on the EPA's Ten Most Wanted List.
- *Plymouth Neon:* I sincerely enjoy doing the Macarena and listening to boy bands.
- *Porsche 944:* I am dating big-haired women that otherwise would be inaccessible to me.
- *Rolls Royce Silver Shadow:* I think Pat Buchanan is a tad bit too liberal.
- *Toyota Camry:* I am still in the closet.
- *Volkswagen Cabriolet:* I am out of the closet.
- *Volkswagen Microbus:* I am tripping right now from something I smoked last night.
- *Volvo 740 Wagon:* I am frightened of my wife.

CASE STUDY: Apple Computer

On a brisk January morning, Kevin Arbogast beams like a child awaiting the imminent start of Christmas. He has traveled more than a thousand miles to wait outside in the cold with nearly 800 others of his faith. It is a pilgrimage he has planned for several years, saving a few dollars here and there and generously testing the limits of his credit card to achieve the journey.

It is hard for a lot of people to understand Kevin. The dedication and zeal he gives to his cause is nothing short of fanatical. The pilgrimage itself seems to most people an extreme measure. Kevin is unphased by such criticism. He is, by all other accounts, a normal, balanced individual. In his mind, the cause deserves the credit for such balance. To others, it is his one eccentric quality.

At the center of his devotion is one man. To Kevin, and virtually all of the other loyal followers waiting in line with him, this man is the symbol of all that they hold dear. His own heroic journey reaffirms that one man with a great idea and the will to persevere can make a difference. No matter how much criticism the world threw at this man, he pursued his dream undaunted. No matter how much attention the world paid to him, he never lost sight of his beliefs and his principles. He stayed the course and changed the world.

As the congregation multiplies in numbers on this blustery morning, symbols of the great leader's legacy are plentiful: articles of clothing, books, magazines, and other paraphernalia. A few yards back from where he stands, another young man plays a video of one of the great leader's speeches on a small, portable monitor. Anticipation is passed about like a cup of piping hot coffee.

Strangely, the pilgrimage Kevin made is not for one of the world's organized religions. The Dali Lama is not the man these people came to praise. Instead, they traveled far and wide to attend the annual MacWorld Expo in San Francisco. The man whose proselytism they eagerly await is Steve Jobs, Apple Computer's founder and CEO.

Every January, Mac enthusiasts from all walks of life converge in San Francisco to see the latest developments Apple has to offer, buy Apple related products, and hear what's soon to come from the man who helped give the world its first personal computer. This event has become such an important part of Apple's existence that all critical, new product launches are timed to coincide with the annual Expo. Each year, Apple and Jobs are expected to "one up" the year before. Fans are rarely disappointed.

Apple is one of the quintessential Legendary Brands. Despite its small share of the market, its customers are textbook loyalists. Some are certifiable martyrs, known to go to great lengths to ensure that a Macintosh computer sits on their desk instead of any other. Others have become bona-fide activists, staging rallies and letter-writing campaigns, "flaming" Web sites, and bringing lawsuits to ensure that Steve Jobs' electronic progeny retain their rightful place in the digital world.

Apple's ongoing consumer bond is tied to a powerful brand mythology that ultimately saved the company. The heroic journey of Apple Computer might just as well have been written by Dante, for it is an epic journey that surprised faithful and enemies alike.

Modern technology, especially technology that appears to think, is often a frightening and foreign concept. In the 1970s, when computers were finally becoming a reality and not the subject of science fiction, people often formed dark opinions of thinking machines. Stanley Kubrick's *2001: A Space Odyssey* perhaps demonstrates the way that many people thought about computers. They likely held this opinion because most computers were out of consumer reach. They were large, expensive machines used only by business. When consumers did interact with them, it was often with strange and unfamiliar tools, such as punch cards.

Apple Computer's founding sacred belief survives to this day: that computers and technology should enable us to do things that can change the world by being radically easy to use. At the age of 15, Steve Jobs and his best friend, Steve Wozniak, built the very first Apple Computer in their garage. It wasn't a very elegant device and it lacked a lot of software functionality, but they succeeded in creating a device that could sit on a desktop, rather than fill the space of a room. Because this thinking machine was built by two suburban teenagers in a garage workshop, they demonstrated that this technology was affordable and within the reach of the average consumer.

Apple Computer started life as a business phenomenon. Prior to Apple, industry giants such as IBM had written off the personal computer as a novelty. They believed the big business machines they built would be the only true applications for the technology. Apparently, they never watched television or listened to the radio. These technologies were also once rumored to be novelties without a consumer future. Consumers bought Apple Computers, schools bought Apple Computers, and yes, businesses began buying Apple Computers. It did not take long for IBM and others to realize that it had better enter the personal computer market or watch a couple of wiry teenagers eat their lunch. The dramatic narrative of Apple Computer was born the day that IBM decided to enter the race.

Steve Jobs is the original and quintessential brand agent for Apple and its sacred beliefs. Jobs dared to take on IBM. The day he stood tall in the shadow of one of the darlings of the American stock market, he truly embodied Apple's sacred belief of changing the world. That narrative continued to unfold throughout the early 1980s. In response to Apple's growth, IBM launched the PC. Using its formidable distribution power and economies of scale, the PC immediately obtained an impressive share of the market, predominantly with business customers. In fairness, IBM gained many share points by expanding the market. Once IBM entered, many business owners began taking the technology seriously. That is not to say that Apple did not experience attrition in its customer base.

Apple responded by doing things differently again. In 1983, Jobs formed an almost renegade division within Apple to redefine the personal computer. His instruction to the team was to create a machine that would be "insanely great." The result came in 1984 with the launch of the Macintosh. This machine changed Apple forever. Macintosh made it fundamentally easier for the user to interact with a personal computer. Rather than memorizing cryptic syntax, users could now point and click from pull-down menus using a new device called a *mouse*. They did not need to configure the machine. Instead, they plugged it into a wall, and maybe connected a printer. Sitting in front of a Macintosh, they peered into a friendly virtual environment that borrowed a lot of things they already understood, like desktops, files, and windows.

Former Apple Software Evangelist Guy Kawasaki described the real power of Macintosh. "Unlike most other personal computers . . . Macintosh ignited a wave of fervor and zeal in early adopters, hobbyists, and college students who didn't care about 'standards,' in third-party software developers, and in Apple employees. Why? Because Macintosh made its users feel more effective. They could do old things better; they could do new things they could not before; and they could do things they never dreamed of."[10]

Apple launched the product by solidifying its brand narrative with a television commercial that aired only once, and yet holds incredibly high recall value even to this day. The infamous 1984 spot ran during the Super Bowl, a savvy media planning decision that proved expensive but effective. Millions watched as the sacred belief system, brand agents, and narrative of Apple came magnetically together for the first time. Playing upon the fears and concerns many pondered because of George Orwell's apocalyptic book, *1984*, the television spot depicted a cold, gray world influenced by an oppressive, big brother. Big brother, of course, translated to IBM. Sitting inside a dark auditorium, thousands of lifeless drones stare hypnotically at a large-scale monitor. On it, big brother spouts meaningless brainwashing about the "information purification directive." Meanwhile, our attention begins to focus on a young woman in colorful clothing, running down a hallway and pursued by men in futuristic security garb. She breaks into the auditorium and throws a giant sledgehammer at the huge display. The image of big brother explodes and the drones are exposed to a freeing blast of energy and radiation. The spot closes with a simple tag line: On January 24th Apple Computer will introduce Macintosh. And you will see why 1984 won't be like *1984*.

Neither Steve Jobs nor the Macintosh product ever surfaced in the 1984 commercial. The commercial implanted the heroic narrative of Apple Computer in the minds of millions, and it was not long before that narrative transferred to Jobs and Macintosh.

Apple's brand mythology cycle found completion with the Macintosh product launch. In an effort to encourage trial and usage, Apple seeded support groups. These clubs of people who owned Macintoshes were designed to help others get the information they needed about the product and keep them happy about their decision to buy a Mac. But these support groups took on a life of their own. They became the first brand communities of the Apple brand. To this day, many of them still exist.

Rituals emerged, too. Apple launched an ambitious product trial program. People were invited to stop by their local Apple retailer and "test drive" a Mac. This ritual created a state of liminality for many people. They entered the retailer either a neophyte computer user or predisposed to some other computer technology, even Apple's own successful line of Apple II personal computers. They left, provision Mac in hand, in a liminal state, not really Mac owners yet, but changed from their previous state. This state continued for a few days while they experienced the workings of the machine. In the end, they either decided to buy one or return to their former state. However, they emerged somewhat changed by the experience. They now knew what a Mac could do.

MacWorld was born. It served the same function as the test drive program by creating a sacred place where every piece of technology related to the Mac was on display. Users could sample hundreds of products and strengthen their relationship with the brand. Along the way they were exposed to rhythmic music and emotionally provoking speeches and demonstrations. MacWorld also brought the brand tribe together and established the social standards of the Macintosh community.

Symbols were an integral part of the Apple brand system. Every Macintosh that shipped included a set of self-adhesive brand stickers. These simple decals of the Apple multi-color logo appeared on automobiles, books, office cubes, and walls. They told people that the bearer was part of the Apple brand culture. They also communicated, implicitly, the Apple narrative. When asked why Jobs chose Apple as the brand name for his company, he said that it was the most fundamental and comforting image he could think of for a computer. What could be more simple and understandable to every consumer than an apple?

The Apple narrative did not stop there, although its next chapter was a dark one. In 1985, Apple's new CEO John Sculley fired Steve Jobs. To loyal Mac users this was an outrage, but to most Americans, the event went unnoticed. Perhaps Jobs was no longer the dominant agent of the Apple brand. Perhaps something or someone else had replaced him. Both assertions are true and incorrect. Jobs was still an agent for Apple. Years after his departure many people still linked his story with the ideals they associated with the Apple brand. However,

Macintosh became a new agent for the brand. The product, and its story became inextricably linked for many users with the Apple belief system. Macintosh became both an agent and a symbol.

Over the next ten years, Apple's story got more bleak. While IBM's dominance of the personal computer market waned (although due more to nimble competitors like Dell and Compaq) a new opposing force emerged. Microsoft and its new operating system, Windows, made Macintosh less distinct in the marketplace. Windows incorporated nearly all of the advanced technologies the Mac OS introduced first, but Windows was easier and cheaper to acquire. In time, it also housed a larger software library. Mac's share of the market dwindled from more than 20 percent of the market to barely 5 percent.

From 1994 to 1996, a strange and tumultuous saga unfolded at Apple's corporate headquarters. But in the end, something happened that would save the Apple brand from extinction. Steve Jobs returned as Apple's CEO and reasserted himself as the quintessential brand agent for Apple and all that it stands for. Apple's advertising was the first to re-establish the brand narrative. TBWA\Chiat\Day, Apple's advertising agency, returned to the central and most sacred belief of both Steve Jobs and Apple: Thinking differently can change the world. Their first campaign, "Think Different," featured historic photographs and film clips of creative thinkers who changed the world. These included Thomas Edison, Albert Einstein, Mohammed Ali, Martha Graham, Alfred Hitchcock, and Pablo Picasso, among others. The product was never shown, in part because Jobs needed time to retool the Apple product line, but also because it was more important to re-establish the dramatic narrative that made Apple a Legendary Brand than it was to show product.

Shortly thereafter, Jobs delivered a simplified line of personal computers that once again redefined what consumers expected from a thinking machine. Apple's new line of iMac's, iBook's, and professional machines were accented by rounded shapes, vibrant colors, and stylish design. Returning to themes they first introduced in 1984, the new machines were easy to setup and configure. Best of all, they were feature-rich and came standard with many options people did not expect from a personal computer, such as built-in DVD drives, Internet connectivity, and plenty of processing power.

Jobs appeared on the cover of every major business publication. His familiar image, dressed in all black, with a confident smile and charismatic glow was a striking difference from what many people would have expected from a company that was not supposed to last. It was also a markedly different image for a technology CEO, especially the disheveled hair, unstylish appearance and awkward demeanor of Microsoft's Bill Gates, the menacing nemesis of Apple.

The future of Apple is still a question that conjures heated debates from rival factions. It is unlikely that Apple will ever regain a double-digit share of the personal computer market. However, the brand has a strong chance of survival if it continues to build upon its brand mythology. Apple's worldview, that the creative people are the ones that change the world, is a theme that resonates truth for millions. Apple's innovative technologies and constant drive to make computers better and different serve as physical proof for this sacred belief. Apple recently took bold steps to let this narrative touch the brand culture that subscribes to it. Branded retail stores are opening in select regions of the U.S. The stores offer an immersive brand experience and a chance to connect with priests and priestesses of the culture (every Apple Store houses a resident "Genius" to help you solve your Mac problem). It is this momentum and commitment to its brand mythology that will ultimately enable Apple to survive for some time to come.

CHAPTER 3

MYTH AND THE NARRATIVE OF LEGENDARY BRANDS

Religions, philosophies, arts, the social forms of
primitive and historic man, prime discoveries in
science and technology, the very dreams that blister
sleep, boil up from the basic, magic ring of myth.

Joseph Campbell
The Hero with a Thousand Faces

Throughout the ages, the myths of man have been the constant companion of creativity. No matter how hard we strive to be original, our creative endeavors are always the product of our shared library of myths. Our social fabric, sacred institutions, and moral boundaries frequently mirror the models dictated by a common mythology. Today, the mythological underpinnings that inspired Sophocles and Shakespeare, Michelangelo and Matisse, live on. They manifest all around our modern world, but most notably in the guise of Legendary Brands.

Myth is the most superior form of storytelling known to mankind, but to understand it and its impact on Legendary Brands, you need a basic understanding of the elements of story. This chapter serves as a guide for the marketer. You will be introduced to the inter-related structures of stories, narratives, legends, and myths. On the surface level, you will gain a working vocabulary to guide you through the rest of the book, for the glossary of storytelling vernacular is not standardized, and many terms are used interchangeably in other contexts. To avoid confusion, we require precise distinctions, which are provided herein. You should note, however, that these definitions are only provided to help you navigate this book. Some terms have different meanings in other material.

Legendary Brands do "boil up from the basic, magic ring of myth." Myth explains their power, appeal, and longevity. For this reason, the latter part of this chapter dips beneath the surface of storytelling structure to help you learn about the power of myth and its crucial influence on the power of Legendary Brands. Storytelling is more pervasive in advertising and marketing than most people realize. Virtually every brand employs at least one element of storytelling, but it is the Legendary Brand's use of myth that separates its adventures in marketing from other brands. An understanding of how and why myth works will help you to better understand Legendary Brands.

THE BEAT

The *beat* is the atomic foundation of every story and narrative—the smallest part of a story that still retains the essence of story itself. The beat goes by many names. You might have heard it called an event, a phrase, an episode, a scene, an anecdote, a statement, or a chapter. Whatever the name, the beat is always a component of a larger story structure.

The beat is a logical construct that demonstrates a cause and effect relationship. Like the basic laws of physics, a beat subscribes to the theory that a subject will remain at rest until something else acts upon it. Without this cause and effect relationship, a story fails to materialize.

Imagine that a widower sits at his breakfast table, reading the morning paper. As he turns the page, he sees a picture of his deceased wife, still very much alive, next to a headline that reads, "Chicago Heiress Weds Hotel Financier." Realizing that the wife he thought was dead is alive and about to be married, the man gathers his things and hurries out of the room.

This is a very simple beat, and a perfect cause and effect relationship. The realization that his wife is still alive causes the effect of the man hurrying from the room. If that man took no note of the article, or ignored it, and kept reading while drinking his morning coffee, we would have no beat.

This imaginary scenario raises another important point about beats: They raise a dramatic question. If the beat stands alone (that is, it is not connected to other beats), it must answer the question. This is not the case in our example. When the beat ends, the audience is left with a very nagging question: What will the widower do? Will he confront his wife? Will he alert the authorities? Will he beg to have her back? Will he stalk the suitor out of jealousy? We do not know the answer, and so tension now exists that must be resolved.

Figure 3.1 provides a graphic representation of the beat. Note that some force acts upon the subject, setting it in motion. For a beat to stand alone, this motion must come to an end or enter a steady state at the conclusion of the beat. To understand this concept, consider the most common form of a stand-alone beat: the joke. Most jokes begin

FIGURE 3.1 The Beat

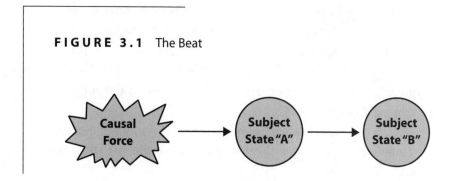

with a setup (the external force that creates the cause) and end with a punch line (the effect). Every time you've heard the phrase, "a guy walks into a bar," you've been introduced to a beat. For the joke to be funny, the beat must end with a clear effect that satisfies your anticipation. Few jokes survive that require multiple beats to satisfy your curiosity.

Marketers have been using beats by themselves for decades. Every outdoor advertisement you find is essentially a stand-alone beat. With so little time to catch the viewer's attention, outdoor advertisers earn your attention by a quick payoff. This form of advertising is perhaps the most underrated of all marketing communications. Consider its simplicity and its ability to make you laugh or take notice from the delivery of a stand-alone beat. While it is true that many of these advertisements do little more than instruct you to turn right on the next exit, the ones that employ the beat are works of pure art and efficiency. The notable masters of the form include apparel brands, alcohol brands, and automotive brands.

Perhaps no Legendary Brand has more resilience with the beat and outdoor advertising than Absolut. Absolut is a brand that employs simple, elegant marketing magic. Every print and outdoor advertisement features an artful depiction of the infamous Absolut bottle design, accompanied by two words, one of them always *Absolut*. One advertisement featured a photograph of a pool shaped like the bottle, followed by the words *Absolut L.A.*. Another ad, featured first in *Playboy* magazine, folded out to reveal a picture of the Absolut bottle disrobed of its familiar markings. The copy: *Absolut Centerfold*. In each of these examples, a story was not presented, but a beat was. Like any good joke, these advertisements feature a cause and effect. It is as if to ask: What if the Absolut bottle was set in Los Angeles? The effect: It would be a swimming pool. The force acting upon the subject is the environment or context it is placed within.

Many television advertisements are stand-alone beats, but the most memorable commercials go a step beyond the beat; they become stories.

STORY: The Beat Goes On

Throughout this book, you will see the word *story* often. Most of us instinctively know what a story is, but might find it hard to offer a precise definition. For our purposes, a story is a three-part linear sequence of events. Aristotle, the ancient Greek philosopher, called these three parts *beginning, middle,* and *end,* but we shall refer to them as *situation, complication,* and *resolution,* graphically shown in Figure 3.2. Notice that within this three-act structure, many beats are delivered. These beats increase the dramatic tension, and later resolve it. The most significant of all the beats, is the climax: the moment in the story when the opposing forces come directly to a head. All stories have at least one beat, the climax, but all beats do not necessarily tell a story. To understand the difference, let us examine the last element of the story, the resolution.

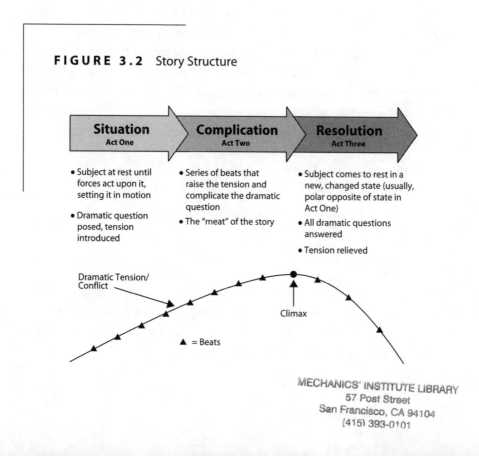

FIGURE 3.2 Story Structure

For a stand-alone beat to qualify as a story, its outcome must resolve all of the audience's unanswered questions. Returning to our example of the widower who discovered that his wife was still alive, the beat does not represent a story. It is a beat because a cause was presented and an effect shown. Tension was created, but it was not relieved. This is the fundamental difference between a beat and a story. A beat can create tension, but not resolve it. The conclusion of a story must always resolve the dramatic tension.

Both a story and a beat transform a subject (usually a human character) from one state of being to another. The most effective beats and stories do this by dramatizing polarity: from ecstasy to rage, from innocence to guilt, from humility to pride, from happiness to despair. Whether comedy or drama, the story engages the audience by showing the cause and effect relationship(s) that make these polar changes in the subject. The difference between a beat and a story is that a beat shows only one change, whereas a story will usually show many. For example, it is rare that a character will transform from ecstasy to rage in one beat. Such a shift in emotional state rarely occurs except in extreme conditions or by acute manic depressive types. To get from ecstasy to rage, most stories dramatize a progression of beats. Each beat causes an incremental micro-change in emotional state that affects the polar change demonstrated by the story. So, for example, a story that presents a subject transforming from ecstasy to rage, might contain five beats:

1. From ecstasy to discomfort
2. From discomfort to annoyance
3. From annoyance to frustration
4. From frustration to anger
5. From anger to rage

Perhaps no other commercial demonstrates how beats are effectively used in this manner, than the award-winning "Aaron Burr" spot created by San Francisco advertising house Goodby Silverstein & Partners for the "Got Milk" television campaign.

We fade in and pan across the dusty interior of an American historical museum that commemorates the fateful duel between Alexander Hamilton and Aaron Burr. Close up shots reveal illustrations of the duel, artifacts from the lives of Hamilton and Burr, and volumes of historical documentation. A radio plays in the background. From it an announcer introduces a familiar quiz-show format promotion in which one lucky listener will be called. If the listener can answer a random trivia question he or she will win a grand prize.

Our attention meanwhile shifts to an awkward young man in his early twenties. He has a lanky, Ichabod Crane physique and a contented disposition. He is totally absorbed in a peanut butter sandwich, spreading a thick layer of peanut butter over a piece of bread. As he takes a bite of the gooey snack, the announcer reads the question: "Who shot Alexander Hamilton?" Within seconds, the phone in the museum begins to ring in sync with the on-air sound effect.

The young man, suddenly realizing this is his lucky day, rushes to the phone, lifts the receiver and, with a mouth full of peanut butter and bread, proudly says, "Aaaain Buhhhhh." Of course, the radio announcer cannot understand what the young man says. Concerned he may miss his big opportunity, the young man reaches for a carton of milk on a nearby table, but it is empty. He meanwhile keeps repeating, "Aaaain Buhhh." Panic sets in. He frantically searches the room for a splash of milk to clear his palette, but it is futile. The radio announcer says with finality, "Oh, I'm sorry caller, time's up." A dial tone. As we fade out, the defeated young man whimpers the name of Aaron Burr. The last image the viewer sees is a simple graphic: Got Milk.

This popular spot told a story through four simple beats:

1. From contentment to excitement
2. From excitement to concern
3. From concern to panic
4. From panic to despair

NARRATIVE: Adding a Point of View to the Story

Many people use the terms *story* and *narrative* interchangeably. In truth, the dividing line is anything but black and white. A story is primarily an ordering—a cohesive and logical sequence of events that demonstrate the change in the state of a subject. It does this through the three-act structure, which we delineated as situation, complication, and resolution. The purpose of this structure is to create rising tension and resolve that tension, leaving the audience with no unanswered questions.

A narrative, on the other hand, adds a point of view to a story. The easiest way to understand the difference is to focus on the root word, *narrate*. A narrative is a story as told by a narrator. Thus, one story could have multiple narratives, each depending on the voice recounting it, and the point of view they select to frame the sequence of events. Narrative is the tool of the marketer; story is the tool of the reporter.

Rashomon, the famous Kurosawa film, is a perfect illustration of this distinction. The story told concerns the rape of a Japanese woman and the murder of her husband, deep within the forests of ancient Japan. However, the story is told four times, each from the point of view of a different witness to the crimes. What results are four completely different dramatic experiences—some tragic, some comic—achieved solely by switching the storyteller.

Narratives can be expressed as an equation: story + theme. The theme is a layer added to the story to instruct, provide an emotional connection, or to impart deeper meaning. For example, a newspaper report describing the events that unfolded in a Nazi concentration camp would not embody the same meaning or emotional connection as the story retold by a camp survivor. The survivor's narrative includes a voice that gives the story a deeper meaning and emotional color.

Marketing is much better at crafting narrative because advertisers generally wish to communicate a point of view that differentiates their brand from the competition. A press release about a new product is usually a story; it attempts to present objective facts. A print adver-tisement, however, is nearly always a narrative because it attempts to persuade you. Most television advertisements, particularly those that utilize voice-overs, are narratives—stories with a point of view.

The importance of narrative versus story will become more clear in the next chapter, where we consider personal narratives and the stories that each of us construct to form our identity. For the moment, remember that a narrative is a story with a point of view, message, or theme.

LEGENDS

Legends are stories and narratives passed down from one gener-ation to the next, usually orally. They are generally believed to have some factual or historical basis. An important distinction about a leg-end is that it has no distinct narrative voice. Because it is passed down, each time it is recounted, the story has a new narrator. This constant change in narration has pros and cons. On the positive side, legends have staying power. As each new narrator shares the story, the narra-tive takes on a completely new life. Some legends last for centuries, and have enormous popular appeal.

The negative aspect of legends is that they are easily distorted. A famous social experiment illustrates how. Ten people are placed in a circle. One person is told a detailed "secret" and instructed to whisper it to the next member in the circle. This process continues with each member whispering the secret to the next closest member. With un-canny regularity, by the time the secret has traveled back to the point of origination, the information is distorted, often to comedic effect. For instance, if the secret began, "Marty spent four hundred dollars on a new toupee so that he could steal the heart of a girl half his age," it might return to the source as, "The young girl Marty was dating stole four hundred dollars from him and ran off with his new toupee." Ob-viously, there is a direct correlation between the distortion of the in-formation and the number of people it passes through.

Legends suffer from the same fate. Over time, they are influenced by their narrators. Their reliance on successive generations of story-tellers, who may be influenced by changing social, cultural, and ethno-graphic conditions, exposes them to interpretation and creative license. The most common form of legend is the so-called urban legend. Most of us have been exposed to one of these at one time or another. A re-cent e-mail chain details the plight of a sad young man who was sup-posedly swept up by a firefighting helicopter while he was snorkeling in a mountain lake. The helicopter was collecting water to extinguish a nearby forest fire. For fifteen minutes, the terrified young man rode inside the darkened belly of the chopper with no way to inform the pilot of his dilemma. His tragic adventure supposedly came to an end as he fell to his death when the chopper spilled its contents onto the raging fire.

I've talked to dozens of people who received this same e-mail, or heard about it from someone they knew. Several people reported that they knew someone who could substantiate its validity. Even though such evidence never materializes, the story retains its appeal. It has a life of its own, woven into social consciousness.

In his book, *The Vanishing Hitchhiker*, Jan Harold Brunvand ex-plains that urban legends must often satisfy three conditions to sur-vive. They must contain a strong basic story appeal; they must have a foundation in actual belief; and they must hint at a meaningful mes-sage or moral.[1]

Legends abound in marketing and can be a tactical weapon or a lingering curse. From a tactical point of view, guerilla marketing tech-niques employ legends to their benefit. Those who employ guerilla marketing attempt to seed their marketing message within popular culture, hoping it will circulate and create a buzz that drives product sales. It is the ultimate example of grass-roots marketing, and if the brand the effort supports is an "edge" brand to begin with, the more distorted the legend becomes, the greater the benefit for the brand. Certainly, Harley-Davidson has enjoyed many benefits from the count-less legends that circle the nation about folk heroes and outlaws that rode in on a Harley.

There can be a devastating downside to legends, however. Some brands have been hijacked by the pervasive, and sometimes absurd, legends that unwittingly formed around the brand.

For many years, Kentucky Fried Chicken battled a nagging urban legend that is completely unsubstantiated. The legend alleged that an unsuspecting couple discovered a deep-fried rat mixed in with their bucket of chicken. Despite numerous attempts to quell the story, the lack of a lawsuit or other demonstrative evidence to validate the legend, and a significant rebranding effort, many consumers continue to believe that this story is based on true events.

Procter & Gamble, one of the world's largest packaged goods companies, faced a similarly daunting urban legend. This one involved the Devil himself. The legend asserted that the founders of P&G were members of a secret satanic cult and that the P&G brand mark contained symbols of the occult. The legend claimed that the seemingly upstanding senior management team engaged in frightful rituals behind closed doors. Again, these claims could not be substantiated with any tangible evidence, and the brand mark could be traced to no nefarious mysticism. Nevertheless, P&G scrapped their historic logo and spent several years, plus a tidy sum of money, to counteract the effects of the legend.

Of course, in some instances, such legends actually improved the brand. Tommy Hilfiger launched the line of clothing that bears his name with the aspiration of creating uncommon fashion for the upwardly mobile man. His apparel was supposed to push men's fashion artfully against the grain. His use of strikingly contrasting primary colors became an instant fad, and a powerful competitive challenge to the otherwise sedentary, nostalgic stylings of Ralph Lauren's Polo line.

The Hilfiger brand succumbed to a legend that changed its fate and created a fortune in the process. It became the fashion badge of the urban gang community. Convicted felons and militant rap artists were seen wearing Hilfiger's signature brand marks. Stories emerged into legends about gang lifestyle, each featuring characters clad in Hilfiger clothing. (Note: the same fate fell upon FILA some years before, and is currently affecting Timberland).

The foundation of the new brand legend attached to Hilfiger contained Brunvand's three precedent conditions. First, it had a strong basic story appeal. To the inner-city audience, the new Hilfiger legend was motivating. Hilfiger was stylish and it had cache. Wearing it began to symbolize success and style. It was also ironic, and the irony did not escape the new audience. They knew very well that this brand of clothing was designed for "rich white guys." This audience felt a sense of entitlement, like eighteenth-century French revolutionists. No longer would the aristocracy own all fashion.

Second, the legend had a foundation in actual belief. There was some evidence to support the story that Hilfiger was the signature brand of gang-bangers. They were seen photographed in Hilfiger clothing. You could see them wearing it on the street, and on the nightly newscast.

Finally, the legend had a meaningful message. For the new brand audience, it symbolized a shift in power. Further, to those who were particularly disgruntled, it contained an air of vengeance, karma, and defiance.

You may have noticed that, whereas stories and narratives have direct marketing execution corollaries, our discussion of legends skews more toward overall brand imagery and associations. Legends come very close to the essence of what makes a Legendary Brand, but legends have limitations, as we have seen. They are very hard to control, and they change much too frequently and easily. They are the less developed cousins of what truly makes a Legendary Brand remarkable—myth.

MYTH: Hard-Wired Stories

Like legends, myths are passed down for generations and, in some cases, they appear to have some root in truth or history. But the similarities end there. Legends pop up like rumors, circulate like wildfire, and ebb and flow based on the current narrator. Legends are frequently circulated as a novelty—a shallow amusement. Myths, stories that never wane from the collective unconscious, provide a meaningful way for people to orient and understand their world. These are story archetypes, tucked away in a hidden realm of our cognitive faculties. Despite geographic dispersion, cultural differences, and the steady pace of cognitive evolution, the history of homo sapiens is marked by the recurrence of an all too familiar set of myths. Though the characters may have different names and slightly different physical characteristics, the stories told about these characters maintain an eerie consistency.

For instance, people are often amazed by the striking similarities between Buddha, Christ, and Mohammad. Some theorize that this deity was one in the same, but another explanation is that the mythic essence of these sacred heroes are part of a narrative that transcends borders and cultural tastes. In short, these myths are as much a part of our cognition as fingers are a part of our hand.

To understand the orientation of myth relative to the other forms of story we discussed, consider Figure 3.3. Along the horizontal axis, we find two dimensions to the story-form, based on who is telling the story: a singular or omniscient point of view, and a collective, or plural,

FIGURE 3.3 Story, Narrative, Legend, and Myth

| | | **Storyteller** | |
		First/Third Person	**Collective/Plural**
Meaning/Emotional Context	**Separable**	**Story** • No clear point of view • Meaning is left largely to the audience • Usually an objective voice	**Legend** • Created through chain of storytellers • Meaning driven by context, storyteller, and ethic/geographic characteristics
	Inseparable	**Narrative** • Voice/opinion of the storyteller clearly linked • Narrator's influence on the story provides meaning and provides emotional context	**Myth** • Story structure rests in the collective unconscious • Meaning linked to timeless morals, principles, and shared beliefs

point of view. The story-forms on the left-hand side have a single storyteller. A story is told from an objective, third-person singular point of view, whereas, narrative is told from a more personal, first-person point of view. The story-forms on the right-hand side have many story-tellers. Legends are passed down, and the story is augmented as it passes from one storyteller to the next. Whereas, myth is a story stored within all of us. Its structure rests in our collective unconscious, and evidence of its ubiquity abounds in every corner of the globe.

The vertical axis differentiates these forms by their meaning or emotional context. The story-forms at the top are easily separable from meaning. Stories are generally objective. A perfect story has no meaning. It is left to the recipient to interpret. Legends frequently have meaning, but it is highly influenced by the context of the legend. Thus, when the legend is told by one storyteller it may have one particular meaning, but then switches to another emotional context when the next storyteller recounts it.

The story-forms along the bottom are much more difficult to separate from their emotional context or meaning. The beauty of narrative is that the story is laced with the storyteller's point of view. *The Great Gatsby* ceases to be *The Great Gatsby* if Nick Carraway's voice is omitted. It becomes an entirely different novel, and the meaning is lost. Similarly, myth is very hard to separate from the meaning attached to it. Every myth that stands the test of time is linked to a timeless moral, principle, or belief. These morals and principles are not very controversial. They are the roots of civilization: do not steal, do not kill, do unto others. . .

Myth plays a very important role in our lives. While myth has always served as the muse of poets and playwrights, it was, until recently, the indisputable explanation for man's existence. Today, in our era of science and technological progress, few of the old cosmological mysteries remain for myth to solve, yet our basic need to experience myth in our lives remains. As a result, the mythic constructs of the past manifest to give meaning to other phenomena in our lives—namely, our ability to socially orient ourselves in a fast-changing world. Where we once looked to sacred artifacts for the power to heal, triumph, or cure the pain of unrequited love, today we imbue these powers on consumer goods that promise to render magic. Where once we modeled our behavior after demigods, prophets, and mighty warriors, today we look to celebrities, athletes, and CEOs for role models, infusing them with heroic attributes. Where once we made pilgrimages to sacred lands, today we journey to theme parks, resorts, and shopping malls hoping to replenish our spirits with the healing devices they embody.

Legendary Brands leverage the power of myth to establish meaning and common ground in the goods and services they represent. Study any one of these brands and you will uncover a storyline that is timeless and familiar. To understand how Legendary Brands tell stories to consumers, you must look no further than that mythic storyline, for it is the root of their tremendous brand equity. In the scientific realm, researchers are mapping the human genome to understand the fundamental underpinnings of human physiology. In our study of Legendary Brands, the mythic foundation is the genome that maps the brand's soul. Myth provides the code by which the consumer mind creates the brand narrative, it is the strategy by which the brand manager sustains an authentic competitive advantage, it is the source of the brand's personality, and it bestows a social life upon the brand.

CONNECTING THE DOTS

Advertising plays an important role in the development and sustenance of a brand's narrative, but once that narrative is established, it has the potential to take on a life of its own. Legendary Brands convey their narratives in spite of their advertising. Their story is told through many channels, some of them much more intimate and experiential than the traditional 30-second broadcast spot.

Legendary Brands tell stories by providing us with just enough prompting to trigger the mind's natural tendency to fill in the missing gaps. Because the myths Legendary Brands convey are part of our collective unconscious, it takes only a single reference point, a clue, for our subconscious mind to retreat to the mental library and piece together the remainder of the narrative.

The visual center of our brain clearly performs this task all the time. Consider the works of impressionist painters. What is painted on the canvas is not a realistic depiction of the subject. Using rough brush strokes and a convergence of colors, they present beautiful representations of natural life. Standing an inch away from the canvas, these works are only dabs of paint. Step back, and order emerges. We see seascapes, still lifes, and artful portraiture.

Perhaps the greatest illustration of this concept can be seen in the post-impressionist paintings of Georges Seurat. The sanguine scenes of nineteenth-century French public life, such as *Sunday Afternoon on the Island of Grande Jatte*, are nothing more than thousands of tiny, multicolored dots painstakingly arranged on a large canvas. In the center of this canvas is what appears to be an aristocratic lady holding a parasol. In reality, it is merely a jumble of pixels. Our mind does the heavy lifting, ordering the pixels into a beautiful and meaningful image.

If a machine were to examine these paintings and report back on what it saw, it would describe the obvious: dots of paint in a semi-randomized pattern. Our brain, on the other hand, computes what the dots of paint represent. Our minds literally trick us into seeing what is not there.

The aural center of our brain does much the same task. This is why we can often understand what is being communicated on a cell phone even when the transmission is interrupted. It takes very sophisticated technology to enable a machine to make sense of only partial sentences, but our brains do it effortlessly.

This tendency of the brain to fill in the missing gaps, string together loose constructs into a complete whole, or extrapolate data from vague clues goes well beyond piecing together what we hear and see. It also occurs in gossip circles, in which an innocent remark or action evolves into an unseemly affair. It manifests on jury panels, causing judges to remind jurors that their only function is to consider the evidence presented, not the meandering conjecture such evidence may presuppose in their minds.

Consider your experiences in the darkened space of a movie theatre. Can you recall a time that you knew what would happen next in the story before it actually occurred? It is doubtful that you had read the script prior to your screening. Yet, you might have found yourself charting the next moments in the plot with remarkable accuracy. How did you do this?

Most of us have endured movie experiences that failed to impress us because the plot was too predictable. Critics describe the formula motion picture, which is said to have a story constructed from a template. Go easy on the screenwriters. They probably had good intentions, for there is truly no such thing as an original story, only an original narrative. Every story ever told was told before, but the same story can be told again and again and continue to hold our attention if the narrator paints it from a different perspective. Thus, the works of Shakespeare continue to be performed, but often in very unconventional narrative guise. Richard III has been presented in the traditional medieval setting, in the context of Nazi Germany, and in stark 1960s minimalist counterculture.

The same mental mechanics that enable us to enjoy a Seurat painting, fill in the missing measures of a symphony, and predict the plot of a motion picture, allow us to receive and interpret the narrative of Legendary Brands. If Jung is indeed correct, and each of us is born with the same library of archetypes stored within our unconscious, then Legendary Brands activate these stored myths by serving up clues that trigger our minds to piece together brand narrative.

Figure 3.4 illustrates how this mental model works. Because the myths referenced by Legendary Brands are a part of the collective unconscious, the primary aim of any brand communications effort is to trigger the myth associated with the brand. Doing so creates a phenomenal marketing efficiency. Once the referenced myth is loaded into the subconscious of the viewer, the brand can isolate its labors to aesthetics and imagery. In other words, the brand is free to focus on the beat(s) of the narrative.

A discussion regarding branding's reliance on myth would not be complete without reflecting on Nike. The myth of sports is one of the most powerful and engaging of all time. The reason events such as the Olympics garner such phenomenal attention stems largely from

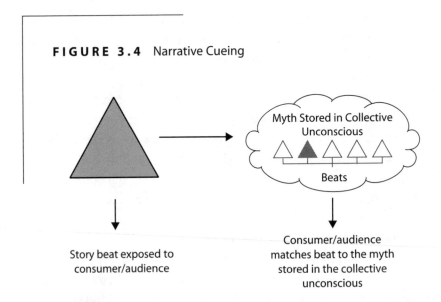

FIGURE 3.4 Narrative Cueing

Story beat exposed to
consumer/audience

Consumer/audience
matches beat to the myth
stored in the collective
unconscious

the universal reverence for athletic competition. The playing field is the perfect physical manifestation of dramatic structure. Only one player or team can win. Conflict is certain. Resolution is anticipated. Every narrative tradition in the world contains a myth that glorifies athletic excellence and the uncertainty that can only be revealed through the act of sport. Athletic competition provides the leveling mechanism that separates ordinary men from heroes. Nike draws upon this myth to create one of the few brand platforms that does not need to work very hard to tell its story.

Joseph Campbell identified a mythic formula, a derivation of the situation-complication-resolution framework that appears in all the great myths of heroic conquest.

A hero ventures forth from the world of common day into a region of supernatural wonder: fabulous forces are there encountered and a decisive victory is won: the hero comes back from this mysterious adventure with the power to bestow boons on his fellow man.[2]

Understanding this framework is key to understanding the power of Nike. The timeless myth of sports always thrusts the hero into a conflict that yields a decisive victory. More importantly, the hero's conquest is deep and meaningful to the culture he or she represents. Nike has followed this framework from the earliest days of its advertising, in some cases taking the heroic framework to its most literal interpretation. In a 1998 Nike commercial that aired during the World Cup, Nike pitted a team of the world's greatest soccer players against a team of demons in a supernatural court of fire. Here, the athletes, setting aside cultural and national differences, saved all of mankind. The spot was popular around the world, though it was seen less in the United States because of its somewhat controversial use of graphic violence.

On a figurative level, Nike has often played upon the call to adventure and excellence that makes athletes into beloved heroes. Nike's love affair with Michael Jordan produced some of the most emotionally charged advertising ever broadcast. Upon the close of Jordan's triumphant title-winning season with the Chicago Bulls in 1998, Nike aired a 60-second advertisement that paid tribute to his phenomenal career. The unusually understated spot featured a musical soundtrack of solo piano, playing a nostalgic melody. Video clips played from Jordan's earliest days as a high school athlete, to his infamous 19 foot leap to the board, to his tear-filled exuberance on winning another championship title. This advertisement triggered the myth of sports. The viewer pieced together Jordan's call to adventure, his triumphs and decisive victories, and his cultural significance. Millions of Americans, particularly those in Chicago, were the beneficiaries of great pride and confidence thanks to the heroic efforts of Michael Jordan. Through its support of and association with Jordan, Nike links that myth to its brand. Consumers of Nike products are encouraged to accept their own call to adventure, to honor the rewards such an adventure can yield for mankind, and to push themselves to their utmost limits in order to return victorious.

MYTH AND MEANING: The Soul of the Brand

The myth behind a Legendary Brand is more than a reference point. It conveys meaning. Myth gives a brand an emotional context. Think of it as the narrative of mankind. It is a story told with a collective voice and shared point of view.

When we were children, we encountered many fairy tales that ended with a moral. That moral taught us a lesson, using the action of the fairy tale as proof. Myths provide the metaphysical equivalent of fairy tale morals. Though less direct, myths teach a lesson. We relish this deeper meaning for the same reason that we attempt to find meaning in life. Myths teach us how to be. They give us guidance. They set examples. It is the meaning locked within myths that is the vital driver of a Legendary Brand's bond with the consumer.

Literary critics have labored for centuries to narrow the field of narrative and myth down to a few common themes. They argue that behind every great story lies one of a small set of timeless lessons, and these lessons are differentiated by their meaning to human cultures.

In his inspiring book on mythology, Phil Cousineau details six myths which he calls the "once and future myths." They are:

1. The myth of the creative struggle
2. The myth of time
3. The myth of mythic power of mentorship
4. The myth of travel
5. The myth of the city
6. The myth of sports

In a flowing narrative that itself is a testament to the power of story, Cousineau argues that all of the great stories that are ever told touch on one of these great myths because they are subjects we feel compelled to examine time and again in our search for greater meaning.[3]

It is no surprise that many Legendary Brands draw upon these six mythic bases. We've already studied the myth of sports and its effect on the Nike brand. Let us now consider the myth of time. Voluminous tales project the human quest to control time even though it is ultimately something beyond our control. Time passes us by without regard to our dreams and desires, kind only to those who pay no attention to its passing.

Cousineau recounts a legend from the Salish Indians of North America. In the story, the trickster Mink steals a clock from the European travelers who had just visited their land. Prior to the arrival of the Europeans, the Salish people had no sense of time. They lived their life as Cousineau said, "In accord with the rhythms of the sun and the moon, the stars and the tides, day and night, light and darkness."

But Mink chanced upon the Europeans and observed their reverence for the clock, a strange object with funny hands and strange markings. He became mesmerized by it, so much so that he decided to steal it so that he might learn more about its great powers. No sooner had he stolen the magic object, then he realized that it carried a curse. He began wasting away his time, staring at the moving hands of the clock when he should've been gathering food. Before doing anything, he found himself checking the face of the clock to mark the time. Every so often, he had to return home to the clock so that he could wind it, lest it cease to record the passing of time. Cousineau writes:

> Low and behold, as the wise commentator, Joseph Bruchac, has noted, because Mink stole time it now owned him and the people. It has been that way ever since. Time owns us the way we used to own the sun.

The myth of time provides deeper meaning to many Legendary Brands. "Time management" is a phrase that is fully integrated into the business vernacular. In recent years, a rapidly growing number of time management programs have emerged, spawning books, software, and the all-important day planner. The brand that stands above them all is Franklin Covey.

Franklin Covey came onto the scene in the early 1980s as two independent companies. Franklin, a company located just outside Salt

Lake City, Utah, enjoyed widespread growth as a result of its very successful day planner and time management system. This system helped people prioritize the events of their daily life. It argued that effective time management was the key to leading more meaningful, productive lives.

Across the valley in Provo, Utah, Steven Covey launched his own time management system on the backs of a book that floated atop the best-seller list for several years. *The Seven Habits of Highly Effective People* revolutionized the way many people led their lives. Covey preached that the key to leading a more effective life was to "put first things first." To do this, he suggested a weekly time management system that helped users put important priorities at the top of their to-do list. Shortly after the widespread appeal of this book, Covey launched his own "Seven Habits Organizer," which quickly became the number two player in the time management market.

In 1998, the two companies merged and became Franklin Covey. In 2001, the combined company had sales of more than $500 million. The company serves more than three-quarters of the Fortune 500, and their customers pay more than a 20 percent premium when compared to similar products sold in traditional office supply chains. Despite this, FranklinCovey customers exhibit a fierce, sometimes zealous loyalty. Like Mink, these people are mastered by their planners. They rarely travel far without them. Franklin Covey is a Legendary Brand with an intense, loyal group of followers. They believe in the meaning behind the brand: Don't let time control you—you must control time. A classic myth with a timeless theme resurfaces in the modern age.

MYTH VERSUS CLICHÉ

The stories told by Legendary Brands are well known and have been told in a variety of different traditions, yet no matter how many times we hear these stories they engage us anew. When we seek an original story, we really search for an original narrative. True, we are familiar with the basic myth, but we never tire from a new and novel retelling. The ancient Greeks awarded the highest honors to the play-wrights and poets who retold familiar tales well. Those who wrote "original" works are now forgotten.

While we enjoy experiencing the same myths over and over through differing narrative, most of us have little patience for cliché. Cliché is narrative photocopying. Myth is a living story that resurfaces in the cultures of the world because of its timeless and life-affirming content. Cliché on the other hand, is the result of intentional efforts to replicate a story.

Legendary Brands always tell stories that feel new and fresh, but are built on universal themes and familiar stories that reverberate like an echo from our primordial past. This combination gives them au-thenticity. Competitor brands often take an easier road and resort to cliché. They make knee-jerk marketing responses that overtly attempt to replicate the success of the Legendary Brand's marketing. To them, it is all just a formula. While such attempts may be met with initial success, the long-term sustainability of such marketing tricks are fleet-ing because consumers eventually see through the guise. Consumers know the difference between the original story and a copy.

Suppose consumers were to accept, even admire, the work of the plagiarist. The plagiarist is destined to be the second choice of the con-sumer. Why? Consumers will compare the work of the authentic brand narrative to the work of the copycat. In essence, the copycat, by design, must take its cue from the original.

To illustrate, consider the Legendary Brand of ESPN. In 1978, Bill Rasmussen launched a small cable channel in the modest New England community of Bristol, Connecticut. He called his channel ESPN. The *E* stood for *Entertainment*, which Rasmussen believed would be a part of his programming, though entertainment content never materialized. Bristol, and its surrounding neighbors, was a community of sports fans, and it was hungry for sports content that went beyond the network coverage of the "big" games. Though the channel had a shoestring budget, it quickly developed a strong local audience due to its cover-age of NCAA events, unique news coverage ("SportsCenter"), and the personalities of its on-air talent such as Chris Berman and Dick Vitale.

ESPN didn't really start off as a Legendary Brand. It was small, poorly funded, and had limited reach. Yet underneath its particle-board exterior lay the roots of a truly Legendary Brand. ESPN was a channel for sports fans, run by sports fans. From the top down, every member of the team loved sports. It was propelled by the timeless myth of sports. Throughout history, we have bathed ourselves in the lore of sports heroes. Usually, this myth unfolds from the conventional perspective of the athlete's point of view. Not so for ESPN. ESPN is told from the fan's point of view. Nowhere is this more evident than in the on-air talent. This was not a network of highly paid, high-gloss commentators. The anchors of ESPN were "regular guys" who lived and breathed sports. These elements, mixed with the actual historic origins of the network, constructed a powerful narrative. ESPN tells the story of sports fans covering the sports world for sports fans. It does it with irreverence, candor, and passion.

Thanks to the cable boom of the 1980s, and a rapidly growing sports industry, ESPN now has international reach and is unequivocally a Legendary Brand. Every cable network in the country must have at least one ESPN channel in order to remain competitive and keep its customers happy. Whether they know the real story or not, ESPN fans perceive a story in the brand that is strikingly similar to reality. It is the story of regular, ordinary people (like the viewers) following and supporting the trials and tribulations of athletic competition.

Contrast ESPN with FoxSports. FoxSports was born of the sprawling News Corp media empire. Rupert Murdoch, known for his savvy understanding of mass media and his keen competitive insights, took notice of the growing phenomena that was ESPN and saw a sound business opportunity. By launching a sports network of his own he could mitigate ESPN's bargaining power on his own cable and satellite holdings. He also knew well that every category has room for at least two competitors. With no one else competing against ESPN, he could easily enter the market, which he did in 1997.

FoxSports is a quality sports network. It has acquired great talent from the beginning, much of it from ESPN. News Corp invested millions of dollars to acquire exclusive broadcast rights to various sporting events. More importantly, it went regional. FoxSports established a local channel in every major market and acquired the rights to cover that market's local sports.

Despite quality and reach, I would argue that FoxSports is not yet a Legendary Brand. Many FoxSports viewers report that they regularly watch ESPN. Most of these viewers have no choice but to watch FoxSports because it owns the rights to their local sports team coverage—often the coverage that is most important to them. These viewers, however, flip channels when the game is over to watch ESPN Sports Center or other ESPN programming.

FoxSports doesn't fit as a Legendary Brand because it doesn't really have an authentic story. It imitates the ESPN brand narrative, and utilizes savvy economic strategy, not brand strategy, to capture viewers. It was born of industry, not from inspiration. It was born of money and media power, not from a relationship with fans. The story of FoxSports is a chapter in the story of Rupert Murdoch, whereas, ESPN is the story of sports fans.

CHAPTER 4

LEGENDARY BRANDS AND PERSONAL NARRATIVE

LIFE WITHOUT STORY

Imagine life without stories. You would never go to the movie theatre. Beloved cinema classics like *Casablanca, Star Wars,* or *Gone with the Wind* would not be a part of your vernacular. Opera and live theatre would not exist. Television, the new American pastime, would seem pedantic. Forget situation comedies, one-hour dramas, soap operas, television miniseries, and made-for-TV movies—the meat of television content. The TV would deliver a stream of facts and only the facts, rather than the glossy, magazine-style format news programming we have now come to favor.

Perhaps you believe life would be better without the distraction of television, movies, and other entertainment programming. But imagine a life without literature. No Hemmingway, no Chaucer, not even Stephen King. Gone, too, would be the fairy tales of Aesop or the Brother's Grimm, those beloved fables known to us from childhood that pepper our colloquialisms and tie to our proverbial wisdom.

While our search for meaning would probably sustain organized religion, our religious experience would lack the enlightening, often poetic verses associated with the Bible, the Torah, the Koran, or the

Sthaviravada. Sacred scriptures would read like a series of random recorded historical events, rather than the epic drama arising from the conflict between heaven and hell, ignorance and enlightenment.

We would still enjoy music but virtually no songs, for lyrics generally tell a story. You would never waste away in "Margaritaville," pine over "The Girl from Impanema," or wax rhapsodic in the verses of Mozart's "Voi Che Sapete."

The bottom line is this: We relish storytelling. It is a popular consumer good with strong demand characteristics, so strong that if stories disappeared tomorrow, we would lose nearly a quarter of our gross domestic product. We would also have a lot of idle time on our hands, as story occupies us for several hours each day.

Stories as Mechanism for Understanding

Life without storytelling indeed seems bleak, but we haven't even scratched the surface of its impact on human culture. Stories serve us in ways that go beyond mere amusement. Without story we would lose our life experience.

For example, without stories you would never enjoy those cherished personal moments occurring from reflection on past experience. Think back to a time when you shared a past experience with friends and laughed so hard it made your stomach hurt. Would it all have been as funny if not for its delivery in story form? Or consider those treasured moments in your life when you learned how your parents met, or when your mother told you about the day you were born, or when you discovered your grandfather's bravery in the war. Rarely are these facts or events revealed in a list of bullet points or in the objective, explanatory phrasing of a dictionary entry. If they were, they would not have the same effect. Recalling them might seem pointless.

The three-act, cause-and-effect storytelling structure that we explored in Chapter 3 mirrors the way in which our minds order and frame life experience. Without the story form, we would find it very difficult to reconsider that experience or share it with others. Where would you begin? Where would you end? How would you sequence the events so that others could understand?

Not only is story a mechanism for ordering and recalling experiences, it is also an important means to the acquisition and interpretation of information. Story is the logical resource most employed by our cognitive faculties in order to learn. Even in our earliest days of learning, our lessons were often delivered in story form. We read books. We learned nursery rhymes. We watched children's television. Our teachers incorporated stories into lessons such as verbal math problems, history pageants, and the contrived stories of early reading primers.

The bottom line: story plays an important role in human experience. In fact, many experts would argue that without story, we have no experience. Story makes coherent otherwise random events. It is the primary means by which we understand and share our understanding of the world. Without stories, we would have a difficult time negotiating life and the experience of living.

Beyond Amusement and Experience

Today, story enjoys an exaggerated influence upon our lives—an influence unprecedented in human history. Our culture demands a story from every object, every place, every institution, and every human being. This phenomenon has led many social critics to refer to the current era as the era of entertainment. It is an age in which we ascribe value to everything around us based upon narrative delivery. We cast laurels upon and live vicariously through celebrities, not because of their character but because of the stories that circulate around them. We flock to themed restaurants, theme parks, and otherwise mundane public spaces (e.g. shopping centers) that are infused with a narrative life often lacking a foundation in truth. We live in newly minted, single-family homes with ever smaller footprints, but greatly enhanced design features that convey the narrative of the American dream—a home of your own. These homes are nestled in planned communities, on land that was once barren, in an attempt to live the modern variation of the ever-popular American narrative of "Main Street, USA."

Even consumer brands are judged by entertainment value. As we saw in the last chapter, the brands that tell us a story earn our loyalty. Those that fail to achieve this objective fade into obscurity or become mere commodities. Faced with such ominous threats, advertisers are forging closer ties to Hollywood and the entertainment industry, fueling increased entertainment copromotion, product placement, and content sponsorship. Some brands now seek to own and produce entertainment properties. As one recent advertising executive explained, advertisers "want brands integrated into plots."[1]

The demand advertisers sense for entertainment value is actually a derivative of a broader consumer movement. Consumers want their lives integrated into plots—narratives, to be precise. Today's consumer shapes his or her identity according to a perceived narrative that serves as a script to the drama of life. Consumers live within what author Neal Gabler refers to as the "life movie." Gabler and many other cultural critics believe that our demand for entertainment has crossed a line. Entertainment has become more real (e.g., the abundance of "reality" television programming), and real life has become more of an entertainment (e.g., NikeTown and the many other entertainmentized retail ventures). The line that once separated these two dimensions is significantly blurred, to the point that it is practically nonexistent.[2]

Shakespeare claimed that "all the world's a stage and all the men and women merely players." Never was that more true than today. Every consumer is truly an actor, performing a part in a life movie. On the surface the notion that we pretend to be somebody else every day of our lives seems rather shallow. In reality, however, it is a natural effect caused by sweeping changes in our culture. In previous times, we focused our energy on production. There was little time to "perform." Our character emerged inwardly through our focus on our individual contribution to society. Today, we have no shortage of contributions. It is difficult to keep up with the rapid changes in technology and discovery. In fact, we produce more than we can consume, a circumstance that causes less social emphasis on productivity and more emphasis on consumption. In this context, sociologist David Riesman claimed we are now "other-directed." Our productivity and contribution is less significant to our self-worth. Rather, our character is influenced by the way others see us. The feedback we receive from our family, our peers, and the media set the parameters for our sense of identity and our social behavior.[3]

When society places less value on what you produce and more value on how you present yourself, where do you turn to construct your character? Increasingly, we turn to entertainment and the media. Like any good entertainment property, narrative is the foundation. Each of us crafts a hidden script that governs our actions, dialogue, and behavior. It is a narrative stored within our subconscious that is constantly evolving. So malleable is this narrative, that most of us will continue to refine it until the day we take our final bow on Shakespeare's global stage. More intriguing is the fact that many of us act upon more than one narrative. Our narrative identity often shifts depending upon the audience. At home with our family, one script is at play. In the office with our coworkers, another script may be at work. Thus, the postmodern consumer now rivals legendary actors in his or her ability to present various characterizations flawlessly to the public.

As consumers, we frequently go to great extremes in order to present our narratives well. To ensure that our image fits the part, we often sculpt our bodies through diets, personal trainers, and even expensive medical procedures. To perfect the delivery of our lines, we often seek therapy, coaching, and self-help programs that prepare us mentally and help us "become the character." Last, but certainly not least, to connote authenticity in our affairs, we consume and employ goods and services that make our character more realistic—to others and to ourselves. We ensure that we wear the right costumes, buying just the right fashion styles and labels appropriate for the character. We use the most authentic props, either decoratively or functionally, to enable the character's actions. We even place ourselves within the right settings, styling our homes to fit the character's habitat or vacationing in locales appropriate to our narrative identity. In fact, vacation destinations are becoming more and more focused on creating an escape experience whereby the consumer can make their narrative life real.

It is in this context that Legendary Brands play a vital role. As consumers base their lives on narratives, and brands attempt to become part of narratives, entertainment and consumption merge. To keep apace with the insatiable consumer demand for entertainment, Legendary Brands must activate a story. While Legendary Brands make the consumption experience entertaining for the consumer, they also enable the consumer to present narrative identity. Legendary Brands actively participate in the narrative life of consumers. Other brands do not.

LEGENDARY BRANDS AND NARRATIVE IDENTITY

Figure 4.1 provides a conceptual model for the relationship between Legendary Brands and personal narrative. Each dimension of the relationship is here presented in a linear sequence related to the performance of narrative identity.

During pre-performance, we prepare ourselves for the roles we will play. From a brand perspective, this is where we select the brands that will be associated with our identity. It is here that we define our brand preferences. We select only the brands that complement our nar-

FIGURE 4.1 Legendary Brands and Personal Narrative

Sequence:	**Pre**	**During**		**Post**
Brand Phase:	Selection	Use		Experience
Narrative Driver:	Theme	Character	Plot	Aesthetics
Consumer Activities:	Role Preparation	Performance		Evaluation / Feedback
Influence:	How we define our identity	How we present our identity to the world		How the world responds to our identity

rative identity or make it more authentic. As we saw in Chapter 2, sacred beliefs are the key to the brand/identity relationship. We seek to align the theme of the brand with the theme of our personal narrative.

Next in the sequence is the actual performance. When we perform, we set three narrative elements in motion: plot, character, and aesthetics. Aristotle claimed that without a plot, there could be no story. If there is no plot in our personal narrative, we have nothing to do. Plot defines our actions and gives the resulting experience cohesion. As we shall see, Legendary Brands are instrumental to the plot's unfolding. They are rarely passive set dressings, but rather active participants.

Characters determine how the plot unfolds. There is a double entendre associated with the role of Legendary Brands in the performance of personal narrative. On the one hand, Legendary Brands are a part of our characterization. The brand makes us more authentic when in character. It gives us confidence or better prepares us for the role. On the other hand, Legendary Brands act as characters themselves. They often serve as mentor, ally, and occasionally antagonist to our character's objectives.

Legendary Brands also contribute aesthetically to our performance. Their presence makes the performance authentic. They serve as props, costumes, settings, and other devices that generate a sense of realism. Though it is a static role, the aesthetic impact of Legendary Brands in the performance of our narrative should not be underestimated.

Finally, in the post-performance phase of the sequence, we take time to reflect on the experience of the performance and the brand's role within that experience. Here, we focus on the feedback we receive from the environment. The feedback we receive may be direct, as in how others reacted to brands used in our performance, or it can be indirect, as in how the brands made us feel during performance. Legendary Brands color our perceptions in a variety of ways.

This brief summary is intended as a general overview to familiarize you with the conceptual model, which will be expanded in greater detail shortly. One caveat is necessary before proceeding. The linear construction of this model is designed only as a learning aid. In reality, these three phases occur simultaneously. We perform the role while we prepare for it because the narrative is our identity. Therefore, even while we are evaluating brands and contemplating their potential effectiveness, we remain "on camera." Meanwhile, while we perform, we receive subtle feedback from the environment that alters our performance. The post-performance reflection of this feedback occurs while we simultaneously select new brands or make changes in brand preferences. This in turn affects our performance, and so on. Narrative identity is complex, and the relationship between brand use and narrative performance is recursive. It is easier to study the model by freezing time for a moment and giving it a linear shape. In this format we can better understand the cause-and-effect relationships. In actuality, however, the model is anything but linear.

PREPARING FOR THE ROLE OF A LIFETIME

What do you stand for? What is the meaning of your life? Can you answer this question articulately, or do you find yourself searching for the right words? Do you ever give much thought to such questions, or do you think they are a complete waste of time? Regardless of your answer, most of us do stand for something, even though we may not contemplate such questions. For each of us, behavior is guided by certain boundaries. They delineate the difference between right and wrong, pleasure and pain, love and hate. In each case, the theme of our personal narrative is at play.

Until recent times, codifying the theme of your life was easier. Tradition, religion, or culture provided the template and all we did was add a dash of color. But in a society that is "other directed" these templates are less effective. We don't have clear answers to what we stand for. We turn to new influences: celebrities, mass media, and Legendary Brands.

Like the myths that underlie a brand narrative, our personal narratives gain meaning from its theme. If you are the type of person who has given some thought to the theme of your life, you probably select

Legendary Brands with great scrutiny. You discriminate between brands to ensure that they align with your own principles and values. On the other end of the spectrum, if you rarely give thought to your theme, you probably select Legendary Brands intuitively or haphazardly. Though your brand selections may appear impulsive or arbitrary, it is likely that the brand communicates values that resonate with you, even though you may not be able to articulate those values. Most consumers fall somewhere in between these two extremes.

Brands even connote narrative theme within the "antibrand" segment of consumers. These consumers profess total opposition to anything branded. By avoiding Legendary Brands, or known brands of any kind, they make a statement about what they stand for. Ironically, a recent study in the *Journal of Consumer Research* found that, despite passionate resistance to Legendary Brands, these consumers often invest a significant amount of time and money in the selection of their brands. This investment often leads the consumer back to Legendary Brands, though the consumer justifies their loyalty for very specific reasons—generally apart from mass culture influence. Being a discriminate consumer gives meaning to their narrative identity.[4]

With life so full of consumption, rather than production, it is easy to see why brand selection can have such an influence on the theme of our personal narrative. It is perhaps the most powerful aspect of the Legendary Brand. Legendary Brands grow to their greatness because of what they stand for. In return, they attract those who stand for the same principles, values, and sacred beliefs. Some of those they attract select them consciously; others do so out of instinct.

Ben & Jerry's Ice Cream has a loyal and enthusiastic following. Despite the great taste and quality of the product, many consumers pay a handsome premium for Ben & Jerry's because the brand supports the theme of their personal narrative. With flavors such as "Cherry Garcia," which pays tribute to the late inspirational and socially conscious singer Jerry Garcia of The Grateful Dead, or "Rainforest Crunch" which uses natural ingredients that cause no harm to pristine rainforests, Ben & Jerry's Ice Cream is a product with a moral stance. Consuming the product, and thereby the brand, is a means of reorienting with sacred beliefs, supporting a cause, or associating oneself with something that matters.

Why would someone pay more than $1,000 for a mass-produced work of art? It seems counterintuitive. Yet, thousands of people pay more than that to own their very own Thomas Kinkade painting. Kinkade paintings start out as originals by the artist, but are then reproduced by machine to supply more than 300 Kinkade galleries worldwide. To each reproduction, a craftsman adds subtle touches of highlight and shadow with paint and brush, giving the reproduction its own unique signature and an artificial authenticity. This formula has inspired thousands of Americans, who have never before set foot in a gallery, to spend considerable amounts of money for a touched up reproduction. Why?

Thomas Kinkade is a Legendary Brand that connects with its consumer base at a visceral level. Kinkade paintings are infused with theme, some of it inspired by religion. Many of these consumers subscribe to a personal narrative of balance, simplicity, and humility. They look onto the canvas of a Kinkade painting and meditate on the tranquil setting it depicts—a simple farmhouse in a green meadow, a lighthouse challenging a coastal tide, or a quiet village adjacent to a mountainside. Though in their daily lives these consumers must hustle and bustle to earn a living, they aspire to a life of greater simplicity and quietness. Their narrative identity longs to connect with words of the ancient Eastern philosopher Lao Tzu:

> Racing, chasing, hunting,
> drives people crazy.
> Trying to get rich
> ties people in knots.
> So the wise soul
> watches with the inner
> not the outward eye,
> letting that go,
> keeping this.[5]

Displaying a Kinkade painting within their home activates the theme of their personal narrative. Even the act of purchasing a Kinkade painting activates the theme. Just as religious people find fulfillment in tithing and giving to their churches, consumers of Kinkade paintings, many with constrained economic resources, view their purchases as spiritual investment, never mind the fact that it has amassed millions of dollars in wealth for the man behind the name.

With regard to the thematic nature of personal narrative and its relationship to Legendary Brands, there is one final aspect that warrants your attention. It is very rare that one brand resolves all of the thematic needs of a consumer. Postmodern consumers are of an eclectic thematic construction, figuratively and literally. From the figurative perspective, we use various brands to codify our worldview. The respect for personal mastery that we gain from Nike might be mixed with the endeavor to push creative boundaries espoused by Apple. In other words, we mix and match the themes of various Legendary Brands to create our own, unique thematic construct. In this sense, the postmodern consumer is quite different from consumers of the past. Those consumers were truly part of a "mass" culture. They conformed. Brand selection remained consistent across a wide range of consumer segments. Being unique and authentic was less important; in fact, it could be a liability.

In contrast, the postmodern consumer selects brands that resonate on a personal level. The brand selections provide a sense of authenticity. By layering brand selections upon one another, we create what we believe is a "unique" character. This enables us to perform a character that is perceived as novel and genuine, despite its reliance on well-known, culturally established brand platforms.

From a more literal perspective, most of us have more than one narrative identity. Thus, one set of brands may espouse what we stand for in the workplace, but a very different set of brands may tie to our theme on Friday night, after hours. In the workplace, we might gravitate towards the no-nonsense styling of Brooks Brothers and its conservative principles. While during the weekend, we might prefer to

align with the theme of Dolce & Gabbana, flaunting those we encounter with provocative styling.

THE JOY OF PERFORMANCE

There is only one word to describe the impact a Legendary Brand
has upon the performance of personal narrative: *emotion*. Whereas the
pre-performance sequence of the model is reflective, the performance
phase is active and Legendary Brands "activate" the performance experience. We enjoy performing. We relish those moments in life when
we feel we are the most in tune with our narrative identity. Legendary
Brands heighten the emotional impact of these moments. They do this
in three ways.

Activating the Plot of Our Narrative

When Legendary Brands activate the plot of personal narrative,
they actually create an experience that aligns with what we desire
from our lives. We often speak of *enablement* when we deal with plot
activation, because the Legendary Brand *enables* us to live our narrative identity.

In Chapter 2, we discussed the concept of liminality. Recall that a
liminal state occurs when people are set apart from their previous
identity. They exist, for a temporary time, in a state of "nothingness."
They emerge from this state changed. Liminality is most often associated with ritual, but it is also connected to the use of Legendary Brands.
Through the liminal state, the consumer touches their narrative identity. It is in this state that plots unfold in our narrative life.

A plot is the beginning, middle, and end of a narrative. It's the
structural architecture of story. A good plot ensures that every event in
the story makes logical sense and that the cause-and-effect relationships are clear. Remove any event from a well-constructed plot, and
the story disintegrates. Life, as lived, is not so neat and tidy. Our lives

are anything but ordered according to a beginning, middle, and end construction. Randomness is an ever-present distraction. Our experiences are not naturally compacted into narrative form, but when we or other elements shape them as such, our narrative identity springs to life. Legendary Brands activate the plot of our personal narrative by giving brand experiences an ordered, compact, and cohesive story structure.

The prime example of this concept manifests in the Harley-Davidson brand. Though we have already discussed this Legendary Brand, it is worth revisiting because of the powerful effect it can have as a plot activator.

The Harley-Davidson brand conveys a narrative of roughness. Most consumers associate it with Hell's Angels, and the open road of the southwestern deserts. It is a brand narrative that equally serves outlaws and men of honor alike. One common denominator is indisputable: the Harley-Davidson brand is imposing. It connotes that those who come across it should treat the bearer with cautious respect, and a touch of fear.

Harley-Davidson has a peculiar relationship with consumers that don't seem to fit its target brand audience. These white-collar riders have Ivy League pedigrees and quiet homes in the Berkshires. For example, C. Michael Armstrong, the charismatic and powerful CEO of AT&T, is said to ride a Harley-Davidson on the weekends. He is one of many who associate themselves with a brand that seems utterly apart from their daily lives. Yet, it is Harley-Davidson's ability to activate the plot of these consumers' personal narratives that explains the affinity for the brand.

These men and women subscribe to at least one personal narrative that rewards rebellion. They build a part of their life around a story that defines them as genuine, authentic, and fully liberated. They are the modern-day equivalent of that great American patriot, Patrick Henry, who exclaimed to the world, "Give me liberty or give me death." Unfortunately, in their daily lives as lawyers, accountants, and senior managers, they are not fully afforded the opportunity to bring this narrative to life. In fact, the narrative identity they seek is interrupted and disjointed by activities and events that often work against its performance.

A Harley is not a quiet motorcycle. It shouts to the world with a guttural, foreboding voice that those who attempt to get in its way will pay the consequences. When Harley consumers kick down on the crankshaft and feel the instant rumble emanating from the more than 1400 cc's of pure American muscle, the narrative truly begins and the plot of the story unfolds. The use of the Harley-Davidson brand provides meaningful bookends to the narrative experience. It ensures that the story is complete. Once brand-use stops, the narrative ends. Thus, the consumer is able to perform the narrative only through the use of the Legendary Brand. The Legendary Brand makes the narrative experience orderly and cohesive.

Activating Our Character

Very few plots succeed without the actions of characters. The great dramas of all time pit dynamic characters against each other. While plot is concerned with action, character focuses on the effect that action will have. The relationship is analogous to chemistry. The action is mixing two chemicals together, but the effects of that action vary greatly on the chemicals used. If you mix hydrogen and oxygen, you get water. If you mix hydrogen and chlorine, you get a toxic acid.

Legendary Brands activate character in two distinct ways. First, they act as a crutch. Fashion brands frequently serve this purpose. J. Crew is one example. J. Crew conveys a narrative closely associated with an Eastern seaboard, preppy lifestyle. Its product catalogues and retail stores personify casually stylish people within youthful, active narratives. At one time, the brand aligned itself with the *Dawson's Creek* television series to further align itself with such characters. Wearing J. Crew apparel activates the character that many of its consumers wish to personify. Wearing it brings out the young preppy within them. It brings the character to life through the imagery it conveys, and the way it makes the consumer feel. The operative word here is *feel*. It is the feelings brand-use evokes from the consumer during the performance that make it essential to narrative experience.

The second way Legendary Brands activate narrative through character is a bit abstract. Stories generally have more than one character. In your personal narrative, there is always at least one character— you. There are, however, other characters in your life: your spouse, your lover, parents, children, friends, enemies, coworkers, and many others. In some instances, a Legendary Brand can also be a character in your personal narrative. This aspect ties closely to the concept of brand agent, which we discuss in Chapter 2. Brand agents, you will recall, stand for a set of sacred beliefs and give evidence to what they stand for.

To understand how a brand can be a character in your life, you need to think for a moment about people you have known that are no longer actively present in your own personal narrative. Though these people may not interact with you on a daily basis, they often continue to influence who you are and what you do. It may be a loved one who passed on, or a friend who is no longer close by. Regardless of the reasons for their inaccessibility, these figures cast a shadow on your identity and your experience.

Legendary Brands, too, can be ghosts in the room. The characters they portray are imaginary, but they influence our behavior. They are role models, instigators, mentors, and allies. At various times in your life you might have asked yourself, "what would my mentor do?" So too, many consumers wonder how the brand character would handle a given situation. Another way of looking at it is to ask, "what's the brand ___ approach to the situation?" Pick a Legendary Brand to fill in the blank and you can probably envision a particular attitude or approach. It's no wonder that Legendary Brands are often referred to by consumers and advertisers as "trusted friends" and "faithful companions."

In most cases, a brand becomes a character in the personal narrative when it is attached to a human agent. Martha Stewart is a person and a brand. Consumers loyal to her line of merchandise bring a little bit of Martha into their lives. The same can be said of Oprah Winfrey and Rosie O'Donnell. Many women feel they have a personal relationship with these celebrities. They feel that they know these women, though they have never met them. In this context, they look to these women as role models, counselors, and confidantes.

Legendary Brands do not require a human brand agent to assume a character role in your personal narrative. Mountain Dew is a Legendary Brand that has dominated the beverage category within "edge" culture. Mountain Dew invests considerable sums of money to associate with extreme sports and a high-risk lifestyle. Though some would argue that it is now so culturally adopted, it is losing its influence, Dew's advertising and brand activities remain irreverent and youthful, with a decidedly counterculture flavor. Consumers seeking to live a similar narrative identity are influenced by the messages from this advertising and branding. The brand can literally take the shape of a character—an ally or friend—who influences decisions, behavior, and other character traits. Standing nervously on the precipice of a skateboarder's half pipe, Mountain Dew is the instigator that encourages you to jump in with your board and try your luck.

Activating Aesthetics

Sometimes, a Legendary Brand activates a personal narrative for no other reason than its presence. When it does, it is acting upon the aesthetics of the narrative. Costumes, settings, and properties are extremely important to the quality of a story. Would *Casablanca* have been as romantic and filled with intrigue if the action unfolded in Akron, Ohio? Would *Little Women* have been as charming if it took place in South Central Los Angeles? Would *Tom Sawyer* have captured our latent childhood fantasy if it were set in Antarctica?

Aristotle included *spectacle* in his precedent elements for a good story. The descriptive aspects that surround our most beloved stories are nearly as important as the action of the tale. But scenery is not the only element that adds to a story, especially when the story is internalized like a personal narrative. We have five, not two senses. Never underestimate their individual powers. It doesn't take words and images alone to activate personal narrative. The subtlest stimulation of the senses can bring it into play: the lingering fragrance of a flower in bloom, the liberating touch of the wind upon your face, the sensual taste of wine on the palette, the sound of a bass player plucking jazz notes at midnight, or the ghostly vision of white linen curtains swaying in a spring breeze.

Legendary Brands bring personal narrative to life by acting upon these sensory touch points. Their presence makes the story more real because a substitute would make it less real. For example, if your personal narrative revolves around you having a refined sense of taste, you would probably not serve Gallo wine at your next party. Though Gallo is the largest producer and distributor of wine in the country, it is synonymous with "jug wine." You are more likely to serve Kistler or Screaming Eagle. These Legendary Brands of the wine world are expected elements in the setting of your narrative. Anything less plays against the story.

Conversely, if your personal narrative is rooted in hard-working, American values, you would probably not drive a Honda, drink Perrier, listen to Edith Piaf albums, or wear a Swatch. Each of these sensory touch points plays against your narrative. The settings and properties that are more likely to bring your narrative to life are a Dodge truck, a can of Coca-Cola, a Bruce Springsteen album, and a Timex watch. These are, indeed, stereotypes, but I use them to illustrate a point. Location scouts, art directors, property masters, and sound editors in the film industry pay close attention to every detail presented on-screen to ensure that the fictional reality presented suspends your disbelief and engages you in the story. Legendary Brands serve the same purpose in the narrative realities of the consumer. In this instance, it isn't about what the brand does or how it makes you feel, it's what perceived authenticity the brand lends to the moment.

The aesthetic quality of Legendary Brands has an influence on two audiences. First, it has an external impact. If you are performing for others, then the authenticity of your performance is critical to convincing them you are who you purport to be. If you wish to portray yourself as an urban hipster, you will probably not convince your audience of this characterization if you in fact live within a traditional Colonial home on Nantucket. Legendary Brands have cultural value, and their presence within your performance sends signals to the audience that your character is consistent.

Second, Legendary Brands impact your own internal grounding with your character. Method actors often seek props and costumes that are authentic rather than fabricated. A method actor playing a transient might visit a shelter and obtain the real clothes of a transient to activate his performance. Legendary Brands serve the same purpose for consumers. Having these brands makes it easier for the consumer to believe in their performance.

RESPONDING TO THE CRITICS

When actors perform on stage or screen, their performance is evaluated by third parties: audiences and critics. If they fail to convince either party, they suffer serious consequences. Either their performance is cut short, or their ability to gain the attention of these audiences dwindles.

Consumers face similar pressure. We must convince others—our peers, family, coworkers. Failing to do so invalidates our identity. Fortunately, Legendary Brands elicit audience response and connect consumer performers with their audiences, yet another factor that distinguishes them from other brands.

Recall that without narrative, we have no way to define our experience. It is through the ordering of events, and the information we choose to include, that we are able to reflect on and share what has happened to us or how we felt. Somehow, Legendary Brands manage to become a part of this ordering. They become landmarks and mile markers that ease interpretation and recollection. They also serve as communications vehicles for others to comment on our performance.

Legendary Brands are frequently included by narrator and audience member alike in post-performance accounting. An audience member might recall the Prada shoes, or the Apple Macintosh, or the BMW

700 series that played a part in the narrative. At first glance this might seem trivial, but consider the fact that the Legendary Brands recalled are often among scores of brands presented to the audience during the same experience. Only the Legendary Brands survive and forge an indelible imprint on our memory. This is largely due to their shared significance and the clarity of the signal they transmit.

Sometimes Legendary Brands generate a direct response—an immediate and noticeable reaction from the audience during the narrative performance. For example, as you interact with colleagues, they might call attention to your new Kate Spade handbag. Such responses interrupt narrative discourse and often take it on a new path. When this occurs, the consumer performing the narrative receives an immediate signal from the audience. This signal in turn impacts characterization and plot.

Legendary Brands also attract audience response in a delayed and more subtle manner. The most meaningful narrative experiences occur with people we know well and interact with often. When these people change their brand-use, or adopt our brand preferences, we receive a signal that our choices are appropriately activating our narrative identity. For example, some consumers take great pride in being associated with a particular brand. They love to be known as a Coach girl or a Abercrombie & Fitch boy. These brands have such an impact that others associate the consumer with the brand and brand with consumer.

When peers try or adopt the same brands, these consumers believe their narrative identity is effective. They believe they are having an influence, either as a trendsetter, or as a role model. It has the same effect as influencing one's opinion about politics, cuisine, parenting, or any other topic. When our peers vary their brand preferences as a result of our brand selections, our narrative identity is validated.

The manner in which Legendary Brands become a part of post-performance experience is subtle, but the fact that they are present at all sets them apart from other brands.

THE GOD PARTICLE OF
BRAND MARKETING

In physics, researchers are on a mission to find the god particle. When discovered, scientists will possess the smallest part of matter that can no longer be divided into component parts. It will be smaller than an atom, smaller than an electron, and smaller than a quark. Many scientists believe that when they finally isolate this minuscule building block of our existence, they will gain an insight into the origin of our universe. Hence, it is known as the *god particle.*

The personal narrative of the consumer is the god particle of brand marketing. Anyone that believes narrative is best left to the bohemians and philistines in Hollywood fails to understand the significance narrative plays in consumer behavior. It is a fundamental part of our psyche and it helps us to understand the world and ourselves. Without it, our world and our experience does not exist.

The stories your brand tells complement this personal narrative. They intertwine with the narratives consumers construct to guide their behavior and their sense of identity. Everything you do with your brand should focus on this narrative construct. It is how you activate the personal narrative that determines your ultimate connection to the consumer.

PART TWO

Part One presented you with the theory behind Legendary Brands. We now turn our attention to managing them. Marketing literature is rich with brand management and proven applications, but managing the Legendary Brand requires a unique approach, dissimilar from conventional branding wisdom. It requires an emphasis on story.

Lack of formula is a familiar theme you will encounter in the chapters that follow. It would indeed be a great accomplishment to offer a comprehensive formula detailing how to create or implement the winning narrative for a given brand. Unfortunately, narratives are not so easily crafted. They resist formula, as do consumers. If crafting great narratives were as easy as aligning x with y, then practically every motion picture would be a blockbuster. In reality, less than 10 percent of the movies released each year make 80 percent of the box office revenue—a testament to the difficulty of creating a story that resonates with audiences.

Narrative development is a craft. Crafts require practice, patience, and persistence. Crafting a brand narrative involves four critical activities.

1. *Listening.* Chapter 5 addresses the critical need for managers of Legendary Brands to listen to their brand audiences. The prevalent way to listen to an audience of consumers is through market research. You will learn about the role of research in the narrative development process, and the specific research methodologies and techniques that are best suited to the task.

2. *Crafting.* Chapter 6 addresses the craft of the narrator. Specifically, we discuss the need for brand managers to develop a brand bible, a device that maintains consistency and outlines all of the important parts of your brand narrative.

3. *Telling.* Chapter 7 focuses on the use of effective communications media to communicate the brand narrative. We study the traditional devices of television, print, and other advertising. We also address the emerging role of media and entertainment.

4. *Nurturing.* Chapter 8 discusses the oft-forgotten task of nurturing your brand culture. It is not enough to develop and tell a great story. Story becomes a sales agent when it is internalized by consumers and affects their behavior. In Chapter 8 you will learn about the ways that consumers become a part of a brand culture, the clustering of consumers into cultural segments by narrative subscription, and the activities brand managers can undertake to nurture such involvement.

A NOTE ON ETHICS

Marketers have an *obligation* to understand the tremendous influence they can have on consumers. This influence, if abused, has the power to mislead and betray consumers, even cause them harm. When it does, the marketing profession deserves the criticism and loathing it so often receives. Also, when this material is misused, it can cost the marketer money. Consumers punish marketers for misrepresentation, often in figurative mobs bearing torches and nooses.

Marketers must make many ethical decisions in the course of their narrative development. An equilibrium exists in the market for Legendary Brands. It is an efficient market, and consumers are much more aware of the meta-behavior than we give them credit for. When they perceive that a brand is misleading them, the market falls out of equilibrium and the brand gets what it deserves. I encourage those using this material to put it to good use. The tide of consumerism now empowers your brand with deeper meaning, which holds you to a higher standard of responsibility.

RELATING THE MATERIAL TO STRATEGY

Finally, for the hardcore student of marketing, I provide the following reference table. It is intended for those who have been raised in the conventional legacy of brand marketing. As you can see, what I propose is directly proportional to the normal marketing cycle. I believe the material presented in Part Two is no different than what has gone before. It is merely presented in a slightly different manner—a manner better suited to the storyteller.

Comparison of Traditional Brand Marketing

and the Narrative Approach to Brand Marketing

Narrative Approach	*Traditional Approach*
Listening	Data gathering
Crafting	Strategic planning
Telling	Communications planning
Nurturing	Servicing

CHAPTER 5

INVESTIGATING

BRAND NARRATIVE

Whether you are managing a venerable Legendary Brand or plotting to create a new one, effective consumer research will play a vital role in your success. Legendary Brands are sustained by constant conversations with the consumer. Conversations require you to listen as often, if not more often, than you speak. To be effective, Legendary Brands must observe the audience response to the stories they tell and learn how the narrative affected the audience. Primary consumer research is the means to this end.

How do you use consumer research to manage a brand? Seasoned marketers scoff at this question, mumble about Q-scores, and pontificate on the latest brand equity study. Many of these marketers regularly commission research to measure the strength of their brand, but few of them really use the research to alter their brand strategy. Part of the problem is that research is frequently commissioned for the wrong reasons. These include self-preservation interests, tactical requirements, and the "warm and fuzzy" feeling that comes from talking with consumers. A more significant problem, however, is that the research initiative was poorly planned or executed, in large part because the marketer is not studying the cause-and-effect relationship between brand narrative and consumer behavior.

Our study of research in this chapter is narrow. We are only interested in firsthand consumer research. This form of research requires skilled practitioners to meet with consumers, talk with them, and generate field data. It should be familiar ground for most marketers. It is a well-documented, staple technique used to determine price sensitivities, brand recall, brand awareness, and the effectiveness of specific advertising and promotional initiatives.

Using consumer research to explore the dimensions of brand narrative, however, is not so familiar. While narrative is perceived by the consumer, it is a difficult concept for most consumers to grasp and discuss. Getting at it requires the marketer to be flexible, creative, and intuitive. When you think of consumer research, your first thoughts probably turn to focus groups and quantitative surveys. Though these are the most popular research instruments in use today, Legendary Brands require you to think broader. While focus groups and surveys have definite value, you need to consider the full spectrum of research tools available to effectively converse with your brand audience and gauge the dimensions of your narrative. The purpose of this chapter is to help you structure an ongoing listening exercise through effective consumer research. It explores the limitations of research, designs for planning and executing research, and alternative methodologies that can be particularly useful.

THE PRISONER AND THE PLAYWRIGHT

Most of us find research intriguing. It can be a fun and interesting aspect of brand management. In all of our enthusiasm for research projects, it is easy to lose sight of their limitations. One significant limitation is that the results of consumer research are not perfect data. Another limitation is that the feedback received from consumers is subjective, and should not always be taken literally. To illustrate these limitations, I shall provide two analogies.

The Prisoner's Dilemma

Imagine that you are a prisoner in a foreign country. You are placed in solitary confinement. Behind two of the walls that border your cell are other prisoners, but the third wall neighbors the guard's quarters. You have no idea which of the three walls adjoin which party, and all parties are strangers to you. You come up with an idea for an escape, but you need the assistance of another prisoner to pull it off, and you have only 24 hours to make it work.

Your first challenge is to determine which wall to use. Two of the three walls at your disposal face fellow prisoners, but one wall faces the guard. Which do you choose? You don't have the time or resources to communicate with each of them, and you know that one wall is clearly the wrong party to speak with. This is the challenge of the re-searcher who attempts to select the right group of consumers to query. You know that not all consumers are representative of your brand au-dience, but you have very little information at your disposal to sort the good from the bad.

Having selected your wall, your next challenge is to get past the communication barrier—the concrete wall. It severely limits your abil-ity to communicate clearly or intimately. You're going to have to be creative. Alas, this is the same challenge faced by the researcher. We may not face literal brick walls, but we do face significant barriers. For starters, people don't always say what they really feel. It isn't that they are intentionally holding back, but rather that people don't necessarily think like they speak. "Any particular thought in our head embraces a vast amount of information. But when it comes to communicating a thought to someone else, attention spans are short and mouths are slow."[1] So says cognitive scientist Steven Pinker. As much as we would like to open up the heads of our consumer audience and look in on their thoughts, we unfortunately have to rely on what they tell us or show us. Many consumers find it difficult to put what they think or feel into words, so you need to select research methods that help them out.

Assuming you find a way to communicate with a prisoner in an adjacent cell, he or she may not speak the same language. While you speak French, she may speak Lithuanian. You've solved the problem of how to transfer your communications, but you haven't solved for interpretation errors. You have the same challenge when you research consumers. Consumers frequently use local vernacular, special vocabulary, dialect, and colloquialisms when they speak. These may be unfamiliar to you or may have a different contextual meaning. To do good consumer research, you have to navigate through this special language.

Finally, assuming that you are able to communicate and speak the same language (more or less), you have to question whether your accomplice really speaks truthfully. You have to evaluate the trustworthiness of the information. How do you know the person on the other side of the wall won't turn you in or kill you once you escape? Further, when you face a fork in the escape tunnel and your prison mate assures you that the path to freedom lies to the right, how do you know if that is correct? Consumers who participate in research projects generally have good intentions. In fact, sometimes their intentions are too good. They want to help so much that their good citizenship skews the information they provide. What they tell you may be far different from how they really feel, or how they would act outside the research house. In a few cases, consumers have an axe to grind with marketers, and they purposefully mislead you. Thus, your task is also to evaluate the accuracy of the information you receive.

I offer this analogy, drawn from the famous Prisoner's Dilemma exercise used in game theory, as a cautionary example. Many challenges prevent you from gaining perfect data. Your goal is to learn as much as you can from your consumer audience. You want to ensure that your brand isn't talking to itself—that it is having an impact on consumers. But you should not consider the data to be the gospel truth. In the end, you must trust your instincts as much as your findings. That means observing more than what people say. You have to know when to ignore the data.

The Playwright's Pleasure

Close your eyes and imagine that you are seated in a darkened theater in the middle of the performance of a play. If you were the author of this play, you would not need to do audience research to know what the audience thought of it. Sitting in the theater, you would have first-hand insights into the power of your prose. To gauge the value of the comedic elements, you would listen for laughter. Did the joke play so well that the actors had to pause for the laughter to subside, or was there merely a fleeting chuckle? When your heroine succumbed to consumption in the arms of her tortured lover, was your audience reaching for tissue, or retrieving the valet parking stub from their jackets?

Playwrights have it easy when it comes to connecting with their audience. They can observe the audience firsthand. Brand marketers cannot make such observations without consumer research. Though an analysis of the sales data may indicate that the marketing efforts are working, the brand manager has little idea why it is working. Was it the latest installment of your advertising campaign, which took your brand narrative into a new conflict, or was it the outdoor campaign that highlighted pictures from last year's story sequence? Is your story appealing to a new segment of consumers that have a latent personal narrative closely associated with your brand, or is your core segment feeling more connected to your brand than ever before? The answers to these questions are often revealed through consumer research.

The theater analogy can be carried one step further in order to illustrate the limitations of research, particularly as it pertains to brand development (launching a new brand, or relaunching a brand with a new narrative). Playwrights don't sit down with audiences in advance of writing their material—at least not in the literal sense. Most of the feedback the playwright receives is in reaction to the material, which means it has to be written first. Some successful playwrights, comedian Neil Simon perhaps the most famous, do a lot of observing before they write. They watch people and situations to inspire their act of creation, but they don't do a focus group and ask people what they want to see on stage.

When you craft a brand narrative from scratch, the role of research is primarily to help you observe the life of your audience. Like the playwright, it is best to create the brand narrative first, then refine it based on the reaction of the audience. Reversing the process leads to absurd concoctions posing as the story of the brand. These consumer-generated stories are generally shunned by the very audience that claimed they were the stories they wanted to be told. Research is like laughter and applause. It lets you know if you are pleasing the audience. Pander to it, however, and the only sound you'll hear is crickets.

ENVIRONMENT INFLUENCES THE RESULTS

Pay very close attention to the environment in which you engage consumers for their feedback. Brand narrative hides in the consumer's subconscious. It represents an intimate relationship between consumer and brand. It is often linked to identity, emotion, and cosmology—all very personal and guarded aspects of our lives.

Psychotherapists and field anthropologists would never interview and interact with consumers in cold, sterile research environments. They know that the subject matter to be discussed can be uncomfortably revealing. Market researchers, however, thrust research respondents into these environments all the time, and expect consumers to reveal very personal information. Some research environments are the most uninviting of places, with stark florescent lighting, uncomfortable furniture, and huge mirrors masking hidden observers and recording equipment. In focus groups, consumers are surrounded by a dozen total strangers and asked to reveal intimate details of their lives. Fat chance!

If you want consumers to tell you about their narrative identity, choose a research environment that makes them feel safe to do so. To go deep, consider one-on-one interviews, or if a group situation is preferred, gather consumers together who know each other. Group interviews in which the respondents have an established relationship (e.g., families, circles of friends, coworkers, etc.) can reveal some of the most helpful insights about your brand narrative.

The modern research facility is convenient and easy on the researcher. The best facilities are outfitted to make observation and recording practical. But even if they are easy on the researcher, they may not be easy on the respondent. Think like a therapist. Some research facilities offer very comfortable surroundings. Instead of a large conference table, these facilities may offer sofas and comfortable furniture. If you are fortunate enough to have access to these facilities, pay the premium.

Further, you might consider avoiding professional research facilities altogether. Conduct your research in the environment of your respondents—in their homes, offices, or social hubs. A coffeehouse can serve as an effective research environment. So, too, can a mall. In fact, depending upon your research objectives, these may be the ideal places to see the brand narrative in action.

PARTICIPATE IN THE PROCESS

You may not be a researcher, but you have an obligation to participate in the research. Far too many brand managers approve research designs and wait for the researcher to report back on the findings. This is a mistake. Whenever possible, make the time to observe the research in action. True, most qualitative studies are recorded on video or audiotape, but recording media miss many of the nuances evidenced in person. Also, when you are present, you have the power to make course corrections. You can advise the researchers and direct them to change the direction of their query.

Ideally, you will have the opportunity to conduct an interview yourself, or lead a field initiative. Not everyone has the training or the talent to do this. You do, however, have the ability to witness it first-hand. Brand narrative is hidden beneath the surface of consumer behavior. You are a detective looking for clues that reveal its presence and its impact. Getting into the field is the best way to understand it.

USING RESEARCH TO MANAGE
LEGENDARY BRANDS OVER TIME

Researching brand narrative is an ongoing process that answers important questions about the brand at various stages in time. Knowing when, what, who, and how to research at each stage is critical. Logic trees are one method to map the critical questions brand managers must answer at each stage.

The tree provided in Figure 5.1 is illustrative. You may structure yours in a different way, specific to your brand's specific stage of development. The only rule that applies to the design of your framework is that you should force binary logic through each branch. In other words, each node on your tree should ask a question that can only be answered with a yes or a no. Though this approach may seem limiting, it prevents you from getting lost in qualitative considerations. Before you know it, you are so confused you forgot what you were trying to research in the first place.

FIGURE 5.1 A Logic Tree

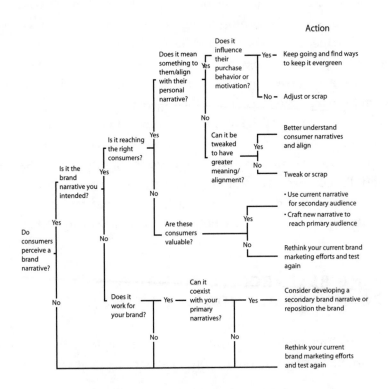

Exploring Narrative Presence

I began my tree by asking a question, "Do consumers perceive a brand narrative?" If narrative is the key to Legendary Brands, then the first task of any study is to determine whether consumers perceive a narrative.

Presence studies are research projects that explore the perception of a narrative by consumers. They require broad, exploratory designs. The goal is to comprehend consumer attachment to the brand, and to see if it has any root in narrative identity. You wish to learn if the brand is telling stories to consumers. For this reason, you approach a presence study assuming no narrative exists.

Coaxing the Narrative

How do you get consumers to reveal the narrative of the brand, if any? If you ask them to tell you what story they think the brand tells, you'll probably get a blank stare. While each of us in our own way is a storyteller, few of us possess a mastery of storytelling. Fewer still are those who can talk about storytelling critically.

The first task is to coax stories out of respondents by exploring their life experience. People love to talk about themselves, particularly when you ask them to recount peak or emotional experiences. Pay particular attention to the words they choose and the way they structure the sequence of events. These can be good comparison points when you later cluster consumers and narrative components.

Gradually, your task is to lead the consumer to the brand experience. The old research maxim applies—it is like peeling an onion. If you were to explore the potential narrative dimension of a motorcycle brand, you might begin by discussing travel. Look to understand how respondents feel about travel. Have them tell you a memorable travel experience. Again, notice how they frame the experience and the words they choose to describe it. You might then raise the topic of road trips and vehicular travel. Gradually, you would lead them to the topic of motorcycles. Ask if they have traveled anywhere on a motor-cycle. Explore the experience. If the respondents happen to be mo-torcycle enthusiasts, your next task would be to explore why they enjoy riding motorcycles. You might then ask them to describe a spe-cific time when they most felt that sense of enjoyment. This process continues until you get to the brand level.

The operative word in this exercise is *experience*. Recall that with-out story, we have no experience. When you encourage consumers to describe events from their past, they are forced to tell you stories. They may not be very good stories, but subconsciously the consumer is moving into a narrative frame of mind. Getting them in this frame of mind helps you (1) understand the narrative proficiency of the re-spondent, (2) dig up the roots of the brand narrative, and (3) identify common themes across respondents.

Regardless of the research methodology you employ, a presence study attempts to find common themes and archetypical experiences. In the example above, you may note that several respondents com-bined a theme of adventure versus stagnation when they described travel and their affinity for the motorcycle. This pattern may lead to a brand theme. Further, if you were to note that several of your respon-dents described a similar, revealing experience, you may have uncov-ered part of the actual brand narrative. Using the motorcycle example, you might hear several respondents describe a test drive the same way. Each might have indicated initial doubts about owning a motor-cycle, but after going on the test drive at the dealership, they knew they had to own one. This pivotal experience may very well be a se-quence in the brand narrative. Explore it.

EXPLORATION METHODS

Focus groups and quantitative surveys are, by far, the most fre-quent research methodologies in practice today. Each of these method-ologies has its merits. Focus groups are relatively inexpensive, quick to design and execute, and qualitatively revealing. Survey research, on the other hand, is often more precise and statistically significant. Focus groups are better at measuring depth of information, while survey research is better at measuring specificity.

Each methodology has its share of limitations, too. Focus groups are only as strong as the moderator conducting them and the screeners selecting the respondents. Survey instruments are only as strong as the questionnaire design.

The use of focus groups and surveys is pervasive. You've probably either used one of these instruments or participated in their use by someone else. For this reason, we will limit our discussion to other designs—designs that are less frequently used but have potentially great value to the keeper of a Legendary Brand. Know that focus groups and surveys are both viable tools that you should, and undoubtedly will, use in your exploration of brand narrative. Their widespread adoption within the marketing industry make them effective and efficient resources. Survey research, in particular, is a valuable tool you will use when measuring the effects your brand narrative has on purchase behavior.

As we previously discussed, the exploration of brand narrative is difficult because people do not necessarily think like they talk. Further, they may have trouble expressing how they feel about brands, and an even harder time articulating the stories they perceive about the brand. The techniques that follow warrant your attention because they make it easier for consumers to reveal how they perceive the brand.

In-Depth Verbal Techniques: The Long Interview

Perhaps the most valuable and overlooked child of marketing research is the long interview, or one-on-one. In recent years, many advertising agencies and research firms have expanded their use of long interviews, but they have not enjoyed the same level of adoption at the corporate level. Usually marketing managers fear that the small sample size associated with the technique will not provide data that truly represents the market.

Statistically speaking, the sample sizes of most long interview studies are not significant. They do not usually have the statistical validity of a large, survey-driven research design. Because it is often very costly to implement a long interview study that includes an appropriate number of respondents in order to be statistically significant, this methodology is invariably neglected. It's a shame, especially because, with the right practitioner, the results of the long interview are often revealing and representative of the larger consumer segment, even in small sample sizes.

The long interview is exactly what it sounds like, a long interview. A sample of consumers is screened in advance according to the research design. Then, a researcher meets with each consumer individually, to discuss a topic. Some interviews are as short as 20 minutes, while others go on for hours, sometimes in multiple parts over several days.

The long interview's place in the exploration of Legendary Brands is critical, especially when you seek to understand the brand's role in the consumer's narrative identity. The process is akin to psychotherapy. The one-to-one relationship provides for a more intimate conversation, and increases the comfort level of the respondent.

Of course, two variables determine the quality of the research: the quality of the researcher and the design of the questionnaire. The two are interrelated. When you use the long interview method, the researcher is the research instrument. Unlike with a survey, the researcher cannot stick to the script and barrel through a battery of questions. The long interview is truly a conversation, and the interviewer must listen carefully and take cues from the comments of the respondent. That does not mean that such interviews should be conducted without a questionnaire. The questionnaire is critical, for it becomes the guide-map from which the researcher artfully navigates the discussion.

The seminal publication on the technique is Grant McCracken's *The Long Interview*. He offers a particularly solid technique for analyzing your data once the interviews are complete, which is altered here for the purpose of studying brand narrative.[2] Your analysis should unfold in five stages. In the first stage, you merely observe what is said in the interview. You note remarks and discussion points that are of interest, but ignore their relationship to other points. For example, you might note that Consumer A mentioned a preference for horror films. Consumer B mentioned liking rock music. Consumer C liked extreme sports. Each of these observations may or may not be related, but that is not your concern at this stage. You are merely noting points of interest.

In the second stage, you develop your observations in three ways: (1) by fleshing out what the observations might mean individually, (2) by comparing the observation relative to other observations found in the rest of the interview, and (3) by comparing the observation to secondary sources or other studies. For example, you might believe that the comments of Consumer A (liking horror movies) relative to the rest of the interview demonstrates a need for suspense and fear. Perhaps this consumer likes to be scared. A review of other studies conducted in the brand category may validate your hypothesis.

In the third stage, you sketch a consumer profile. You look at your observations more abstractly, and try to piece them together to create an archetype, or at least a characterization that is likely to be relevant to the brand narrative. For example, your observations above (coupled with others we have not presented) may lead you to construct a narrative identity linked to rugged heroism. At this stage, you might begin relating the observations to myths, culturally significant legends, or other comparative narratives. You also begin to position your brand in relation to the consumer profile. Where does the brand fit within the narrative? In this instance, you might find that the consumer narrative compares to the hero in a comic book series—with two-dimensional foes and extreme dramatic situations. The brand might occupy a position of enabling the hero. If your brand was Mountain Dew, for example, you might hypothesize that the brand somehow augments or activates this extreme heroism.

In the fourth stage, you test your hypotheses. Do the relationships you've constructed between your observations accurately depict the narrative identity of the respondent based on the data collected in the interview? Are there other solutions? For example, is it possible that Consumer A likes horror movies because the consumer actually enjoys seeing violence? Perhaps the consumer has violent tendencies and the horror films are a way to safely explore such thoughts. In this context, maybe Mountain Dew plays the role of counterculture rebel—an accomplice to a perceptual crime. Stage four is a chance to circle back and ensure that you've done your homework and not been led astray by initial observations.

Finally, in stage five, you look for the patterns between the interviews. It is at this stage that you define the narrative of the brand, doing so by relating it to the brand's position within the observed character profiles. Your task is to define archetypes, themes, genre, and/or narrative templates. For example, you might determine that one theme of the Mountain Dew brand narrative is heroics versus death. The narrative template revolves around an extreme hero being beckoned to potentially fatal challenges, an acceptance of the challenge, followed by a frightening but life-affirming transformation.

The process above is illustrative, but McCracken's five stages provide a thorough methodology for translating deep interview material into brand narrative. Whether you are the researcher, or the analyst who must review the work of the researcher, it is beneficial to apply this rigor to your analysis.

Observational Techniques: Narrative Inquiry

In the physical sciences, most theories are proved through observation. Marketers are less inclined to trust observations. Instead, they often seek data to analyze. Yet sometimes the best way to explore brand narrative is to observe it in action. Narrative inquiry is a technique that allows you to do so.

Narrative inquiry is not a standardized research methodology. In fact, the definition of the technique varies widely. For our purposes, it is the study of how people narrate, meaning that the focus is on the discourse. When you utilize a narrative inquiry study, your objective is to observe how consumers recount their experiences, including their word selection, phrasing, event sequencing, and delivery.

The simplest form of narrative inquiry is to review written materials. The consumer is given an assignment, either a lengthy essay-style questionnaire or a simple question to be answered in a few paragraphs. The researcher then studies the material to discern what the consumers have said and how they chose to say it.

For example, suppose you are the manager of a computer hardware brand. You wish to determine whether your brand narrative is meaningful to consumers. You ask consumers to write a 500-word essay about the most meaningful experience they ever had with their computer. Twenty-five consumers respond to your query. You note that more than half of the consumers chose to talk about their first experience connecting with someone else via the Internet. These consumers attribute the connectivity to their computer. One consumer says, "When I heard that voice tell me I had mail, I was just so psyched. It was so easy, and I thought it wouldn't be. If a dummy like me can use it, anybody can!" From this observation, and others like it, you can glean a lot about personal narrative. First, we can conclude that the consumer finds most technology to be complicated (". . . I thought it wouldn't be. . ."), but also that an inability to quickly learn how to use technology makes the consumer feel inadequate (the self-reference to being a "dummy"). From the text, you can sense the excitement caused by the brand (being "psyched," using an exclamation point, and general tone).

The limitations of this technique should be obvious. Grammatical proficiency will vary greatly between respondents. Some respondents do not write the way that they would talk. Writing provides many respondents with the opportunity to edit and change the material that is not reflective of the original thought.

Despite these deficiencies, a written inquiry should not be dismissed. You must factor limitations into your analysis, but data such as these can be a strong supplement to your other research. A written narrative study can also tie nicely with promotional programs, although you must consider self-selection biases.

The second method of narrative inquiry is more difficult to implement because it requires very skilled researchers, but it yields fascinating results. These studies analyze in-person interviews with respondents, usually in pairs or small groups of people who know one another. The respondents are guided through a conversation about life experiences related to the brand. After the interview is complete, the researcher reviews the conversation to examine the ways in which the respondents interacted and constructed their personal narratives. For example, when one respondent repeatedly interrupts another or completes the other's sentences, it may be an indication of "co-tellership." In their book, *Living Narrative,* Elinor Ochs and Lisa Capps explain that co-tellership has both negative and positive aspects. The negative aspects are that high levels of co-tellership may skew the narrative recollection or stifle narrative expression. On the other hand, co-tellership may create a debate between the respondents over what really happened in the past brand experience. This gives the researcher the opportunity to observe conflict and its relationship to the brand. It also generates greater detail, because one respondent elaborates on the comments of the other, recalling information that might otherwise have been omitted. Finally, the observed interplay provides the researcher with consumer information beyond what is said. For example, suppose one respondent frequently interrupts and corrects another in your study. Assume also that the interrupter is your loyal brand user. This domination of conversation or the pursuit of accuracy may tell you something about your consumers, particularly if you observe this pattern of behavior in other interviews.[3]

Such narrative inquiry studies hold great potential value for the explorer of brand narrative. They complement traditional focus group and qualitative studies well, and provide structural balance to the narrative. They are particularly well matched to studies designed to profile your consumer segments—the people living narratives your brand activates. The interplay between respondents also allows the researcher to delineate between the constructed identity of the speaker and the perception of that identity by the companion.

Nonverbal Techniques: ZMET

Perhaps the best methodology for your research is one that does not use words at all. As we discussed earlier, evidence suggests people do not think with words. Putting thoughts into words is a translation process. For this reason, research methodologies that use nonverbal response mechanisms are often invaluable, particularly in brand narrative studies. Some of these methodologies include asking respondents to draw pictures of a brand experience, caption illustrations related to a brand-use experience, arrange or manipulate photographs and other images associated with a brand, or act out a scene from a brand experience. Each of these techniques allows the respondent to communicate with something other than language. The problem with these techniques is that they are open to interpretation. They are also dependent on the capabilities of the respondent.

One technique that has gained a lot of attention is the Zaltman Metaphor Elicitation Technique, or ZMET. Developed by Harvard professor Gerald Zaltman, ZMET is a research methodology that captures nonverbal thought by having respondents construct visual metaphors. The participants are asked to take photographs or collect images from various sources that express the meaning of a given topic. Usually, the participants have several days to complete the assignment. The technique then leads to an eight-step process that includes storytelling, collaboration, and image manipulation. The end result is a visual metaphor, with corresponding interview data, that articulates the consumer's thoughts about the subject.[4]

ZMET is gaining a following in the marketing community because of its analytical rigor and its incorporation of nonverbal responses. Its potential use in the study of brand narrative is promising because it allows you to study consumers' metaphorical representations of the brand, and because it uses storytelling to achieve its purpose. The technique is patented and practiced only by licensed practitioners, making it more difficult and costly to access. Nevertheless, as it continues to grow in popularity and credibility, ZMET is one of a handful of new research methodologies that are well suited to Legendary Brands because it taps the subconscious level that masks brand narrative.

AN INTERVIEW WITH LIN MACMASTER: CEO of Strategic Partners Group

Lin MacMaster is the founder and CEO of Strategic Partners Group, a marketing research and strategy firm based in McLean, Virginia. Strategic Partners Group has uncovered pioneering insights for brand-leading clients such as AOL, Coca-Cola, Disney, and Kodak. Her firm is a specialist in right-brain research methodology, a proprietary framework well suited to the discovery of brand narrative.

Larry: What is right-brain research methodology?

Lin: Right-brain research methodology is rooted in cognitive psychological methodology. It is used to uncover rational and emotional drivers and ultimately consumers' motivation for the decisions and actions that they take. It was first practiced by Dr. Richard Maddock, based on 25 years of psychiatric practice. Its basis is the belief that there are five core motives that account for 70 percent of the decisions that consumers make. The other 30 percent is accounted for by rational and logical behavior. The five core motives include:

1. Survival motives (spiritual, physical, territorial, and sexual)
2. Orientation motives (person, place, time, circumstance)
3. Expectation motive (trust, hope, conviction, future, happy endings and resolution)
4. Adaptation motive (desire to adapt and be like others)
5. Play motive (fun and creativity)

Larry: How is right-brain research methodology conducted?

Lin: It is conducted in a one-on-one, one to one-half hour length interview. It uses relaxation and repetition so that, in some ways, it is like being in a hypnotic state. When consumers are fully relaxed, we have the ability to take them back to moments in time when they made a decision about a specific brand. We are able to gain all of the emotional content of that decision and how the individual rationalizes the transaction.

During the course of the interview, the respondent "gives" the interviewer subliminal cues. Most of the cues are developed in childhood, hence when we take individuals back to their first experience, they more often than not will go back to their childhood for their very first experience.

Larry: Can you provide any examples?

Lin: For Madison Square Garden, individuals relived their first memories of Madison Square Garden, and how it was a rite of passage. It was their first time being able to go somewhere without a parent. It was feelings of freedom. These were life-defining moments. They also recalled being with the family as kids, and all of the positive feelings that flowed from that experience.

In each case, these experiences were recounted with specific cues in terms of "it made me feel like I had arrived," "that I was special," "that there was no place else like it." All of these cues align with a specific motive.

Larry: What makes right-brain research methodology effective in brand narrative studies?

Lin: Storytelling is a form of personalization. Stories help consumers process their lives. As David Wolfe has said, "every good storyteller knows that the way to reach people's interest is to capture their hearts before getting into the minds." Marketing is more about appealing to people's dreams, fantasies, and feelings that relate to who they are and where they want to be in their lives. It's about personalization.

So, if we were to look at brands, how do brands help people process their lives? How does this brand create meaning for me in my life? It is through personalization. The right-brain research methodology cuts through all of the rationalizations that a consumer has about the product or service and gets to both the emotional and rational drivers that define how consumers process their lives and how products and service fit within. The interview is emotionally based and the affinity reveals itself through the emotion. The respondents tell their stories in the process.

Larry: When should right-brain research methodology be used?

Lin: Right-brain research methodology is best used in understanding the consumers' relationships with brands, especially the needs related to the development of an offer or specific communications message. It is an excellent means to uncover hidden needs and motivations for product use.

6

CRAFTING BRAND
NARRATIVE

. . . care for shimmering set, active plot, bright
characters, change of pace and gaiety should
all show in the plan. Leave out any two, and
your [story] is weaker, any three or four and
you're running a department store with only
half the counters open.

F. Scott Fitzgerald in a letter to John Peale Bishop,
1935 *Letters*

Story is strategy. In many ways, the two concepts are the same. A strategy is a carefully crafted sequence of events. So, too, is a story. Strategies are the product of rigorous logic and thinking, but the best of them are also inspired by imagination and creativity. So, too, are stories.

As the steward of a Legendary Brand, you must learn to trust story as your strategy. The minute brand managers ignore the narrative of the brand, and craft strategy with the language of the banker or corporate financial officer, the power of the brand evaporates. Yes, brand narrative must translate to financial results, but the voice that gives it structure and endurance must be that of the storyteller.

Crafting a brand narrative, and nurturing it over time, is your most important task. You may not consider yourself a storyteller, but you are. Veteran television producer Norman Lear claims that storytelling "is a gift we all have." He cites children as the clearest example of our natural narrative gifts. "Kids have stories to tell every day of their lives." Much of our everyday storytelling ability results from instinct, but the craft of narrative can be learned and applied.

In this chapter you will learn how to create a brand bible. The brand bible governs the sacred and profane dimensions of the brand. *Bible* has a secondary meaning, too. In the entertainment industry, television producers construct series bibles to guide the development of television programs. A series bible chronicles all of the dramatic twists and turns of a series from its pilot to the present. It also provides background material on characters and tangential story arcs.

Creating a brand bible is not an exact science. It is a creative process that requires your unique variation on a theme to bring it to life. Think of yourself as a chef studying the culinary arts. Chefs do not impress their guests by following recipes. Instead, they master the tools of the trade and then use those tools to explore their own palette and imagination, combining ingredients to create a signature dish. What follows is a chef's reference for the storyteller. You need not use every technique. Each serves a slightly different purpose, but all of the ideas and methods presented can help you define and memorialize your brand narrative.

A CRITIC AS YOUR GUIDE

The best framework to structure your narrative thinking was written 3,000 years ago by Aristotle, the Greek philosopher, and part-time dramatic critic. His essay, *The Poetics*, is still widely used today by writers ranging from copywriter to screenwriter. Aristotle wrote the material as a counterargument to an attack on poetry by Plato. There is no indication that he ever intended it to be a rule book for dramatists, yet his critical analysis of what makes great drama and poetry powerful is as relevant today as it was in ancient times. He deduced that a good story can be deconstructed into six parts:

1. Plot
2. Character
3. Reasoning (theme)
4. Spectacle
5. Song
6. Diction

For the purposes of constructing a brand narrative, I have condensed these to four parts: plot, character, theme, and aesthetics. Aesthetics includes any part of the brand that stimulates one of the five senses. Spectacle (what you see), song (what you hear musically), and diction (how words are constructed to convey meaning) are important elements for the visual and performing arts. Brands, however, can also stimulate taste and touch, and these can be powerful narrative devices. For example, the taste of a Mondavi Cabernet Sauvignon is just as important to its brand narrative as the design of the winery's label—maybe more so.

Figure 6.1 shows the four elements that we can consider when thinking about brand narrative. Most Legendary Brands are strong in each of these dimensions, but any one of them can be isolated to craft a narrative. Depending upon the way your mind works, one of these dimensions may spark your creativity more than others. By focusing on aesthetics, for example, you may inadvertently define your plot, or vice versa.

Many other parts of *The Poetics* will often be your reference in this chapter, and others that follow. In addition to the four story elements above, we will also return to the three-act structure, the role of the beat, and the importance of archetypes and myths. These were first presented in Chapter 3, but will be heavily applied to the material herein.

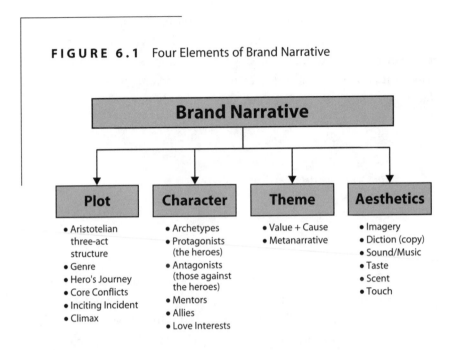

FIGURE 6.1 Four Elements of Brand Narrative

CREATING MATERIAL FOR A BRAND BIBLE

A brand bible is the marketing equivalent of a family scrapbook, a book of shadows, and a personal diary combined. It can take many forms. Some brand bibles are voluminous and paper-bound, while others are concise and mounted on foam-core boards. Some are digital and live in the form of PowerPoint slides. Still others fill an entire room with props, renderings, and other paraphernalia. You may wish to use the four story elements as the "chapters" of your bible, but many brand bibles never overtly address them. Some brand bibles include a mission statement, a statement of purpose, a credo, a song, or a set of principles. Others have few words, are filled with pictures, and resemble a gallery exhibition catalog. Regardless of the choices you make on the form and content of your brand bible, its purpose remains the same: A brand bible should be the ultimate sourcebook of the brand team. Do not worry if it is too cumbersome to be useful with third parties or senior levels of management. That is not the purpose of a brand bible. Though it will be culled to inform those parties, the brand bible is a resource for the team bound to the longevity of the brand.

The first step in the crafting process is to think about your brand and decide what is needed to understand, define, and communicate the brand narrative. Ask questions, such as:

- What are the forms of communication the people in my company will best respond to?
- What forms of communication suit the style and personality of my brand?
- What will help me and my team get grounded in the story of the brand?
- If my team disappeared tomorrow, and all that was left behind was this brand bible, what would it contain that would help the new team sustain the brand story?

If all else fails, ask the classic questions journalists use every day:

- *Who* will read the brand bible?
- *Why* will they care about its contents?
- *What* must it include to resolve their needs?
- *Where* will it reside?
- *When* will the users most likely refer to it?
- *How* will it most often be used?

The Box

Most writers, myself included, fear only one thing: a blank sheet of paper. While a blank sheet promises a wealth of possibilities, it also offers nothing. Empty vessels are simultaneously liberating and confining. For established brands, the brand narrative already exists but hides in the shadows. Your task is to define it. This is usually easier than launching a new brand and literally starting with a blank sheet. In either case, you may initially find yourself staring at a blinking cursor on an empty computer screen. Whether crafting a narrative for an established brand, or defining the narrative for an upstart, *the box* will relieve the tension you might initially feel about starting from nothing.

The box is a concept that imposes limitations on the narrative landscape. It is a simple idea. Draw a box on a sheet of paper. Everything inside the box is part of your brand narrative. Everything outside the box is not. For example, "beautiful and beneficial" is inside the box for Neutrogena. Any beauty or health products that do not accentuate the body's natural beauty or that can potentially cause harm (such as pore-clogging cosmetics) are outside the box. If you were to define Neutrogena's narrative landscape, you would be limited by "beautiful and beneficial" as an in-the-box criteria. The narrative structure requires an emphasis on health and beauty working together—not "face paint" and "astringents." You would probably not use the story of Cleopatra as a narrative archetype for Neutrogena. Our archetypal image of Cleopatra involves liberal use of mascara and artificial cosmetics (some illustrations have depicted her in gold face paint). It is widely perceived that such use of cosmetics is damaging to the skin. Thus, Cleopatra is probably out of the box for Neutrogena's brand narrative.

By limiting that which does not exist within the narrative of your brand, you define the brand narrative itself. Also, limitations challenge you. Some of the greatest works of art and engineering resulted from the imposition of limitations. When we are given clear boundaries, our natural instincts are to push against them. When we do, the result is usually breathtaking. The works of painter Pablo Picasso, architect Frank Lloyd Wright, and filmmaker George Lucas are but a few examples of artists who changed the world by pushing against the boundaries of their medium.

A large factor driving Apple's resurrection resulted from the daring ways the new product and its advertising pushed against the established boundaries confining Apple. When competitors were playing and winning a low cost game, Apple responded with an emotional appeal to the creative aspiration in each of us. They redefined what a personal computer meant in your life—they can be used to play and mix music, edit a home video, or create family photo albums. Apple even asserted that computers themselves can be beautiful. They do not need to look dull and gray. They can have color.

As you use the box, think of many factors, not just one. What aesthetic elements (color palettes, visual design, etc.) are in the box of your brand narrative? What themes are in the box? What character archetypes play an important role and in what kinds of plot structures? Spend equal amounts of time defining what lies outside the box. This simple framework will guide you throughout.

Characters: The Brand's Living Influence

Narratives are most engaging when the audience can follow compelling characters overcoming great obstacles. We care about great stories first and foremost because we care about the people in them. Stories that fail to give us characters we care about usually fail.

Characters of brand narrative exist in three separate but interrelated dimensions. The first dimension is an abstraction. It considers the brand as a character, in a mythic narrative. It usually does this by representing the brand as an archetype. The second dimension is literal. It considers the consumer and the character(s) they play in their personal narrative(s). Finally, the third dimension considers brand agents and their relationship to consumers and brand.

Considering the brand narrative from these three dimensions creates a system of checks and balances. Thinking of the consumer as a character ensures that you address the narrative needs of your consumer segments so that your brand can play a meaningful role in their daily life performances and your brand agents are relevant. Focusing on the archetypal character dimension ensures that you do not try to be all things to all consumers, preserving the brand's unique point of view and personality. Focusing on the brand agents ensures that you have created the narrative link between brand and sacred beliefs.

Brand as archetypal character. "From the unconscious there emanate determining influences which, independently of tradition, guarantee in every single individual a similarity and even sameness of experience, and also of the way it is represented imaginatively."[1] Famed psychologist Carl Jung asserted that ingrained within each of us is an archetype, a mask of sorts that is instantly recognizable to others and governs our behavior and personality. Although each individual wears the mask differently, Jung believed the commonality of character traits between those wearing the same mask was uncanny.

Today, Jung's theory is having a major impact on marketing. Margaret Mark and Carol S. Pearson's book, *The Hero and the Outlaw*, asserts, in proper Jungian tradition, that brands represent archetypal character. According to Mark and Pearson, brands such as Harley-Davidson are instantly recognizable as an "outlaw," inciting rebellion or living the wild life; while brands such as Calvin Klein may play the role of the "lover," seducing others and living for the glory of sensual pleasure.[2]

Mark and Pearson identify 12 separate archetypes applicable to consumer brands. Though not referring to brands, Joseph Campbell defined fewer archetypes, focusing most of his attention on the Hero, but also identifying the Mentor, Threshold Guardian, Trickster, and Shadow. Jung himself was even vaguer, giving a great deal of attention to a few archetypes he believed had the most psychoanalytic value, specifically, the Mother, the Child, and Father. He left plenty of breathing room for others to define narrower archetypes.

It matters not which framework you choose. Archetypes are a convenient means to an end. By defining the archetype associated with your brand, you reveal clues to the narrative. For example, MTV has defined youth culture for more than 20 years. It has not accomplished this feat quietly. MTV reinvents itself every year, and each time it rocks and shocks. It was on MTV that President Clinton was asked if he wore boxers or briefs. A review of MTV's history, its aesthetic environment, its programming, and its relationship to its audience quickly reveals that MTV embodies the archetypal character of the Rebel, Outlaw, or Trickster—you choose the label. It is the brand equivalent of the smug, wiry high school iconoclast who sits in the last row of class making wisecracks and organizing pranks. It is a brand that means no serious harm, but will always push the envelope. It is serious about certain matters ("MTV Rocks the Vote," a campaign which encourages voter registration and advocates voter participation), while irreverently apathetic about others (the "MTV Movie Awards," which mocks Hollywood as much as it honors it). Thinking of MTV as the archetype of the Rebel makes it very easy to consider the brand narrative. The stories that involve this kind of rebel emerge effortlessly, and if they don't, you have a wealth of source material to draw upon as your template. You can reread *The Catcher and the Rye*, or *A Separate Peace*, or *The Outsiders*, to name a few.

Jung developed his analysis of archetypes as a tool to understand the behavioral patterns of his patients. Identifying the archetypal model could help him and his patient address and resolve negative character aspects and behavioral problems. Your use of archetypes provides a similar purpose. The archetype a Legendary Brand represents provides a character model that should guide the brand's behavior. Once you have identified the archetype, your next task is to codify it in your brand bible. You should answer questions such as:

- What motivates this archetype?
- What beckons this archetype into a confrontation? What kinds of conflict are you likely to associate with this archetype?
- How does it interact with the other archetypes? For example, is it more willing to fraternize with other rebels, is it a loner brand, or does it mix it up with "average guy" archetypes?
- In what environments would you be likely to find this archetype (e.g., would it dine at a deli, a fast food restaurant, or the latest hot spot in the Zagat Guide?)?

There are many other questions you can ask. Your purpose is to give the brand a character description. You don't need to be specific and give the character a name and a specific character history because the archetype is not a character, but a representation of a commonly held character type. Shakespeare's Romeo, Henry Fielding's Tom Jones, and Woody Allen's Alvy Singer (from *Annie Hall*) are all of the Lover archetype, but each is quite different as an actual character. Fleshing out the specific character of the brand is a task you will undertake in the communications process, when you design your brand campaign. Just like your campaigns, the specificities of the brand character may change many times over the course of history, but the archetype remains the same.

Your brand bible can codify the archetype in many ways. Use photographs to show the types of people that fall within the set of the archetype. Prepare a reading list, and identify the character in the cited works who represents the brand in the story. Go through catalogs and circle the clothing or merchandise the archetype would favor. All of this will later help you to place the brand within the brand narrative.

Realize, too, that few brands have only one archetypal dimension. Many times a brand can be either one archetype or another. Sometimes it can be both. Romeo is both a Rebel and a Lover. Similarly, Apple is both a Rebel and a Creator. Be sure to explore the different archetypes consumers might perceive about your brand, and give due consideration to the hybrid archetypal forms your brand is likely to assume.

Consumers as characters. Arguably, the most important character in your brand narrative is the consumer. Consumers populate the landscape of your brand narrative, but they also integrate your brand as a character or element within their personal narrative, or life movie. A symbiotic relationship exists that requires your understanding because it is a relationship that will be integral to your marketing planning.

In his book, *Aspects of the Novel*, E.M. Forster delineated the difference between biography and characterization. Forster argued that literary works that did nothing other than recount the actions of a person were historical in nature, or biographies. Thus, a book that traced the actions of Queen Victoria was a work of history, because it did not allow the reader inside the Queen's head to understand her thoughts. Forster claimed that such a work is wholly different from a book that reveals how the Queen felt and thought. Only a narrative device, he argued, could reveal such information.[3]

The problem with most marketing plans is that they limit their scope to the first of Forster's assertions. These strategies identify what consumers do, but they ignore how they feel or think. For example, a marketing plan might indicate that the brand's average consumer is between the ages of 24–40, with 60 percent female, and an average household income of $45,000. Some plans might give greater detail, adding that this "average" consumer enjoys home renovation, buys Mary Kay cosmetics, and votes Democratic. While all of these observational facts are interesting, they do not reveal how this consumer thinks or feels.

Consumers must be an important element included in your brand bible. Take the time to sketch consumer biographies that allow the team to get inside the head of your core consumers. To create such biographies, draw upon various forms of data, including purchase data, demographic data, and psychographic data. Use the research methodologies outlined in Chapter 5, among others, to gain a greater understanding of the cognitive and emotional aspects of your consumer characters. Your biographies must reveal more than what these consumers do. They must help the team understand why the consumer characters behave as they do.

Unlike the archetype sketch, consumer biographies should not be too abstract. In fact, specificity generates the best results. Cluster your consumers according to common personal narratives and/or the way in which the brand participates in their life narrative (more on this in Chapter 8). Give each character a name, being careful to choose names that generate instant archetypal connotations. Assign a photographic image to the character, casting him or her in the role. If you do nothing else, giving a face and name to the character are often the strongest representational devices that convey meaning. While they do not specifically detail feelings or thought processes, the bias within each of us completes the profile.

Of course, you should go further with your consumer biographies. Specifically, answer the following questions:

- *A day in the life . . .* What is a typical day like for this consumer character? Get creative and describe a full day from the minute the alarm goes off in the morning until he or she turns in for the night. In fact, you could even go a step further and describe what he or she dreams about. Help your team walk in this character's shoes for a day.

- *Perception of the brand.* If you were to ask this consumer character to define the brand as an archetypal character, how would he or she describe it? If you have defined more than one archetype for your brand, or there are archetype blends, you might describe which of these this consumer would perceive.

- *Self image.* How does this consumer character see himself or herself? Clip pictures out of magazines or other photographic materials to give a portrait of how the character imagines himself or herself. This creates particularly meaningful insights if the picture you have chosen to represent the character varies considerably from the pictures the character would choose. It demonstrates their aspirations, or their delusions! You should also discuss the consumer's personal narrative(s). What scripts govern their lives? Perhaps your consumer character perceives herself in a *Broadcast News* narrative at work, but a *Sex, Lies, and Videotape* narrative at home? Most important, where does the brand fit within these narratives? What role does it play?

- *Brand behavior.* What other brands are meaningful to this consumer? Show the entire spectrum of brand loyalty, but don't stop there. Explain why these brands earn the consumer's loyalty. What is it about them that creates the affinity? Are there patterns? Are any of the patterns applicable to your brand?

In addition to narrative descriptions, you might want to use standardized scales to distinguish the differences between your consumer characters. Figure 6.2 depicts an excerpt from a hypothetical consumer character study. Note that in addition to descriptive data, this example also incorporates a scale that shows how savvy the character is about politics and other political criteria.

Brand agents as characters. The third and final approach to characters is to examine your brand agents. These can include your

FIGURE 6.2   A Character Profile

Character Profile | Chris
Age 28

Characteristics:

Political Knowledge	●●○○○
Voting Participation	●●●○○
Television Usage	●●●●○
Social Consciousness	●●●○○

- A **liberal democrat** who voted for Bill Clinton in 1992 and 1996

    - *Despises Republicans*, but has a difficult time articulating why

    - Believes the government has an obligation to provide more social services, particularly to children in poverty

- Familiar with the political headlines, but light on the details

    - Aware of latest scandals

    - Filters out much of what she perceives to be "partisanship"

    - Believe the media **exploits and distorts** political affairs

- Believes politics is local

    - "Too much attention is paid to Washington, D.C."

    - "The difference is made in your home town. If I get involved, it will be at the local level."

Character Profile | Chris
Age 28

Consumption Behavior:

- Buys brands that appear to be youthful and "good for her".
- Purchases are style-driven.
- Likes her purchases to connote a sense of fun, but also be practical
- Enjoys indulgences like trips to the day spa or wanton shopping sprees

She listens to…

She watches…

She consumes/uses…

(continued)

FIGURE 6.2   Character Profile, continued

Character Profile | Chris
Age 28

Heroes and reflections of self image...

Inner Self:

- Struggles against getting old and out of touch with the things that mattered to her when she was young

- Wants to be more socially active and find a cause

- Admires women who can be **confident, strong** and **sexy**

- Conflicted: aspires to a simpler life grounded in social issues -- but enjoys the superficialities of consumption [and aware of the contradiction]

Sarah Jessica Parker (and the persona she portrays in "Sex in the City")

Jodi Foster

Alanis Morissette

employees, the founder, celebrities associated with the brand, even fictional characters. Any entity you have used to represent your brand is an applicable agent for character study. If your brand has not yet utilized a brand agent, imagine that you have an unlimited budget and select the agents you believe would be most appropriate.

If you were to create a brand bible for the Warner Brothers entertainment brand, one character worth profiling is Bugs Bunny. Bugs is a brand agent who plays an important role within the Warner Brothers brand narrative. Similar to the consumer biographies above, Bugs's bio should describe what he does as well as how he feels and thinks. What makes him so mischievous? His bio should also describe how he fits within the Warner Brothers brand narrative. What role does he play? Because he is a brand agent, and brand agents give proof to the sacred beliefs consumers attach to the brand, you should also describe this relationship.

It might seem easy to complete such an exercise for a famous brand like Warner Brothers, but how do you do it for brands with less obvious brand agents? Suppose your brand is very new, and you don't have a brand agent. Ask yourself, if you were to select one celebrity to be your spokesperson, who would it be, and why? Celebrities are a great way to add character to the brand narrative, even if you never contract with them. Making the statement that a specific celebrity is the appropriate agent for your brand, and describing why that is so helps a broad swath of the team (and your consumers, should you ever choose to utilize the celebrity in your marketing communication) to reach common understanding about the brand narrative. For example, Priceline.com went from a faceless brand to a brand with meaning once it added William Shatner as a brand agent.

Plot: The Moving Parts of Story

Good stories have well-constructed plots. Though we touched on plot in Chapters 3 and 4, it warrants re-examination. One of the best summaries of a "good" plot can be found in David Howard and Edward Mabley's book, *The Tools of Screenwriting*.

1. The story is about *somebody* with whom we have some empathy. (Note that this first point highlights the importance of strong character development.)
2. This somebody wants *something* very badly.
3. This something is *difficult*, but possible to do, get, or achieve.
4. The story is told for maximum *emotional impact* and audience participation in the proceedings.
5. The story must come to a *satisfactory ending* (which does not necessarily mean a happy ending).[4]

Drawing from genre and myth. Recall the concept of the box. The box limited our scope by differentiating between that which was a part of the brand narrative and that which was not. As you consider the plot of your brand narrative, use the box to limit your scope. Thinking about the genre and myth associated with your brand is a useful application of the box.

Story sage Robert McKee[5] delineates a number of genres, subgenres, and hybrids, which are partially presented and related to certain Legendary Brands in Figure 6.3.

Figure 6.3 does not state that Marlboro is the brand representation of *The Searchers*, or that Microsoft is the brand representation of *Wall*

FIGURE 6.3 Genre and Brand Narratives

Genre	Film Example	Brand Example
Action-Thriller *(characters face supernatural or unusual foes in a fight to the death—the fate of the world often hangs in the balance)*	*Aliens*	PlayStation
American Cultural Epic *(an honorable character pursues a long-term quest against the changing cultural backdrop of American life)*	*Forrest Gump*	Coca-Cola
Buddy Movie *(an enduring friendship develops through a series of comedic incidents—in the end both characters are changed forever)*	*Big Daddy*	Budweiser
Dark Romance *(a couple's romantic hedonism is tempted by taboo and danger)*	*Eyes Wide Shut*	Calvin Klein
Education Plot *(the main character makes a deep change in his/her view of life—from negative to positive—and learns about a timeless principle)*	*Jerry Maguire*	MasterCard

Genre	Film Example	Brand Example
Family Movie *(a family faces a life-changing event—often laced with comedic exploits—which brings them closer together in the end)*	*Father of the Bride*	Kodak
High Adventure *(explosive action, rugged heroes, and exotic locales)*	*Raiders of the Lost Ark*	Jeep
Maturation Plot *(the coming-of-age story wherein the main character grows up)*	*Almost Famous*	MTV
Metropolitan Romantic Comedy *(people find intimacy and fall in love amidst the craziness of the big city)*	*When Harry Met Sally*	Pottery Barn
Modern Epic *(David vs. Goliath; the individual vs. the state or big money)*	*Tucker*	Apple
Musical *(reality of a comedy or drama represented through the inflection of singing and/or dancing)*	*Grease*	Gap
Punitive Plot *(the main character achieves success but is punished)*	*Wall Street*	Microsoft
Sports Challenge *(an athlete faces his or her most daunting physical challenge, but usually discovers the true test is psychological and against themselves)*	*Ali; Chariots of Fire*	Nike
Western *(cowboys on the open range, stoically facing hidden dangers)*	*The Searchers*	Marlboro

Street. Rather, it identifies a specific narrative genre, demonstrates how that genre was applied to a specific film, and how that same genre influences the narrative of a sample Legendary Brand.

Just as archetypes are a helpful way to define the character of your brand, genres provide a helpful means to create the plot of your brand narrative. By selecting an appropriate genre, you define the parameters of the box. For example, if you determine that your brand narrative fits within the film noir genre, then you should have a pretty clear understanding of what is and is not a part of your plot. Mystery and suspense will be very important, while whimsical musical numbers probably will not be relevant. Film noir plots usually revolve around characters with a somewhat shady background; they are sometimes referred to as *antiheroes*. The antihero of a film noir is often reluctant to accept the challenge posed by the narrative. (Think of all the old detective stories depicting a washed-up private eye who refuses an assignment only to be drawn in by his implication in a murder.) The plots are filled with plenty of subterfuge, usually associated with a sexy love interest—modern day sirens who cause lustful infatuations that lead to death. If your brand narrative is linked to the film noir genre, your plot must subscribe to these genre conventions.

Your brand bible should define the relevant genre or subgenre of your brand. Visual imagery can be invaluable. Select still images from motion pictures, television programs, or other performing arts to provide visual clues to the genre. Draft a narrative description of the genre and how it relates to the brand. Cite examples of storylines that are appropriate for the genre you have selected.

Perhaps the most valuable genre association is myth. In Chapter 3 we explored the close relationship between Legendary Brands and classic myths. It is in this phase of your crafting that myth should be a key focal point. Dust off your library card and explore timeless works of literature or mythology. If you were the manager of a cosmetics brand, you might chance upon the legend of Ponce de Leon and the quest for the Fountain of Youth. You might believe that this myth provides an inspiring backbone for your brand narrative. Perhaps you apply this mythology to the genre of the education plot. Your brand archetype is a Creator who previously sought alchemy as a means to beauty, but learned that true beauty results from the use of natural ingredients that come safely from various corners of the globe. Your brand tells the story of a quest for the fountain of youth that resulted in nature itself. Indeed, this is precisely the narrative of The Body Shoppe.

Consider three-act structure. We reviewed Aristotle's concept of three-act structure in Chapter 3. Recall that all stories contain a situation (act one), complication (act two), and resolution (act three). The three-act structure should be familiar to anyone who has worked in the advertising industry. For decades, advertising has relied upon a proven three-act formula similar to the following:

1. *Situation*: The consumer has a pressing need.
2. *Complication*: The consumer chooses Brand X to resolve the need.
3. *Resolution*: Brand X saves the day and the consumer is delighted.

Whether artfully done with top-notch creative effects, or "on the nose" with production values one step above community access cable, this formula continues to play out in broadcast advertising. It is Aristotle's three-act structure reduced to thirty seconds.

One way of getting to the core of your brand narrative is to think in three acts. Profile your consumer(s) before interaction with the brand. What is life like? What do they do? Where do they exist? This is act one.

Next, identify the complications that cause the consumer to interact with your brand. Complications need not have a negative connotation. Don't assume that brand interaction results because something awful is pressing upon the consumer. This may be the case, but it may be that other factors instigate brand interaction, such as a desire for pleasure, the need to connect with others, or the opportunity to give back to the community. Each of these factors has generally positive associations, yet they can create a complication in "life as usual" that triggers brand interaction.

This transition is known as the *inciting incident,* or the point of no return. It bridges acts one and two and sets your main character on a journey. Understanding it is often the key to understanding how consumers relate to your brand, what motivates them to prefer your brand, and when consumers occasion to use your brand.

Just as you must know what the inciting incident is for your brand narrative, you must also be well acquainted with the climax, the bridge between acts two and three that brings your master conflict to a head. How is your dramatic question resolved and what is the resulting changed state of the consumer? Understanding this is the key to understanding what sustains your brand's bond with the consumer over time.

Your three-act structure should also identify the many story beats, or changes in character state. Recall from Chapter 3 that a beat is a change in a subject from one state to another. Many beats make up a story. Robert McKee elaborates on this concept with the analogy of *the gap.* He believes that "story is born in that place where the subjective and objective realms touch."[6]

To McKee, great stories capture our attention because the participants are faced with a series of choices that increase their personal risk. In other words, the stakes are raised with each act of the participants. With each choice, the participant in the story can only know so much (the objective). They are faced with a decision and the outcome of that decision is unknown (the subjective). This mental precipice intrigues us and keeps our attention.

As you craft your brand narrative, pay attention to the gaps. At each point in your story, what is the gap the consumer faces between the objective world and subjective reality? If you are the manager of a legendary auto brand, you may think about your consumers as they approach their vehicle. The gap may be between safety (the objective world) and the risk of a collision (subjective reality). That gap may influence the consumer's brand preference, which makes it part of the narrative. On the other hand, the gap may be between pedestrian reality (the objective world) and the chance to experience speed and nimble handling (subjective reality). This speaks to an entirely different narrative.

You can choose to define your three-act structure literally, or in metaphorical terms. Sometimes, thinking in abstraction yields a more enduring brand narrative. Remember, you are not writing commercials. You are writing the basic story that underlies your brand. Keep it simple. Imagine a participant, or participants. Identify what triggers a dramatic question for them. Make the participants work to answer the question, and throw more conflict at them. Resolve the question and identify how the participants changed as a result. Do this in five bullet points, or fifty pages. The choice is yours.

Draw from the hero's journey. Modern storytellers owe a great debt to Joseph Campbell. Campbell noted that all of the great myths of the world shared a common theme—the quest of the hero. Campbell noted that this universal "monomyth" followed Aristotle's three-act structure, which Campbell defined as "separation-initiation-return." But Campbell didn't stop there. In each of these acts, he defined a common series of events or incidents, which presented themselves again and again, in countless cultural traditions.

The archetypal hero's journey, or monomyth as Campbell referred to it, usually involves an unsung hero who is called to adventure. The call is initially refused, but some force catapults him or her into an adventure with very high stakes. During the adventure, the hero faces death. In some cases, he or she actually dies. But the character returns from the edge of death with a secret or a special gift (Campbell called it "the elixir"). The hero returns home with secret/gift in hand and leaves his or her mark on the culture.

The most important aspect of the hero's journey is the descent—the hero faces his or her own mortality. Even in stories where physical death is never a threat, the hero usually faces a figurative death—it may be the loss of career, creativity, family, etc. Like the famous story of Orpheus in the underworld, it is the hero's journey through a personal hell and the return from this journey with a new perspective on life that gives the story its power.

Legendary Brands usually link to the hero's journey, most frequently as a symbol of triumph over death. Nike's swoosh is a meaningful symbol because it represents a commitment to self-challenge. Nike's products represent the secret/gift retrieved by the hero. The same can be said of the Apple Macintosh, Starbucks coffee, and Volkswagen Beetle.

As you craft the plot of your brand narrative, think of your brand's products as a secret or gift retrieved from a high-stakes adventure. What was the life and death conflict? What does your product and your brand mean to the hero of this journey? How is it enlightening? Tracing this route often helps to construct a brand narrative.

Refer back to sacred beliefs and known brand agents. In Chapter 2 we discussed the brand mythology cycle and the link between a worldview of sacred beliefs and a brand agent. We showed that narrative is the binding agent that brings these two entities together. As you craft your brand narrative, one very powerful resource to draw from rests in the known sacred beliefs and brand agents attached to your brand.

To this day, Hewlett-Packard still owes a large part of its brand narrative to the men from which it is named, and their legendary garage. GE's brand narrative continues to have some link to Thomas Edison, and the man who reinvented it, Jack Welch. In both cases, the story of the brand agents (the founders and managers) is at least one of the brand narratives.

If one of your brand agents is a person, don't assume that the brand narrative is simply that person's biography or pubic persona. Look beneath the surface. What mythic character does that person resemble? Is she a Prometheus, craftily subverting the secrets of the Gods to mortal man, or is he a Solomon, wisely reserving judgment in his rule of the people?

Explore the belief system surrounding your brand. The plot of a narrative centers on a dramatic question. This question often has philosophical roots. We'll explore these more when we discuss theme; however, the sacred beliefs that link to your brand may point to a dramatic question. This can be an effective starting point for your brand bible.

Consider more than one narrative. Many brands actually have more than one narrative. In many cases, multiple narratives tie back to an übermyth, but not always. In the early stages of your brand bible development, a few narrative lines may surface. Explore them all, or rank order them so that you can give the ones that seem most relevant due attention.

If several narratives do exist, and they are fairly distinct, it is probable that theme plays a dominant role in your overarching brand narrative. When theme plays a role, your narrative is much more abstract and linked to philosophical or phenomenological questions. This condition is a blessing and a curse. It is a blessing because it provides you with the greatest possible liberty to explore and develop your brand narrative. The possibilities are limitless so long as you stay within the boundaries of the overarching question. However, too much liberty can be a curse. Because your landscape looks more like Australia than Hawaii, it is harder to manage the terrain. Your brand narrative is more susceptible to erosion, irrelevance, and undifferentiated ubiquity. By the time you have discerned such problems, they may already have reached a crisis state, whereas the brand with a more constricted narrative will generally discern such issues before they get out of control.

Theme: A Reason for the Brand

Theme is the *why* of your brand. It gives the brand meaning. One could argue that only Legendary Brands offer a theme. All other brands lack that sense of meaning, relying on other qualities to differentiate themselves (e.g., quality, reliability, cost). Legendary Brands connote meaning, and this meaning governs the narrative. The stories that Legendary Brands tell (large and small) serve to emphasize the theme of the brand.

Governing theme. What is the governing theme of your brand? The answer to that question is likely to be a statement that defines the uniqueness of the brand. You might call it a mission statement, the elevator pitch, a position paper, or a point of differentiation. Make your statement of the theme concise and memorable. Robert McKee refers to the theme as the controlling idea. He says, "a controlling idea may be expressed in a single sentence describing how and why life undergoes change from one condition of existence at the beginning to another at the end."[7]

McKee defines the controlling idea as Value plus Cause. The Value expresses what changes. For example, in *Romeo and Juliet*, life-fulfilling love leads to death—*love kills*. The value change is from life to death. The Cause expresses what brought about the change in value. In Romeo and Juliet, the cause is the prejudice and hate of an ancient family rivalry. That gives us a full, controlling idea: life-fulfilling love leads to death when we allow prejudice and hate to govern our actions.

MasterCard's governing theme is so powerful they actually state it in their advertisements: "There are some things in life money can't buy. For everything else, there's MasterCard." If we were to put this in the form of a controlling idea, we would say, "Life is fulfilling (Value) because MasterCard lets us focus on what matters most (Cause)." The value change is from emptiness to fulfillment. Those who focus only on money are destined to live a life of emptiness. MasterCard causes the change from emptiness to fulfillment because it allows us to focus on the "priceless" moments that enrich our lives that no amount of money could ever buy.

It may take you a while to define your brand theme. You may have to flesh out other details, such as the characters and the plot before the governing theme begins to truly emerge. It is often easier to define the governing theme, or controlling idea, once the bulk of the narrative is defined. Once you do articulate the governing theme, memorialize it often. Tack it onto your computer display. Laminate it and carry it in your wallet. Paint it on the walls of the team conference room. This is the statement that will serve as your litmus test for future marketing efforts.

Subordinate themes. One theme may not be enough for your brand. Great stories often have many. In addition to its governing theme, *Romeo and Juliet* thematically depicts the power of true love. MasterCard's governing theme dominates its brand advertising, but it also communicates a subtle subordinate theme—money dominates our lives (Value) when we don't manage it well (Cause). MasterCard is a brand that resonates most strongly with middle America. Many of its core consumers do not live the executive life espoused by American Express, nor do they leap blindly into indulgences like the Visa card user. MasterCard customers manage their money well and with purpose so that credit problems do not take the focus off of the meaningful parts of their lives. One MasterCard advertisement targeted college students. It did not encourage them to get a card and run up a balance on all the cool stuff they could buy. Rather, it glorified the freedom gained by obtaining a good job and being self-sufficient. The advertisement linked to a promotional program that awarded 12 eligible college students a high-profile internship in the music industry. The subordinate theme prevailed.

Aesthetics: Narrating through the Senses

The narrative of Legendary Brands often reaches the consumer most potently through sensory clues. Brand narrative communicates to its audience in a manner that can be far more intimate and sensual than any movie, play, or book.

Starbucks is a Legendary Brand that tells its story well by captivating the senses. Every Starbucks embodies a distinct imagery that transcends the mere installation of the familiar logo. One generally enters a Starbucks and knows instantly that it is a Starbucks and not some other coffeehouse. The story is communicated by the visual design—what we see: natural materials, earthen color palettes, internationally eclectic styling.

Starbucks doesn't stop there. Our sense of smell is triggered immediately. When asked to recall an experience at a Starbucks, few consumers would forget the smell of freshly ground Espresso being force-saturated by scalding hot water.

Starbucks coaxes the ears. You can sense the sound of whistling espresso machines at any run-of-the-mill coffeehouse, but how many of these feature the eclectic soundtracks distinctly played at a Starbucks. These musical selections are closely tied to the brand narrative, and they are so popular that Starbucks created its own line of branded compact discs.

Starbucks also activates the sense of touch. The furnishings are plush and comfortable—overstuffed velvet couches, solid wood coffee bars with rich textural features, and a full line of coffee-related merchandise. Like any good themed-retailer, Starbucks provides you with a rich opportunity to touch the brand.

Lastly, of course, Starbucks rewards the taste buds. You can taste the brand, and when you do, you may touch the far reaches of Sumatra, the rainforests of New Guinea, or the warm tropics of Columbia. All the while, you also taste the French roasting tradition, the stringent Seattle blend of coffee-brewing, and the childishly reminiscent comfort of warm milk.

Brand narrative is often conveyed with the traditional tools of advertising and promotion. Style, imagery, sound cues, and artful use of the spoken word combine to conjure the narrative association. The effectiveness of such tools explains why they make up the largest part of a typical marketing budget. However, Legendary Brands must forage beyond the conventional audio-visual resources to connect with consumers and tell their tales.

Construct an image library. Perhaps the easiest, and often the most fun, part of constructing a brand bible is the process of making an image library. When you make an image library, your goal is to collect as many different photographs, illustrations, visual designs, renderings, and other visual items that communicate a dimension of the brand. One good photo album containing visual concepts of your brand's narrative attributes will train a new team member faster than any creative brief.

Mine stock libraries and clip from magazines to build the narrative imagery of your brand. With the growth of the Internet and the abundant access to software tools, it is very easy to find, augment, and present images that suit your brand narrative. You may seek out these images with preconceived ideas. You can sometimes stumble upon an arc of the brand narrative by browsing haphazardly through an image bank. Images possess a kind of magic for many people. Sometimes it requires visual exploration to drive the textual narrative. You may not know what all the different images mean, but somehow they communicate the brand. Use that visual stimulation to generate narrative by studying apparent plot activities (e.g., pictures of people running freely on the beach or of a woman crying on a park bench), character biographies, or thematic elements.

Create a brand soundtrack. This may seem odd at first, but a good soundtrack can often stimulate your thinking. Starbucks has a brand soundtrack, why shouldn't your brand? You may not be able to sell it to consumers the way Starbucks does, but you can use it to motivate your brand team or reground yourself in the sensory narrative of the brand.

Build a "war room." Anyone who has visited an advertising agency recently has probably chanced upon a client "war room." War rooms have been en vogue for some time now, and for good reason. They provide a space for the marketing team to develop their ideas in an unstructured environment. They also prove to be a great place for the team to meet, because they offer an environment that is infused with the brand.

As you start the process of crafting a brand bible, your first task may very well be to establish a war room. Size doesn't matter. It can actually be a corner of your office or cube. What matters is that you demarcate space exclusively for the brand narrative. Anything you come across that seems to convey the narrative should be placed into the war room.

Some war rooms are very structured, with an order that is very linear. Other war rooms look like a college dorm. They have a myriad of images, quotes, clippings, and three-dimensional objects strewn about.

The only thing that matters about a war room is that it creates an environment that helps the brand team orient with the brand narrative.

Other sensory exercises. Crafting an image library, laying down a soundtrack, and demarcating a war room are among the most helpful activities you can exercise to explore the aesthetic elements of the brand narrative, but there are others. You may choose to explore aesthetics through tastes by staging a brand potluck, or winding down with a brand Happy Hour (although hopefully aware that such an exercise will have decreasing returns to scale). At the Epcot theme park in Walt Disney World, Coca-Cola hosts an exhibit that allows park guests to sample fountain beverages produced by Coca-Cola from around the world. Whether it is the fruity, pineapple flavor favored in China, or the bitter, palette-cleansing variety preferred in Italy, guests can literally sample the different manifestations of the Coca-Cola brand.

You may also choose to explore touch aesthetics. Does your brand narrative require earthy textiles like suede and wool, or does it call for the refined poise of silk and satin. Finally, you could explore the smell of the brand. Once you get past the requisite joking around in your brand team, you can explore whether or not your brand narrative conjures the woodsy smell of cinnamon and hickory, or the perfumed essence of vanilla and musk. None of these exercises are group bonding field trips; they trigger your imagination and land the narrative.

Other Components of a Brand Bible

You should use the suggestions in each of the four dimensions above to craft material for your brand bible. The idea is not just to ideate, but to produce tangible materials that can be shared by the brand team and used to generate real marketing extensions. How you choose to record and memorialize the results of each of the exercises is up to you.

You may include certain other elements that enhance the productive use of your bible.

Glossary. As your narrative unfolds, it will define its own terms, jargon, and vernacular. Some narratives produce a vast and elaborate terminology all their own. Consider the *Star Trek* television and film franchise. You could fill several volumes with just the unique words and phrases it has produced. Hardcore fans have gone so far as to learn fictional languages linked to the narrative.

Your brand bible should include a glossary so that you can define the distinct words, phrases, and other jargon that stems from your brand narrative.

Annotated narrative history. While the central narrative of your brand should be sustained over an extended period (Coca-Cola essentially tells the same narrative today that it told nearly 100 years ago), the variations on your narrative theme will change with the times, consumer taste, and strategic initiatives of your company. Few companies keep an active account of these various narrative offspring. When they do, they are usually managed by an archivist that has absolutely no relation to the brand team.

Think about it. The average senior brand manager has a life expectancy of less than ten years on the same brand. Legendary Brands like Coca-Cola, Kodak, and GE have been around for decades. During their existence, these brands have outlasted a bevy of senior marketing executives, weathered through countless agency reviews and account transitions, and relaunched with all-new positioning more than once. Without a living record, what sustains the continuity of the brand narrative during each of these changes?

The series bible of television chronicles every narrative development of the program. When the writers are looking for a new twist or turn, they often resort back to the bible for inspiration. There, they may find some unexplored plot twist that was started awhile back but never developed. Shouldn't you do the same for your brand? At a minimum, keep, in one place, a record of all the brand advertising campaigns and significant brand endeavors.

PROCESSING AND SHARING YOUR BRAND BIBLE

Bottom-Up versus Top-Down Approach

There are basically two ways to go about crafting your brand bible. You can start from the top down, which is more strategic and hierarchical, or you can build from the bottom up, which is more organic. The choice depends upon the style and capabilities of you and your team.

The top-down approach is appealing to many because it sounds sexy when you explain it to your boss or client. To build the bible from the top-down, you usually start by defining the governing theme, then selecting the parallel archetypes and genres. Using this high-level concept of the brand narrative, you work your way down to flesh out the 12 stages of the three-act structure and craft aesthetic elements.

The top-down approach is a viable and rigorous endeavor. When it works, it tends to produce a brand narrative that is logically consistent at every level. That's what makes it so appealing. The analytical process that is used to produce the end result translates very well to the conventional process of crafting strategy, which makes it easier for the senior manager who must manage up. If you are crafting from the top down, you can provide feedback to your superiors or clients quickly, and keep them apprised of your progress without raising too many eyebrows or causing general uneasiness.

Unfortunately, crafting from the top down is hard. It requires you to define upfront many elements that do not reveal themselves until you have conducted analysis at lower levels. Many storytellers have a hard time writing a story by starting with a governing theme. For these storytellers, the theme is ephemeral, meaning one thing on Day 1, but something very different on Day 22. They let the theme define itself through the finished product.

If you have difficulty thinking in this manner, it is perfectly acceptable to begin from the bottom and work your way up. When you employ this approach, you start off as an explorer. You begin with aesthetic exercises, constructing a war room, culling from an image library, or profiling individual characters. From these activities, certain patterns begin to emerge which form the spine of lower-level narratives, in a sense, scenes from the hero's journey. Over time, these aggregate and you are able to discern the governing theme and the archetypal myth that govern your narrative.

The bottom-up approach works well, but it, too, has its drawbacks. For one, it can be lengthy. Because you don't know where you're going, you may take a couple of misleading paths. That can cost precious time. Second, this approach does not always satisfy senior management. Whether you are an agency or in-house marketing team, you may face some opposition when you tell your client that you don't have the strategy yet, but you built a really great war room. Finally, some people get lost in this approach. Its lack of structure can be a liability. You think you're headed in the right direction only to learn you went nowhere. The bottom-up approach requires self-discipline, even though and specifically because it indulges the creativity of the practitioner.

Translating Brand Bibles to Formal Corporate Strategy

At the end of the day, your brand bible must serve a purpose. This is not a self-exploration exercise and it is not intended as a bonding ritual for your team. This document or presentation must gain a useful longevity—a living strategy.

At Disney, I once watched the button-down chief marketing officer of a Fortune 100 company present his proposal to a group of Disney's creative executives. He did something absolutely brilliant. He retrieved an oversized, mocked-up storybook. Each page of the book detailed another element of his proposal, but it was written in story form, illustrated and designed to look like a fairy tale. He was speaking Disney's language, and he sold his proposal that day. He succeeded in translating his corporate marketing strategy into a form that Disney understood and revered.

Unless you are working at Disney, the chances are that the people you must influence do not speak the language of storytelling. Storytelling is a vernacular that will help you and your team manage the brand, but it will not always help you manage your superiors and external constituents. Your brand bible is not the document to wheel out at board meetings or financial reviews. It is, however, the source material that eases your preparation for those meetings.

APPENDIX: An Illustrative Brand Bible Development Process

Ideally, this chapter would end with a case study from an actual brand bible development project. Unfortunately, there are two pitfalls to such an exercise: First, brand bibles are the equivalent of strategic plans, and thus not material most companies wish to share with their competitors. Second, each project is unique, with its own set of issues and opportunities. For these reasons, I opted to illustrate the process with a fictional company and a hypothetical assignment. This format allows me to avoid inadvertent disclosure of confidential information, prevents against any biases you may have toward the marketing strategy of a given company, and allows us both to explore a wider range of exercises in the brand bible development process.

This hypothetical assignment will be led by the members of my team at Cabana Group, my marketing agency. Though the assignment is fictitious, the people and the techniques employed are very similar to those put to use on real client assignments. Any similarities between the hypothetical company and my clients are coincidental, however. This example is really an amalgamation of experience with occasional dramatic touches to keep you interested.

A Narrative for Communications

Our hypothetical client is a telecommunications company that recently acquired several regional players to forge a nationwide wireless and wireline communications network. I chose a telecommunications company because, after the breakup of AT&T in 1984, no telecommunications service company appears to have Legendary Brand status. Few telecommunications brands mean anything to the consumer beyond price and quality of service. It's not entirely the fault of industry brand managers, however. Telecommunications service delivers intangible value. When it works well, it is transparent, as it should be. The only time consumers are aware of the brand is when they have a problem. This makes Legendary Brand status an extraordinary challenge.

Our hypothetical company will have historic roots that were well publicized (to make the assignment a little bit easier). It is also well capitalized, and the company's senior management believes investment in the brand will deliver long-term benefits. Anyone who has ever worked with a telecommunications company knows that I am delving into pure fiction on this last point, but it is easier to imagine that the brand owners are investing in long-term benefits because a constrained budget would add different influences to our example. Most brand managers have limited resources, which would require rank ordering and other prioritization of the ideas we will develop in our illustration.

Day 1: Stalking the Narrative

Our objective is to develop the narrative that will guide everything the brand does. That is no small order. Our work will guide the company's advertising, promotion, sponsorships, packaging, and public relations. The company's chief marketing officer introduced our team to the leaders of their advertising agency, who will participate in the process. Kay Walsop, the company's Senior Vice President of Brand Management, will also be a key participant.

A conference call initiates the assignment. Our client recently switched agencies and is now represented by one of the best creative shops. They are represented on this call by Vijay Patel, the agency's Vice President and Management Supervisor on the account, Ian Forster, the agency's planning director, and Ben Ford, the agency's legendary Creative Director. Kay leads the discussion.

We are told that the agency must deliver the first round of new brand advertising in three months, when the company plans to introduce a new service that utilizes new collaborative technologies.

Given the timeline, we agree that our narrative development must wrap up in three weeks. We discuss some obvious themes. First, we believe there is value in the company's history. Kay is worried that a focus on the heritage of the brand might make it "your father's Oldsmobile." We assure her that we do not plan sepia-toned imagery as a major theme of the brand narrative, but we hypothesize that consumers will have strong recall of the historic roots.

We also believe there is a narrative that focuses on the value of communications. Ben groans and points out that creating a new round of saccharine ads featuring people in Argentina connecting with people in New Jersey will not do anything for the brand. We agree. The media is cluttered with telecomm brands that promise to break down national and regional boundaries. They produce imagery of people holding hands across borders. There's no story there, particularly because most users of wireless phones have no desire to call outside the country.

The conference call lasts three hours, some of it procedural, some of it dedicated to narrative brainstorming. We end it somewhat defeated. There does not appear to be any concrete narrative to draw upon. Our team divides and conquers. I will dig into literature, secondary research, and our in-house library of myths. My goal is to develop some archetypal representations of the brand and define the genre or guiding mythology. My lead planner, Jim Sheehy, will organize a primary research effort and explore the consumer narratives, if any. Meanwhile, Catherine Davie, our team assistant, will begin coordinating sessions with the agency and the client. She will also gather all of the legacy data from the client and construct a narrative history, paying particular attention to previous advertising and design initiatives.

Day 5: The War Room Comes Together

Several days pass. It is Friday afternoon. Jim just completed his first round of one-on-one interviews with consumers. He has two more rounds scheduled next week. The first round was held in and around Los Angeles. He interviewed a total of 20 respondents, and conducted two focus groups. The respondents included those that were current customers of the brand, those that used wireless services, but not our brand, and those that were intending to purchase wireless services.

Jim uses an artful technique for getting to the narrative. He begins his sessions with several clippings and images on the table. The images include pictures of people talking on wireless phones. They also include pictures of people communicating in other ways. After some introductory remarks and some general query, Jim asks the group to describe their thoughts on the pictures. It starts off very broad. One respondent mentions that the woman shown in one picture appears "stressed out." Jim probes this further and the respondent mentions that the woman pictured is probably using her cell phone to call home and explain why she is running late.

Jim uses this as a platform to get the group talking about cell phone usage. Thus far, the brand is not mentioned once, except for one respondent's comment that he subscribed to the brand. Jim opts not to pounce on this brand recognition yet. Later, he returns to it when the group turns its attention to wireless brands.

The first round of focus groups and one-on-one interviews yield few striking results. Expected observations surface, such as wireless devices being an "enablement" device, and a tool to help people "connect" and be more "productive." We expected comments such as these, but they don't help us much in terms of constructing the brand narrative. Only one insight emerges from these sessions that may be of help to us. One respondent in a one-on-one interview revealed that she uses her cell phone to plan clandestine activities in her life. Even though wireless communications are less secure than wireline communications, this woman revealed that she used her wireless phone to communicate with her former boyfriend. She did this so her current boyfriend wouldn't find out. She also revealed that she only gave her cell phone number to a carefully chosen group of people. What was interesting to us was the hint of privacy and exclusivity she revealed. She may well be a statistical outlier, but her session revealed a hint of intrigue and subterfuge. Something in this struck us all as a potential component of brand narrative.

I went next. My first exercise was to review classic literature and the works of Bullfinch, Campbell, and other chroniclers of myth. I decided to tackle the obvious first and research the narratives of mythic messengers and communicators. The obvious story was that of Hermes, the messenger of the Greek Gods. I thought it a bit "on the nose" but there were some interesting overlaps with Jim's early research. For one thing, Hermes often delivered messages in secret, or disguised himself to help Zeus out of a bind. I thought I might be stretching, but the team liked it.

I also revealed several other classic myths, legends, and stories that pertained to messengers. For instance, I discussed the legendary intelligence system setup by Sir Francis Walsingham during the reign of Elizabeth I, which used an intricate network of spies, children, and secret rendezvous to protect the crown.

We played with each of these stories for awhile. Others on the team added their own memories of stories about the process of communications. Then Catherine presented the material she had gathered about our client's real narrative history. Kay was on hand, too, to provide color commentary.

It turns out that the founders of the core company were practically criminals in their early days. They stumbled on to the concept for the business while phone *phreaking*, or using pirating technology to place free, unauthorized calls. Most of the original founders were no longer with the company, but one sat on the board. Kay explained that the phreaking heritage was ancient history and off-limits. To the rest of us, it was a god particle for the narrative.

Ben and Vijay intermediated. They argued that we would not directly emphasize history, or link the brand with criminal activity. Rather, we would exploit the narrative of innovative thinking, experimentation, and breaking the rules—all in the name of bringing people together. Well, we weren't so sure about the last part. Ian and I helped to shape this idea into something Kay could stomach. We explained that the archetypal Rebel character could be the link to the unusual observations Jim unearthed in his research. The brand, not the found-ers, could be seen as rebels advancing consumer technology. Still un-certain, Kay allowed us to proceed. We moved on to history.

On one wall of the war room, Catherine had laid out a complete history of the company, which looked something like a broom on its side. From the late 1970's to about 1996 the company had a fairly lin-ear development. Then came the period of acquisitions and the narra-tive fanned out into different directions.

I suggested that we keep moving with our core insights: the real history of the founders, the clandestine communications narrative re-vealed in the consumer research, the archetype of the Rebel and the communications myth of Hermes, et al. We also agreed that we needed a good sound genre to give the narrative structure. Ian and I planned to meet the following day and brainstorm the genre implications.

Day 8: Three Narratives Emerge

Jim phoned from Paramus, New Jersey, where he had just com-pleted another round of research. He employed some experimental techniques, this time using more imagery to coax narrative out of re-spondents. He discovered some interesting insights about where our client's brand stood in relation to other brand narratives. One of our client's fiercest competitors skewed towards a narrative of hope, opti-mism, and apple pie. They definitely came across as the "American" brand of communications. That did not disturb us too much because our client's narrative really held no patriotic or national associations, nor did we believe such associations would help it.

Jim found a few new instances of the clandestine narrative. This time it was a mid-forties business executive who used his cell phone to contact client prospects that were not approved by his management. Jim also found that many consumers viewed the brand as a bit "sub-versive." This insight came from their descriptions of people who might use our client's brand versus other brands. Jim laid pictures on the table of five different hypothetical consumers. For instance, one of the pictures showed an older man with a big, warm smile. He wore a polo shirt and appeared in good health for his age. Most respondents picked him as the kind of consumer that would buy the "American" competitive brand. The majority of respondents picked a young, slightly scruffy, but intelligent looking man as the consumer most likely to subscribe to our client's service. They said that the young man looked like a loner, and he would probably want our brand because it came across as anticonformist, or antibrand. We suspected that this belief stemmed from an Internet advertising campaign our client ran a couple of years ago, but the research findings were unclear.

Ian and I believed the appropriate genre for the brand was that of "the heist." This genre is evidenced in many motion pictures, such as *Robin Hood*, *The Sting*, *Sneakers*, and *Oceans 11*. In it, a group of people, mostly societal misfits, conspire together to take something away from a mark. The *mark* is usually a despicable or unlikable character, which makes the actions of the misfits acceptable to the audience. We believed that the genre worked for the client's brand because the giant telecommunications industry would make an appropriate mark that consumers would love to see robbed.

Meanwhile, Catherine set off to collect images that matched some of the narrative passages Ian and I pieced together. She also connected with Jim on a daily basis to begin gathering images that would depict our consumer clusters. Three narrative arcs were piecing together.

1. *Misfit innovators.* This narrative most linked to the actual history of the client. It was the story of scientists and engineers that didn't fit anywhere else so they banded together to create projects that appealed to their interests. In the process, they stumbled on to consumer innovations that benefit us all. They suspect authority, so they keep in the background of the company. But when you buy the product, you actually support their cause.

2. *Messenger of the gods . . . and other heroes.* This narrative focused on the connection capabilities of our client's products and services. The central character of this narrative was the consumer,

who had important information to deliver. Just as Hermes had winged shoes and the wand of caduceus, our consumers have client technology. The story units of this narrative would certainly revolve around the power to deliver information and influence events.

3. *Communications clique.* This narrative again featured the consumer as its central character—actually, a clique of consumers. We went a little overboard with the clandestine narrative. We pictured a comic book saga of people "in the know" linked by the communications network of our client. It harkened back to the days of the phreaking founders, but morphed into an ongoing story of innovation that enables people to stay ahead of oppressive, capitalistic mega-corporations pushing first generation technology onto consumers.

We realized that these three narratives were only weakly perceived by consumers. Some consumers were aware of the founders, but none of them mentioned the phone phreaking. Some recognized the client as an innovator, but it was only a weak recognition. The secretive aspects of the clique narrative surfaced in discussions with consumers, but not to the extent that we fleshed it out. Like any good writer, we needed to take some dramatic license to create the brand narrative.

Day 10: The First Rough of the Brand Bible

To illustrate these narrative extensions, we constructed a Power Point presentation for each story. We told the story with images from stock libraries. For each narrative, we profiled segments of consumers that could currently articulate the narrative or that we believed would subscribe to the narrative, once established. We also put together a soundtrack, which we played while walking Kay and the agency team through the presentation.

The team generally embraced the concepts and we all recognized that there were some common themes. Ben worried that the second narrative might have few opportunities for advertising. It was not so much that there were no stories to tell, it was more that the advertising would come across too similar to the advertising of our competitors.

Kay was enthusiastic of the work, but concerned that it might not play well with her boss, the chief marketing officer of the company. He was scheduled to review our work next week. She felt that we needed a backup plan, which we were all reluctant to do because time was short to begin with. Vijay, Ian, Jim, and I took turns arguing on behalf of our direction. She agreed to give us another few days.

Days 11–13: Preparing for the Big Pitch

We again divided and conquered. Jim took all of the data from the research and prepared five consumer biographies. We sketched these out in PowerPoint, with four slides for each archetypal consumer. The first slide gave a general bio of the consumers: Who they were, what they did, what kind of behavior they engaged in. The second slide profiled their self-image. We used images of famous people to provide an instant visual clue as to how these consumers saw themselves. On the third slide, we showed the kinds of brands they bought. Profiling consumption behavior gave us the opportunity to show our client the collection of brands that accompanied them. Finally, our last slide provided a short description of how this archetypal consumer used the brand, viewed the brand, and weaved it into a personal narrative. Obviously, we were looking to the future. Because few consumers could actually articulate a brand narrative, we built this last slide as though we had accomplished our mission.

While Jim worked on the consumer profiles, Catherine worked with the ad agency to assemble a brief video reel for each narrative. We selected electronic and house music for a soundtrack, lending a high-tech and underground quality. To this, we added still images from the agency's stock library depicting scenes of urban life and wily but charismatic characters. We complemented this with similar video footage to create a two-minute music video for each narrative. The idea was to set the tone before we walked the CMO through the board that outlined the narrative progressions.

While this was coming together, I worked on the boards. I went back to three-act structure and the Hero's journey. For each of the narratives, I outlined the dramatic progression. For instance, in the Clique narrative, the inciting action was always a piece of information that must be transmitted. The conflicts could vary in any story arc, but the inciting incident would always be the acquisition of some important intelligence.

During this same time we reviewed all of the touch points our client possessed to tell the narrative. We had no doubts that the agency could develop a great television and print campaign to support our themes, but we had doubts about some of the other activities.

The client's stores (branded retail facilities where wireless service plans were sold) were about as generic as you could imagine. To compound the problem, many of these facilities were franchises or licensed operations in which the client had minimal control. We prepared a strategy brief that outlined how the client could bring the narrative to retail. This included investment in special displays and merchandising décor. We also thought that the client could create a fictional underground reality game. We would distribute clues throughout various advertising media, which would lead consumers into hidden areas on the client's Web site and within displays in its retail facility. For example, a consumer might enter a special pin into a display phone at a retail store and listen in on a secret conversation. Much of this would have to wait until the ad agency finished its creative work, but we thought it an interesting extension of the narrative.

We reviewed the client's sponsorship portfolio. Most of its investments were in sports. This did not make much sense to us. Kay argued that it was for purposes of reach and hospitality benefits, but we argued that the quality of the impressions was poor. We realized that it might take a few years to get out of these long-term relationships, but we encouraged the client to consider shifting part of the portfolio to entertainment sponsorship and sponsorships of "subversive" but appropriate events and activities—such as nightclubs and music experiences. One area we thought the client should address immediately: product placement. We believed the client should begin telling its story by strategically placing its product in films, television, and other media outlets that matched the brand narrative—programs such as *The X Files*, *Alias*, and *24 Hours*.

Day 15: The Big Pitch

Kay clearly believed we had the right direction for the brand. Apparently, we did a good job of instilling the narrative in her. She led the presentation to Alan Jasper, the client's CMO. She took him through the high-level brand strategy, including the activation points by which the narrative would influence behavior. Then she handed off to the agency, who ran the narrative music video. When it was done, I took Alan through the boards. Then Jim walked him through the consumer research, which supported our claims.

The moment of truth came. Alan loved it. He believed this gave the brand a point of distinction and the "legs" to develop multiple advertising and promotional extensions. He also believed that the client's CEO would adopt the idea of "misfit innovators." Apparently, the company faced internal inertia after the round of acquisitions. The engineering and development teams were stuck in a corporate rut, and the CEO recently preached the concept of breaking rules. He saw the narrative lines we drew as a way to motivate those inside the company, and he wanted us to do some follow-up work to develop an internal branding campaign to this end.

A NARRATIVE DRIVES THE STRATEGY PROCESS

Granted, this case example is entirely fictional, but it is representative of a brand bible effort. In this particular instance, the bible was less concrete. We had PowerPoint presentations that were printed and archived as a narrative guide. We also had audio-visual elements. As a follow-up assignment, we would naturally combine these elements into a presentation that could be used to indoctrinate new employees, agents, or others in the narrative of the brand.

Using our model, the advertising agencies and related design firms would draw upon the brand narrative to develop the identity package and the design environment—all of which would tie back to the hidden story. The agency would also use the brand narrative as the guiding framework for each new campaign. Though the agency might create a number of different broadcast and print executions, each new campaign would fit within the narrative model we designed.

CHAPTER 7

COMMUNICATING BRAND NARRATIVE

In practice, most keepers of Legendary Brands do not explicitly think about brand narrative, brand mythology, or brand bibles. That these Legendary Brands do indeed tell stories is a consequence of keen intuition, not conscious planning. When brand managers or advertisers contemplate the narrative structure of brands, they frequently focus their attention on the effects generated by the narrative. You are likely to hear them discuss a *core benefit, brand footprint, brand imagery, value proposition,* or *consumer equity.* There are dozens of other labels that exist to describe the consumer benefits brand narrative generates. These benefits can be mapped analytically using a variety of frameworks. But brand narrative is not a benefit. It is the engine within the brand that creates the benefits.

The people who are closest to the narrative of the brand are those within the brand's advertising agency. Like consumers, advertising agencies intuitively sense the presence of a brand narrative. Unlike consumers, agencies are more consciously aware of a brand's ability to tell a story, but they often focus their attention on the stories told by the current advertising campaign. It works some of the time, but the brand narrative is usually deeper than the scope of one campaign. Assuming the campaign is the narrative is akin to going on an archaeological dig and marveling at your discovery of an ancient statue, when in fact the statue rests atop a ten-story castle still hidden beneath the next layer of sediment. Advertising agencies are very good at isolating a piece of what consumers sense about a brand narrative and generating an advertising campaign that reflects it. But they often stop there. As a result, brand mythology is tapped accidentally or through a great deal of trial and error. When the campaign is exhausted they are back at square one.

In the agency world, the adoption of account planning has advanced the discovery process considerably. Account planning is a research-driven discipline originally born in the U.K. and introduced with great fanfare in the U.S. by Jay Chiat at the Chiat\Day agency in the 1980s. Account planning combines consumer research with strategic planning. The planner's task is to serve as the "voice of the consumer"— an advocate within the agency that ensures the advertising speaks to consumer needs. Planners are supposed to reveal consumer "insights," which are structured in a creative brief, the purpose of which is to give the creative team a starting point. Planning is designed to make creative development more efficient and effective. To a large extent, it has succeeded. But most planning groups neglect brand narrative. As a result, even the best account planners will admit that there are several instances in which the creative content that ultimately propels the brand has little to do with the insights revealed by the creative brief. Jon Steel, one of the most revered account planners, summed it up best in his seminal book on the matter, *Truth, Lies, and Advertising*, ". . . a solution is *more likely* to come from a creative person than from a planner or account person."[1] It is not so much that planning fails, but rather that planners study the effects of the brand rather than the cause.

Historically, Legendary Brands have been sustained by the work of creative personnel who excel at trusting their instincts and using what they sense to craft advertising that reveals brand narrative through related imagery and aesthetic devices. These aesthetic devices make the narrative recognizable to consumers. In a sense, the creative output forms a common vocabulary between brand and consumer. Just as the words in your grammatical vocabulary are not your thoughts, but rather devices you use to transfer what you think to someone else's brain, the creative output of agencies are devices which transmit brand narrative. Surprisingly, these devices are usually selected by instinct, experimentation, or just plain luck. For all their demonstrable talent as storytellers, most advertising agencies do not systematically define brand narrative. They chance upon it.

Change is mandated. There are more brands on the landscape than ever before, and a particularly rapid increase in the emergence of Legendary Brands. Consumers are confused, frustrated, and exhausted by the myriad of brands clamoring for their attention—all of them asserting that they have the consumer's best interests at heart. It's little wonder that antibrand movements are becoming widespread. Consumers face a cluttered, noisy, overdeveloped marketing terrain. Their response is to rebel or retreat. In such an environment, it is much more difficult for an advertiser to locate a narrative vein by trial and error.

More challenging is the rapidly developing merger between entertainment and marketing. Never before have the two worlds flirted with such commitment, but their marriage has executives from Madison Avenue to Wilshire Boulevard in a state of euphoric anticipation. Both industries sense that a sizable dowry will result from entertainment-marketing hybrids. Unfortunately, early attempts at breeding have produced only crude mutations. Audiences are suffering as brands increasingly loiter within the content of motion pictures and television programs. Product placement deals, in which advertisers pay money or some other consideration to have their brand prominently positioned on the sets of dramatic action, are becoming so predominant that they have given rise to a whole new batch of drinking games. The object is to count the number of brands that appear within a program. While some of these brand integration attempts have enjoyed minor successes, other have failed famously. For instance, Coca-Cola's sponsorship of the television program *Young Americans* on the WB network featured gratuitous and often intrusive camera angles that ensured Coke-branded products and vending machines were in several scenes of each episode. Despite significant hype and promotion, the series lasted less than a full season.

Ample evidence suggests that marketers are correct, and that the marriage of entertainment and marketing is the next frontier of brand development. But the current methods of settling this frontier will never succeed. Brands are not wallpaper. Advertisers are trying too hard to make entertainment content follow conventional marketing discipline. They demand frequent brand exposure, prominent positioning, and literal integration of branded product within the content. This practice disrespects audiences, and insults their intelligence. Audiences are media savvy, and they see through such obvious abuse of editorial license. The practice also foolishly neglects the reason advertisers wish to participate in entertainment content in the first place. Audiences love entertainment because audiences crave a good story. Advertisers must learn that to have a meaningful role with entertainment content, they must give rather than take. Storytelling is their gift. The brand should enhance the storytelling experience, not detract from it. At a minimum, it must be transparent—but transparency does little to achieve advertiser objectives. Rather than tax audiences, brands can contribute to the stories told by entertainment properties. It is the narrative dimension of Legendary Brands that allows for deeper integration within content. Advertisers must think from a new perspective—the perspective of the storyteller.

This chapter will not show you how to create good advertising. It will not provide a formula for participating in entertainment content. The design of advertising programs is beyond the scope of this book, and content integration rarely succeeds from a formula. The objective of this chapter is to change your approach. Every time your brand touches a consumer, it must communicate the narrative of the brand. This chapter shows you how to bring this mindset to the daily task of marketing management.

THE ABSTRACT AND THE LITERAL

Communications planning according to a brand narrative does not limit your options or constrain your creativity. It does not mean your advertising must stick to one linear model for all time. If you choose to execute in this fashion, you should expect stale, predictable campaigns that exhaust themselves quickly.

Figure 7.1 offers a simple categorization to help you understand the different ways that brand narrative manifests in advertising. Note, for reasons of simplicity, my use of the term *advertising* herein is applied loosely, to include all forms of marketing communications—from package design to broadcast advertising and beyond.

Abstractions

A fair amount of the Legendary Brand advertising you witness is an abstraction of the brand narrative. *Abstractions* highlight aesthetic elements associated with the narrative: the form, palette, style, movement, conflict, or theme. An advertisement in the form of abstract representation is like an Andy Warhol painting: By itself, the subject

FIGURE 7.1 Distilling Narrative into Communications

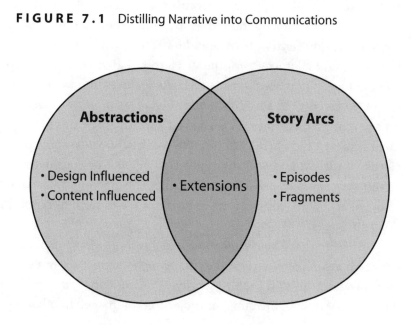

seems very one dimensional, but the narrative influence associated with the subject gives it depth.

Some abstractions are strong on artistic value but low on content. Target's recent campaigns are a clear example. The advertisements showcase several products sold in Target stores that have a common color palette. The commercials play upon this palette in stylistic fashion: people dancing around in colored costumes with painted faces, frenetic product shots, colored liquid spraying about the set, animated colorization of the Target brand mark. Target's brand narrative pays tribute to everyday brands—the brands that are not so legendary. Target positions itself as the affordable but hip place to acquire those brands. Its narrative therefore revolves around a place where dramatic action unfolds, like the drive-ins, record stores, and soda fountains of the 1950s. The advertising, in an abstract format, conveys this narrative.

Abstract advertising can also focus on content or product features. Legendary Brand Southwest Airlines generally employs advertising that highlights its fares. While product focused, these advertisements narrate with richness and humor. The objective of Southwest's advertising is to encourage people to live life to the fullest, be a free spirit, and "roam about the country" because Southwest makes it affordable to do so. Through abstraction, they are able to emphasize this benefit while not losing sight of their brand narrative, which is closely linked to the wit and character of founder Herb Kelleher (Kelleher's executive photograph on Southwest's Web site features him in an Elvis costume). To accomplish this goal, Southwest relies on style, imagery, and tone to remind consumers of the brand narrative. The design environment achieves the narrative objective using whimsical color palettes, clever wordplay, and stylistic typography. Some of Southwest's best advertising exists in print, where it utilizes an irreverent design environment and witty copywriting to tie narrative to simple communications messages.

In their book, *Marketing Aesthetics*, authors Bernd Schmitt and Alex Simonson comment on the use of such abstract design environment. They claim that brand identity often contains *expressive themes* that refer to content, meaning, or projections of image.[2] In other words, the design environment associated with the brand's advertising can act as a powerful abstraction of the brand narrative.

Story Arcs

In Chapter 3, we examined the various parts of storytelling, from the beat to the myth. Recall that a beat is the smallest part of a story that continues to demonstrate a cause-and-effect relationship. Stories are comprised of a sequence of beats that together form cohesive, compact, and logical action. Advertisers have used beats for years to create engaging communications that demonstrate cause-and-effect relationships associated with the product or brand.

A *story arc* combines beats to present only a part of a story. Much like a scene or an act in a play, or a chapter in a book, an arc is rarely a complete stand-alone story. An arc may leave its audience with unanswered questions, or it may fail to provide a complete, cohesive retelling of events. But an arc provides greater detail than a beat. Whereas a beat shows only one change in state, an arc shows more than one change. Because it provides more detail, it has a stronger relationship with the story it serves.

Story arcs provide the marketer with freedom to create fresh advertising campaigns without telling the same story each time, all the while preventing them from straying too far from the underlying brand equity. The marketer selects an arc from the brand narrative and uses it as a template for the communications design.

Episodes

An *episode* is a story arc that is ostensibly self contained. Episodes have a compact beginning, middle, and end structure that allows them to stand on their own, even though they are actually a component of a larger narrative fabric. Episodic advertising replicates the narrative of the brand in a compact retelling. Each advertisement delivers a story that metaphorically represents the brand.

For example, ESPN and its agency, Wieden + Kennedy, have been using this form of advertising for years to market SportsCenter, the popular news program of the ESPN network. The overarching brand narrative of SportsCenter revolves around the story of the newsroom and its relationship to macro events in sports. The reporters at Sports-Center are supposed to be "regular" guys immersed in the mythic world of sports. This juxtaposition of ordinary man amongst the gods and heroes of sports creates humor. How does an average person relate to a "no hitter" or an eight-figure signing bonus?

SportsCenter communicates this brand narrative with short, simple story arcs. One television advertisement, titled "The Kid," opened with anchor Bob Ley recounting how hard SportsCenter works to recruit new on-air talent. He provides one example in which Sports-Center recruited a "new kid" right out of high school. The kid showed great promise, until he got behind the desk. Spoofing the oft-heard story of baseball players who are pulled too early out of the minor leagues to go to the "show," the commercial goes on to show a teen-ager named Seth Hays sitting behind the anchor desk. He interrupts anchor Jack Keith's reporting on baseball player Jimmy Key's performance. The kid says, "Jimmy Key . . . what is he 40? I could hit him. Did you see last night's game? Didn't it suck? It sucked!" The spot concludes with the kid announcing his resignation and Ley remarking, "He just came out too soon." The SportsCenter brand narrative is transcribed through a detailed story arc.

In another spot, titled "Cornerman," SportsCenter played off of the rigor between rounds at a boxing match, comparing it to the grueling work of the anchors behind the SportsCenter desk. The spot opens with Rich Eisen seated behind the anchor desk, telling the audience he'll return right after a commercial break. A bell rings and crews descend upon him like a boxer retreating to his corner in a match. Water is poured over Eisen's head while his face is greased up with petroleum jelly. A husky "old school" coach gets in Eisen's face giving him tough counsel on his performance. Eisen starts to complain, "The teleprompter was going too fast. I'm losing my voice." Lou, the coach, shouts, "Get him some tea!" at which point an aide produces a china cup filled with tea. Eisen whines, "Cut me, Lou," to which Lou replies, "Come on, don't be a lollipop." Another bell rings, the crew retreats, and Eisen is back in front of the camera as anchor. Again, the brand narrative is conveyed by artful use of story arcs from the SportsCenter brand narrative and the mythology of sport.

Each of these episodes tells a story that is a microcosm of the ESPN brand narrative, which differentiates between ordinary people and the heroes of sport. When the anchormen are depicted in the same context as a sports hero, the difference is demonstrated to comedic effect.

Fragments

Fragments are story arcs that focus on only one part of the brand narrative. Unlike an episode, which shrinks the entire narrative and presents it concisely, a fragment sacrifices the larger plot structure so that it can show greater depth on one memorable conflict or inflection point—a moment in the story that is critical to the substance of the narrative.

Nike often uses fragment arcs to convey its brand narrative. Nike serves all athletes, amateur and professional, men and women, young and old. Though it began life as a brand for distance runners, it now represents football, baseball, basketball, soccer, cycling, and a cadre of other athletic disciplines. Nike's advertising focuses on a stage in the monomyth and applies it to the advertising context. This provides a sense of universality and maintains consistency across product lines. In one effective television advertisement titled "If You Let Me Play," Nike showed a series of young girls describing the benefits to their character and their health if they are allowed to participate in athletics. Each girl had only a few words to add to the next, collectively composing a compelling poem with one voice:

If you let me play,
If you let me play sports,

I will like myself more;

I will have more self-confidence.

If you let me play,

If you let me play sports,

I will be 60 percent less likely to get breast cancer;

I will suffer less depression.

If you let me play sports,

I will be more likely to leave a man who beats me.

If you let me play,

I will be less likely to get pregnant before I want to;

I will learn what it means to be strong if you let me play sports.

This haunting commercial selected just one arc from the many stages of the hero's journey: the refusal of the call. The hero is the young girl willing to accept the call to competition, but constrained by some external force. Within each of these girls lies the power to become a hero. The power of this advertisement is that we are watching a fragment arc sliced from the beginning of a bigger narrative. In this case, the fragment arc is extracted from one of the biggest inflection points in the narrative, the point at which the hero decides to accept the call to adventure and cross the first threshold testing their stamina.

Extensions

Extensions are the least structured form of advertising that concretely represent the narrative. Extensions are the cousins of abstractions and fragments, yet they are neither. They are not an abstraction because they focus upon literal elements of the brand narrative. They illuminate a particular character, or a particular location, or secondary events that relate to the narrative. Some extensions create an entirely new story that is separate but linked to the narrative, much like a spinoff is related to a television series. Extensions are not fragments either, because their focus is either too diffuse to be considered a story, or the story they tell is unrelated to the core narrative.

Coca-Cola's "Life Tastes Good" television campaign was a series of extensions. One advertisement showed a young South American woman preparing for her wedding. Several other women surround her, adjusting her gown and primping her hair. In front of her, a young girl stares in awe, then carefully hands the bride a bottle of Coke with a bent straw. The bride smiles and drinks.

There is not much story in the above advertisement. It lacks strong conflict. The advertisement works, however, because it allows us to study a moment in greater detail. It is like an animated portrait. Most advertisers would refer to it as "lifestyle" advertising. It is also a narrative extension.

ALIGNING FORM WITH STRATEGY

The first step in planning your advertising is to identify your communications objectives. Begin by considering the impact you wish to have on consumer behavior. What do you want the consumer to do? For example, the behavioral objective of your advertising could be to drive sales of an underperforming product line, perhaps during a key period. Second, consider the emotional impact you wish to have on the consumer—how do you wish to make the consumer feel? The emotional objective is tied to the consumer's personal narrative; it is often achieved by activating a part of that narrative.

Drawing on these two objectives, you can now consider which parts of the narrative apply. Subsequently, you can decide how to communicate the narrative excerpt, and in what media. The ideal process looks something like that presented in Figure 7.2.

In postanalysis, this appears to be the methodology for a recent Gap campaign. Gap's energetic brand narrative speaks to the personal derivations of mass culture. Gap designs and manufactures fairly ubiquitous articles of clothing: jeans, t-shirts, and casual wear. The brand narrative revolves around your ability to make a personal fashion statement using practical, classic articles of clothing. It has always linked its narrative to culture, music, and simplicity. Gap's narrative

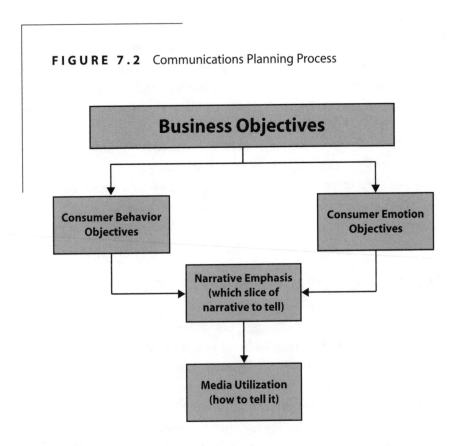

FIGURE 7.2 Communications Planning Process

glorifies classic casual wear, which it shows in a variety of contexts and historical periods—each time adorning the shapers of popular culture. The underlying theme is that it is not the clothes, but the people who wear them, and the way in which they wear them, that affects fashion and style.

In the early part of 2002, Gap witnessed declining sales in core product categories: denim, khakis, and white shirts. Historically, these were flagship product lines for the apparel retailer. Gap launched a summer campaign designed to achieve two business objectives:

1. *Behavioral Objective:* Stimulate sales of denim, white shirts, and khakis
2. *Emotional Objective:* Appeal to the need of being stylish

Three advertising executions were launched to achieve the objectives. The campaign drew from Gap's core brand narrative, mixing music, celebrities (particularly those who shape cultural opinions), and simple design to reflect upon popular culture. The first installment was titled "Two White Shirts" and featured actors Christina Ricci and Dennis Hopper. Two different versions of the advertisement ran, one with an instrumental soundtrack by the Beach Boys, and an identical spot scored to "I See the Rain" by The Marmalade. Veteran filmmakers Joel and Ethan Coen used black and white film stock, and deep focus photography, executed in one continuous shot, to capture an intriguing hint of story. The spot fades in with a close-up of Hopper, donning dark sunglasses and lounging on a deck chair near a swimming pool. He is dressed in a white, button down shirt and a plain pair of pants. As the camera dollies back, Ricci's arm comes into view, holding a cool drink, which Hopper nonchalantly accepts, sipping casually from the straw. Ricci, barefoot and simply dressed in a white, button down shirt and khaki pants, looks down upon a chess board which stands between Hopper's deck chair and her own. She pauses for a moment, casually patting her thigh with her hand, then reaches down to make her move on the chess board. She turns, sits on the adjacent deck chair, dons her own pair of dark glasses, and casually crosses her legs. We fade out on a wide shot of the two celebrities lounging, both staring effortlessly at the chess board, neither in too great a hurry to make the next move.

Surprisingly, the campaign raised some controversy. A few critics decried what appeared to be a Lolita relationship between Hopper's character and Ricci's. As Hopper is old enough to be Ricci's grandfather, this interpretation caused some consternation. In truth, the Coen brothers showed us only a hint of the dramatic action, and left the rest for us to conclude for ourselves. The spot worked because it served Gap's business objectives while also drawing from its narrative. By showing celebrities like Ricci and Hopper lounging in Gap apparel, especially in such a casual setting, Gap demonstrated that even the most famous and stylish wear Gap—and they look great. Specifically, the commercial showed how well a simple white shirt can make you look. This commercial created a postcard moment of quirky romanticism, but in so doing it glorified a simple piece of clothing. The new campaign appears to have worked. Shortly after its launch, Gap reported its first month of profit following several months of disappointing sales declines.

Marketing is an art and a science. The inspiration for great advertising is not always derived from linear processes depicted in the previous example. Sometimes, a creative idea—one tactical execution—leads the process. When it does, you will have to trust your instincts and be guided by the narrative forms that surface during the creative process. This is why it is critical that you have an in-depth understanding of your brand's mythology. You can "go with the flow" with greater confidence if you understand the depth of your brand narrative, and the ways in which it can be abstracted, arced, or extended.

Proceed with caution, however. The series of Gap campaigns that preceded "Two White Shirts" were overly influenced by creative form. Gap spun out dozens of artful advertisements, all very stylish, but most of them had nothing to do with the brand narrative. As one senior Gap executive exclaimed, "We sabotaged ourselves!" After awhile, consumers lost their connection to the Gap brand. Gap's new campaign is guided by the narrative, largely because it was conceived with solid business objectives and a keen understanding of how those objectives aligned with Gap's brand.

ALIGNING FORM WITH MEDIA

The final part of the planning process presents a strategic challenge. You must decide which form of advertising media best matches the narrative form you have chosen to communicate. In practice, this is often determined by a reductive process. You begin thinking about narrative, but are constrained by media requirements, which in turn change your thinking about narrative form. Chaos theory may present the only true formula to explain the process.

Matching the form to the appropriate media is mostly an art. Certain creative ideas just lend themselves naturally to specific forms of media. Apple's "Think Different" campaign relied heavily on historic photographs of people who changed the world. These classic photos lent themselves to print and outdoor advertising. Of course, print and outdoor advertising were also strategically relevant to Apple's business objectives. These media outlets have historically generated the highest return on investment for Apple.

Several nonnarrative factors will influence your media selection decision, including the cost of the media relative to the size of your marketing budget, the reach of the media and its relationship to the media habits of your target audience, and the functionality of the media relative to the product features and benefits you wish to demonstrate in your advertising. These factors are well documented in a variety of other marketing texts. Your media decision will often dictate whether you present your narrative as an abstraction, episode, fragment, or extension. Aggregate historical patterns provide vague rules of thumb. Episodes and fragments generally work best in fluid media, such as television and radio advertising. Extensions and abstractions are frequently more effective in static media, such as print, outdoor, and other design environments. However, you could just as easily argue to the contrary in both cases.

Great painters possessed no formula to help them decide between oil on canvas or oil on wood. Sometimes their decision was dictated by their patrons, sometimes by economics, and sometimes purely by whim. However, all of the great artists took the media into account and fashioned their work to best suit the media, and vice versa.

Entertainment Media

In the current marketing environment, most marketers select entertainment media by default. The media is already married to a narrative. Motion picture marketing opportunities are usually presented to advertisers once the script is complete and the picture is racing through production, if it has not already completed principal photography. This leaves advertisers with only one solution: attempt to jury-rig the entertainment content to suit business objectives. Is it any surprise that integration attempts are heavy handed?

Pre-emptive approaches have proven just as ineffective. When the word hits the street that your brand wishes to invest in entertainment properties, you can expect talent agents and producers to descend upon you en masse with projects that they claim will give you "star power." Most of these people are not marketers, and they have no idea what your business objectives really are. What they offer you is the opportunity to associate your brand with a "blockbuster" entertainment property or celebrities. When the time for execution arrives, your brand's role continues to be pedantic.

This form of brand integration is rarely the most effective use of the media. Occasionally it creates brand benefits, but these often arise from unique situations in which the entertainment property required the integration of the brand in order to remain authentic.

Legendary Brands should participate in entertainment media when that media serves as a viable narrative form for your brand message. For example, Steven Spielberg's motion picture *Minority Report* was a fitting media extension for Lexus. The Lexus brand narrative places form ahead of function. It is associated with refinement. The sacred beliefs of the brand dictate that engineering should be transparent—it serves a purpose. Lexus automobiles have reflected this narrative through elegant, but quiet, design features.

In *Minority Report*, which takes place in the year 2054, Lexus teamed with DreamWorks pictures to style the Lexus vehicle of the future. The 500 horsepower futuristic vehicle played an integral role in the film. Lexus designers worked with the producers to create a realistic looking vehicle that artfully incorporated the Lexus brand identity. Referred to as a MAGLEV vehicle, the integration remained true to the Lexus brand narrative. As depicted in the film, the interior design of the futuristic Lexus MAGLEV were quiet, soothing, and refined, yet tastefully branded and consistent with the rest of the film's art direction.

During the film's run, Lexus showcased the 2054 model on the home page of its Web site. Clicking on the vehicle whisked the consumer to a cobranded Lexus/*Minority Report* Web site that engaged the user in an interactive experience, driven by a narrative mirroring the conflicts of the film. Even this mini-narrative gave the Lexus brand a relevant, and credible role. The Lexus vehicle served as the escape mechanism in the user's encounter with antagonists.

Effective as it was, the Lexus initiative relied heavily upon product placement. The true frontier of entertainment marketing will provide the opportunity for *narrative placement.*

You can probably recall many television advertisements you have enjoyed that gave only a brief amount of time to brand or product placement. Many of these only show the brand or product at the end on a title card. Despite this limited brand exposure, you can recall the advertisement and connect it to the brand. Why? You connect the two because the narrative depicted in the advertisement was linked to the narrative of the brand. The same mental mechanics can work for brands in entertainment integration.

Successfully integrating your brand narrative within an entertainment property requires advanced participation. In fact, some brands may soon wish to develop and produce entertainment properties on their own, rather than wait for the right opportunity to arise. To illustrate how this could work, let's consider a hypothetical example.

Suppose one of Starbucks' business objectives was to stimulate greater store traffic from teenagers and young adults. Suppose also that the emotional objective of this endeavor was to make teens feel more adult and worldly. The Starbucks brand narrative imbues an international flavor, a love of exploration, and an eclectic sensibility. Let us assume that teens who have an affinity for Starbucks seek to activate similar narrative aspects in their own lives. They long to travel, they wish to explore their mental and physical capabilities, and they seek to develop a character that is unrestricted by local custom, geography, or a narrow social context.

Starbucks could select an episodic approach to its narrative, using creative media to illustrate the narrative of adventure and exploration.

To make it meaningful, Starbucks might team up with MTV and produce a new reality television series that follows a group of teens who travel together through foreign countries. If it chose to get very literal, these teens might venture through countries that are coffee producers. Perhaps the action of each episode unfolds in coffee houses or their equivalent (and not necessarily Starbucks branded venues).

To activate the association between Starbucks and the program, it would not be necessary to force product placement (the teens are always carrying a Starbucks cup). One alternative would be for Starbucks to bookend each episode with advertising media, to make an immediate impression. The advertisements serve as the proverbial title card. To safeguard this impression, Starbucks might require MTV to grant it category exclusivity during the broadcast, meaning that no competitor could air a commercial during the program.

There are subtler ways of linking the program to the brand. Because the narrative association is natural, Starbucks could introduce elements of the television program into its coffee houses, particularly those that are located in areas with a significant teen population. Hopeful explorers could apply to participate in the program within their local Starbucks coffee house. Cause-related marketing programs could benefit student learning initiatives and aid for underdeveloped countries. Featured coffees sold in stores could hearken back to locales depicted on the program. In-store video monitors could replay recent episodes. The number of ways in which the program and brand could intertwine is limited only by the imagination and the budget. The reason such a program could prove successful is because it is driven by solid objectives and integrated at the content level. Starbucks would not participate in the program as a mere prop. Program and brand would be partners in storytelling, each lending authenticity to the other, and each giving the consumer a gift.

AN INTERVIEW WITH TY MONTAGUE

Ty Montague is the cocreative director of the Wieden + Kennedy agency in New York city. He is the current guardian of ESPN's "This Is SportsCenter" campaign, featured in this chapter. Besides the fact that his career has included work on some of the world's leading brands at premier advertising agencies, Ty is also a staunch advocate for a new approach to advertising, and speaks frequently on the topic.

Larry: How is brand advertising changing?

Ty: There are companies in the world that are wedded to this old model of creating communications that interrupt what people are really interested in. Companies that think this way are going to have a hard time in the future. They used to be in control because the media environment was originally created to be commanded and controlled by them. That is changing. Command and control is shifting into the hands of consumers.

There is a small group of companies who are just now beginning to get good at communicating with people in a different way—a more collaborative way.

Larry: How is the new approach collaborative?

Ty: It has to do with the questions you ask when you sit down to plan a piece of communication. All ad agencies approach the process today by asking themselves, "What do we want

people to think and feel about this piece of communication?"
They ask, "When we are finished communicating with people,
what do we want the result to be?" That is a one-way, a-to-b way
of communicating. I heard someone say that markets are
"conversations." That is absolutely right. Present day advertising
agencies do not treat markets as conversations. Most treat
markets as monologues. The proper question should be, "What's
the most interesting thing we can say to ignite a conversation
with the people we want to be talking to?" And then, "What is our
plan for responding to them once they respond to us?" For lack of
a better name, I call this new model of advertising Participative
Communications.

Larry: Can every brand engage consumers in something
more than a monologue?

Ty: I believe they must. Brands have to find a place in
people's lives. There is a deeper story to just about everything.
Most brands aren't exploring them because they are defining
themselves by the objects they produce. Ultimately, I don't
believe people are going to sit through 30-second commercials
that fail to explore the story. They're not going to have to. It's
more about giving, than taking. It's actually giving to get. You
have to create communications that actually enhance the
meaning in someone's life—that gives them insight into
themselves. Tell a story someone finds interesting, and they'll
invite you in.

Larry: So many marketers are trying to achieve what you describe by integrating into movies and TV. Is this the answer?

Ty: Most of what we're seeing right now is nonparticipative. Marketers are attempting to push into a new medium—film—with the same old model. They're using a monologue style of communication. To be truly participative, you have to put the viewer first. You have to say something that's interesting to them. Ask, "What are we giving them in order to get their attention and respect?" Consumers are reaching a saturation point because most marketers don't understand the difference between product placement and actually getting at the essence of a brand and telling that story within the film in a way that people really want.

8

BRAND CULTURE

O**n a lonely** bluff in England, the remnants of a lost story stand sentinel on Salisbury Plain. The giant rocks of Stonehenge are a mystery left behind by the ancient Druids. Very little is known about the rites and rituals that were performed within the giant stone rotunda, but we are reasonably certain such rites were connected to a cosmological or mythological narrative. The many people who built Stonehenge believed in it so strongly they erected the massive temple using only primitive bronze-age tools.

Half a world away, surrounded by the Pacific Ocean, Easter Island is home to a population of giant stone moai, their vague faces guarding secrets that promise to speak volumes if only we can solve the riddle of their existence. We wonder why the ancient Rapu Nui labored with limited technology to hew the figures from solid rock and haul them to the borders of their remote island. For all that we don't know, we are pretty certain that the moai's existence relates to ancient stories—probably stories told around a fire by wise chiefs to faithful tribe members.

Throughout history, people have gathered together and created cultures bound by a foundation of narrative. Each of us, individually, seeks a narrative to explain our world. We naturally gravitate to others who share the same narrative explanation. This congregation of people with shared narrative perceptions creates a culture. People who believe that the right to bear arms is "God given" congregate in the culture of the National Rifle Association, which has a narrative linked to personal liberty. Some of those NRA members live in Texas, a state with its own distinct culture so independent that many Texans believe they are part of a separate nation—an annex of the United States. These proud members of the Lone Star state know well the narrative of the Alamo. Texas is a part of the United States of America, which houses a culture of people who subscribe to the narrative of "life, liberty, and the pursuit of happiness." Cultures exist on many levels, but they always rest on the foundation of a shared narrative.

Marion Harper, Jr., the former president of McCann-Erickson, once said, "Advertising is found in societies which have past the point of satisfying the basic animal needs." Legendary Brands are found in cultures that lack the ability to satisfy basic narrative needs. As a brand manager, you must care about these narratives. Your brand leads or participates within a narrative that brings people together. For if the cultures of the past could be inspired by story to move giant stones with a minimum of technology, certainly your brand story can inspire a culture of people to do something as simple as consume your product. The stewardship of brand cultures is the topic of this chapter.

DISPELLING MYTH

Brand cultures are immensely appealing to brand managers, but greatly understood. Before proceeding, let me dispel three closely held myths.

Brand Cultures Are Begotten, Not Made

If you believe that you can set out to create a brand culture, think again. Brand cultures are organic entities. Even when all the precedent conditions are just right, a brand culture may never emerge. When a marketing team tries too hard to forge a brand culture, it is often at the expense of brand equity.

Brand managers must think of themselves as gardeners. You can plant the seeds of a culture, fertilize, water, prune it into the shape you desire, and protect it from pests. However, only nature can determine the actual yield. The bottom line is this: There are many things you can (and probably should) do to encourage the development of a brand culture, but most brand cultures are born from circumstances outside the control of the manager. Like human identity, a brand culture is the product of nature and nurture.

Perhaps the best metaphor is the city. Cities like San Francisco, New York, and London developed over time to become Legendary Brands in their own right. They were not settled to become the metropolitan giants they are today. They were not master planned. Though each has its own individual urban challenges, for decades, in some cases centuries, they continue to captivate and inspire us. Each of these cities is more than a city; it is a cultural center.

In contrast, consider recent cities like Santa Clarita, California, and Celebration, Florida. Each was designed according to a comprehensive master plan. While beautiful, clean, and efficient, they are not particularly inspiring. They have often been criticized for their artificial feel. Some critics say they lack a soul. If they do lack a soul, it is largely because they were engineered from something other than a narrative held by a culture of people. They contain no cultural authenticity, despite the façade their progenitors meticulously tender. When wishing for a brand culture, think Pinocchio not Pygmalion.

Brand Cultures Can Be Nurtured, but Not Controlled

As marketers, we take great pride in the strength of our brands. The stronger the brand becomes, the more we are compelled to control it. We devise systems and policies governing the activities that might impact brand equity. In many companies, brand managers are referred to as the "brand police," individuals who control what others can and cannot do with the brand marks and intellectual properties.

While employees in your company may obey the brand police, your customers will probably fail to recognize the authority. Brand cultures, particularly American brand cultures, resist control. You are best to remember that a culture is made up of people—in this case, people with very strong emotional and personal attachment to your brand. Your efforts to control this culture will often be seen as a profane intrusion of personal expression. In short, you will come across as a different kind of brand police. This police force is oppressive, arrogant, and opportunistic. You might as well do your job in riot gear.

Disney faced a public relations nightmare in 1989 when a day-care center in the town of Hallandale, Florida, just miles from Disney's theme parks in Orlando, painted depictions of Mickey Mouse and Donald Duck onto the exterior classroom walls. They received a nasty cease and desist letter from Disney demanding immediate removal of the character infringements. This letter found its way into the national press. Within days, Disney's competitor, Universal Studios, came to the rescue and furnished studio artists to paint Universal characters (such as Woody Woodpecker) pro bono, in place of the unauthorized Disney renderings. Disney believed it was safeguarding its valued intellectual properties, but to the average American consumer it appeared that Disney was holding Mickey Mouse hostage—unreasonably withholding a national treasure from innocent children.

Though you cannot control your brand culture, you can nurture it. You can provide it with tools and resources that make participation in the culture meaningful and enjoyable. You can encourage the members of the culture to participate in the narrative in their own way. You can reward the culture for its faith in the brand and the underlying narrative. When the brand culture strays, participating in activities that appear to conflict with your business objectives, you can counsel and encourage change, or you can ignore them. You can cut off the flow of benefits and counterprogram. For example, Disney had a legitimate concern in the above situation. Suppose the daycare center became the subject of a child molestation case. The display of Disney characters on the facility might implicate Disney in the scandal, yet Disney would have had no control over the facility to prevent such a public relations disaster. Still, Disney could have approached the issue from a different perspective. It could create a program that distributes standardized character art to any legitimate daycare center that requests it. This not only gives Disney some control over what is displayed, it also constructs a new marketing channel. Disney could use the relationships forged with daycare centers to market its products and services.

As the brand steward, you must be a sincere and honest advocate for the brand, rather than a smug dictator. Think Lincoln, not Mussolini.

Brand Cultures Own the Brand, Not the Other Way Around

When a brand culture emerges, ownership of the brand transfers to the culture. Sure, you may own the trademarks, the copyrights, and the financial benefits. You may pay the advertising bills and you may hold the secret brand strategy. But the heart and soul of your brand is owned by your culture. Once it adopts it, shares it, and makes it a part of its life, you are its servant—a *steward* of a public asset.

The relationship between Legendary Brands and their corresponding brand cultures is not dissimilar to the relationship between corporations and their common shareholders. Many a CEO will testify to the power of seemingly small, shareholder voting blocks. Though individually each of these shareholders may own a dozen or so shares of the company's stock, collectively they speak with a powerful voice. These small voting blocks have thwarted the best-laid plans by CEOs who refused to listen.

Your brand culture has the power to take your brand to the destination it desires. This is a phenomenon unique to Legendary Brands. Because the brand culture cares so much about what your brand stands for, they feel inherent ownership of it. You can fight them, but if you do, you risk starting a civil war that only leaves scores of the faithful dead in the trenches. A brand beset by the backlash of its culture is a brand with lost equity. Your best strategy is to serve your culture wisely and well, even when it seems their actions may lead to ruin. In my experience, the bad seeds in the brand culture eventually go away. When they do not, it is usually because the narrative foundation of the brand was weak to begin with.

HARLEY-DAVIDSON AND "HELL'S ANGELS"

Harley-Davidson is a brand I often mention in this book because of its powerful narrative. There is little doubt about what *Harley* means in the mind of most consumers. However, Harley-Davidson is a brand that frequently flirted with trouble.

The most common association with Harley-Davidson is the Hell's Angels, an organization named in honor of the 303 Bombardment from World War II. Hell's Angels have a reputation linked to trouble. In fact, the group has often appeared in the press for criminal activity. The group's imagery is rough—linked to bars, diners, and taverns in the badlands. It is often imagined riding in packs, descending unexpectedly upon a diner, and stirring trouble—or at least, that is the image painted in various films and television programs.

Hell's Angels helped and hindered the Harley-Davidson brand. On the one hand, they made the brand a legend. They raised brand awareness and imbued it with the rugged, libertarian personality it holds today. On the other hand, Hell's Angels threatened to limit the brand. It faced the real danger of being too closely linked with outlaws, criminal activity, and trouble.

As fate would have it, many white-collar riders enjoy the association with the outlaw imagery, and it has ultimately helped the brand. Still, it is an example of a brand culture taking a brand

on a new narrative course beyond the control of its management.

At the end of every theatrical play, the cast returns to the stage for curtain calls. There's an old saying in the theatre: curtain calls are your chance to thank the audience, not the opportunity to exact applause. The audience always applauds. Sometimes they give a standing ovation. It is an immensely gratifying experience for the cast, but it is only a residual benefit of the curtain call obligation. The actors are there, first and foremost, to thank the audience for their attention and patronage.

Your brand culture does not exist to serve your needs. You exist to serve theirs. When you interact with the brand culture, you should be thinking of ways to thank them, rather than looking to them for signs of gratitude. Think Gandhi, not Marie Antoinette.

KNOWING YOUR CULTURE

Are you the same person today you were ten years ago? Do you have the same aspirations? The same desires? The same self-image? Few of us can answer yes to such questions. Ten years ago you may not have been married, but now you are, or ten years ago you might have been married, but now you are not. You may have been in a different job or career—or you might have been in school. There are a number of events and life changes that can occur in a relatively short time. People change.

The biggest mistake managers make is to assume that the brand culture remains static. In earlier chapters we examined the narrative life of consumers. Postmodern consumers live a life movie, which is a narrative concept that defines identity and governs behavior. But just as actors grow older and change the kind of roles they play on the big screen, consumers grow older, too. As they do, they star in different life movies. Add to this the generational effect, meaning that each new generation in the consumer population is affected by different narrative stimulus, and you face a brand culture that is a constantly moving target.

MTV may be the best at understanding its brand culture. MTV has one of the highest executive turnover rates in the television industry—but that is just the way they want it. Their management training program is reminiscent of the science fiction film *Logan's Run*, in which a futuristic society executes members of the population on the day they turn 30. MTV hires very young interns who are quickly promoted to programming executives. These executives know what programming suits the audience because they are a part of it. Once they age to a level where they are no longer in sync with the next generation of audience members, they move up to nonprogramming jobs or out of the company.

Part of your brand management system must include a periodic assessment of your brand culture. You can use the techniques discussed elsewhere in this book. Narrative research methodologies described in Chapter 5 should be frequently applied to get at the narrative life of your consumers. Take care not to assume that the current batch of consumers thinks and feels the same way that the preceding batch did.

Develop consumer character profiles like the ones described in Chapter 6. As you profile more and more consumers, you will begin to see patterns. These patterns represent the consistent narratives your brand activates within a culture of consumers. Whereas much of our attention up to this point focused on the narrative of the brand, your attention to brand culture must focus on the narrative of consumer segments. These segments will shift and evolve over time. Your task is to keep up.

Researching and profiling the segments of the culture are not enough. Get out and observe the culture in action. Far too many brand managers never observe the brand in action. They may read about the narrative guiding the culture, but they would have a hard time identifying it in public. The senior management team at Wal-Mart makes frequent visits to all of the company's stores—in every part of the country. When they visit, they come unannounced and dressed like consumers. They roam the stores and observe behavior.

Finally, immerse yourself in the culture. Don't settle for research data. Don't settle on the observations made roaming the aisles. Become a part of the culture. Every single employee at ESPN is a sports fan. In fact, job candidates receive offers only if they satisfactorily pass a quiz testing their sports knowledge. At Wieden + Kennedy, ESPN's advertising agency, new recruits for the account are selected based partially on their passion for sports.

You cannot truly understand the dynamics of your brand culture unless you throw yourself into the crowd and join them in their narrative journey. It is by far the best way to understand the life movie at play between them.

MAKING BRANDS INDISPENSABLE TO CONSUMER NARRATIVES

In Chapter 6 we segmented your customers according to patterns of personal narrative—not by demographics or other metrics. For example, one segment of your customers may live a personal narrative that mirrors a daytime soap opera. They see themselves in a life where everything is glamorous and overdramatic. Your brand is a necessary part of that drama because it, too, is over the top and glamorous. Yet another segment of your audience may live a completely different narrative. This segment may live a narrative that believes there is no value in "second-best." In their lives, everything they do and everything they consume must be the best. They must work for the best companies, have the best education, raise the best family, and consume the best products and services. Though the demographic data between these two segments is probably very similar, the narratives are quite different. One is infused with drama and the other is infused with rationalism.

Legendary Brands succeed because they activate the narratives of their brand culture. This is why it is so important for you to understand the nuances and subcultures associated with your brand. It gives you the power to stage your brand in meaningful experiences that bring the consumer's narrative identity to life. Legendary Brands *activate* narrative identity.

There are many elements that can activate consumer narrative, but two dominate the spectrum: semiotics and ritual.

Semiotics and Brand Activation

For our purposes, semiotics are the signs, symbols, and very specific design executions that represent the brand narrative. For simplicity, we shall call them *symbols,* but realize that a symbol in this context can include a color palette just as easily as it can include a brand mark. The Nike swoosh is a symbol, but so too is the crisp Garamond typeface consistently associated with Apple brand communications.

The artful and strategic placement of brand symbols is a powerful way to seed the development of a brand culture. Note the two words that preface that sentence: *artful* and *strategic.* Conventional marketing calls for brand managers to spread a blanket of brand symbols. The wisdom associated with this marketing strategy is that the more consumers see the symbols, the more they will recall your brand, and the more they will be inclined to use your brand upon the purchase occasion.

Unfortunately, the carpet bombing technique of symbol dispersion leads the brand towards irrelevance more than it does brand activation. Armed with a sizable marketing budget, a brand manager can effectively disperse the brand mark over a wide territory, and consumers *will* recall seeing it. But this strategy leads to ubiquity. Consumers are so accustomed to seeing it they take it for granted. Also, the fact that the symbol appears anywhere and everywhere does nothing to reinforce the brand narrative or give it greater meaning. In a sense, the symbol becomes more marketing noise.

Nothing evidenced this phenomenon more than the dot-com frenzy. Nascent companies with millions of dollars in seed capital hired the best and brightest advertising and design agencies. They constructed clever brand marks, and then dispersed them. Oh, how they dispersed them! Billboards, bumper stickers, T-shirts, direct mail, e-mail, television advertisements, bus stands, buses, taxicabs, newspapers—you name it, these marketing managers exposed the brand symbols anywhere and everywhere. Today, most of those brands have evaporated. Despite the exposures, most consumers cannot recall what these companies did in the first place. They may recall seeing the logo, but they have difficulty remembering what it stood for.

By no fault of the brand manager, great brand symbols can be overexploited. Coca-Cola is a powerful Legendary Brand with a pervasive collection of brand symbols (the contour bottle, the brand mark, the polar bears, the Sundblom Santa, etc.). In recent years, Coke actually limited the exposure of certain of these symbols. The reason: they were so pervasive they weren't being seen. Coke sought ways to reduce overall exposure and make the exposures that remained relevant and activated.

As brand manager, your job is to see that the brand symbols appear in places where the narrative is actually unfolding. For example, Quiksilver is a Legendary Brand for surfers, snowboarders, and skaters. Its brand symbols, which are instantly recognizable in these communities, only appear on products and other items that are actively a part of the lifestyle. You will find the Quiksilver logo on boards (surf, skate, or snow). You will also find it artfully integrated into the clothing made by the brand. It appears in tasteful executions at events staged by the company—events that include surf music, board competitions, or other activities that allow consumers to live the brand narrative.

QuickSilver truly has a brand culture. It was an early supporter of legendary skateboard champion Tony Hawk. It stages events each year that showcase emerging surf, ski, and skate talent. Its symbols lend authenticity to these experiences. They have a meaningful role. In fact, die-hard enthusiasts judge the legitimacy of such events based upon the presence of QuickSilver symbols. Activision, the video game manufacturer, secured an alliance with QuickSilver to use its brand symbols within its skateboarding video games—further adding an authenticity to the experience. QuickSilver doesn't carpet bomb. It treats its brand symbols like currency.

Symbols in the hands of the faithful. There is an exception to the rule, however. You will sometimes find brand symbols in obscure locations that appear to have nothing to do with the brand narrative, but it is perfectly acceptable. This happens when you give the consumer the brand symbol, and allow them to place it wherever they choose. This is frequently accomplished with stickers and decals.

Stickers and decals are often controversial in the brand marketing community. They are also often undervalued. There is good reason for both of these facts. Stickers are controversial because they have a way of showing up in places brand managers fear to tread: bars, bathrooms, jalopies, prisons, slums, etc.

They are undervalued because, for most brands, they are never used. Most consumers are not looking for a way to adhere your brand to their life, unless, of course, you are a Legendary Brand and your narrative stands for something integral to their belief system. If this is the case, your brand symbols may appear close to the narrative activities whether you provide them or not.

In the packaging of every Macintosh, since the first day the machine was offered to consumers, at least one Apple logo sticker is enclosed. Remarkably, a lot of these stickers are actually used. They are affixed to workstations, automobiles, notebooks, and any other place that the loyal Mac user wishes to tell the world he thinks "different." Nine times out of ten, the sticker appears in a place that is closely associated with the consumer's acting out of the brand narrative.

When you put your brand symbols into the hands of your brand culture, you empower them to show you where it is most meaningful. It does not have to be a sticker or a decal. It can take many forms, but in each case you can observe what consumers do with it.

Christopher Williams, in his book, *A Kick in the Seat of the Pants*, recounts the story of an architect who planted grass between a series of buildings he designed and constructed. He waited for several weeks to see where the grass was trampled by the paths of people moving between buildings. After observing this, he then instructed the contractors where to build the sidewalks. The same principle applies to brand symbols. When you put them into the hands of your culture, you can observe where they put them to use, and calibrate your other brand activities accordingly.

Slow burn. Occasionally, your brand symbol(s) will resonate with your audience in such a way that their exposure gets beyond your control. Most brand managers hope for such rapid and widespread consumer adoption of their intellectual properties. When this happens, however, you must redouble your efforts to monitor the brand.

Symbols are perhaps the most easily adopted link between consumers and brand narratives. Symbols have great power to communicate a multitude of ideas about a belief system in a finite lexicon. A symbol is like an electron, a tiny part of a bigger whole, but containing enormous amounts of potential energy. Your job as brand manager is to ensure that your symbols do not become so active that they cause a brand meltdown. Most of us know this phenomenon as a *fad*.

Fads rarely stand the test of time. When consumer tastes shift, and the fad is no longer the fad, consumers have a way of shunning the source. In most cases, the shunning is worthwhile. We have all experienced untalented musical artists that enjoyed their 15 seconds of fame for more than a year. When the joyride ends, we are all too happy to bid them good riddance. Occasionally, however, good people and good products succumb to the stigma of fad.

When brands fall victim to fad backlash, it is usually because the brand managers put all of their proverbial eggs in one basket. As one group of consumers rapidly adopted the brand, the manager gave that segment its entire focus, rather than developing the brand within other segments or exploring what cultural narrative was being activated by symbol inclusion. Assuming that the brand has substantive value, and it is linked to a true set of sacred beliefs and brand narrative, this should not happen.

You can avoid the downside of a fad, and consumer burnout by taking a few preemptive steps.

1. When the first signs of rapid adoption appear, focus your efforts on new segments. Use the opportunity to divert some of

your resources to emerging or undeveloped segments of your target consumer base. Introduce brand symbols to this base in a new or different context.

2. Now is the time to do more research and profiling. Take clues from rapid symbol adoption and get into narrative of the consumer's identity. Why is the symbol important? What is it activating?

3. Rapid adoption is a sign that the first story arc from your brand narrative works. Use this opportunity to introduce a new story arc or build up the next level. Changing the story arc is a good way to keep the competition at bay, and to sustain the consumer excitement. Without changing the story arc, you risk becoming a "one hit wonder."

4. Leave them wanting more. When the use of your brand symbols overheats, voluntarily pull back. Your senior management will likely think you are insane. However, it is far better to disappear with an audience wanting more than it is to retreat while they throw tomatoes. Great musical artists know this strategy well. Their managers are careful to stage the release of the artist's albums so that fans can work up an appetite for new material.

5. Plan your communications strategy around significant events in your culture's life, in addition to the significant events of your brand platform. Most companies carefully plan to expose their brand marks in tandem with new product launches and important press events. Few, however, consider what else occurs in the culture calendar. If you have profiled your culture well, you should be able to anticipate such events. Knowing what is on this calendar can help you expose your brand at calculated, meaningful times. It can also help you to avoid overexposure, particularly if your brand will play second to another brand that also affects this culture.

Nothing makes marketers happier than to see consumers volunteering to wear, post, and display their brand symbols. It is a clear sign that a culture is forming around your brand narrative. It indicates that what you stand for means something to people.

Expose your brand marks carefully. Integrate them into communications media in a way that is relevant to the brand narrative. And by all means, allow your consumers to make them a part of their life in their own way, without your interference.

Consumer Ritual

Brand narrative comes to life and brand cultures form quickly when brand use exists within a consumer ritual. For many years, marketers ignored the ritual aspect of brand consumption. Recently, however, the ritual dimension of consumer behavior has gained a great deal of attention.

Rituals are the dramatic re-enactment of a myth. There are essentially two types of ritual: sacred and mundane. Mundane rituals are similar to habits. For example, you might brush your teeth, shave, weigh yourself, and drink a cup of coffee each morning before you take your shower. This is a morning ritual for you. It is not a sacred ritual, however, because it is not attached to any great meaning, nor is it linked to a narrative. It is a mundane ritual, incorporating a series of habits and behavioral activities.

Sacred rituals occupy different cognitive space. They have deeper meaning and cultural significance. They are comprised of a set of actions that serve to activate a narrative or myth. For example, gift giving at Christmas is a ritual linked to religious dogma and family tradition. Graduation ceremonies are sacred rituals linked to a rite of passage and the transformation from the ignorant to the wise.

Brands are often a part of mundane rituals, but rarely take advantage of sacred rituals. For example, shaving with a Gillette Mach III razor is perhaps only a habit for many men. Some men might make it part of a mundane shaving ritual. Suppose they shave with a Gillette Mach III razor after soaking their faces for five minutes in warm balm and applying a coat of thick shaving cream imported from London. These activities are quite different and apart from the razor's participation in a sacred ritual, such as a group head-shaving ceremony mark-ing the completion of basic pilot training for an F16 squadron. If such a ritual were to exist, the brand would participate within a ritual that is infused with meaning and emotion.

Ritual components and types. In the best material on the sub-ject, "The Ritual Dimension of Consumer Behavior,"[1] Dr. Dennis Rook wrote that, "Ritual experience relies on four tangible components: (i) ritual artifacts; (ii) a ritual script; (iii) ritual performance role(s); and (iv) a ritual audience."

Brand participation in consumer ritual is typically, but not exclu-sively, through the devices of ritual artifacts. For example, to partici-pate in a H.O.G. ride, you need to own a Harley-Davidson motorcycle. You put this artifact to use to enact the ritual narrative. Sometimes brands participate in consumer rituals, but they are not the only brand used. Godiva chocolates are one of many artifacts that may be used on Valentine's Day, but any chocolate qualifies as an artifact for the Valen-tine's Day ritual.

The specificity to which your brand is required in the ritual speaks to the strength of your brand narrative and the relevance of the ritual to it. Figure 8.1 illustrates the ritual artifact hierarchy. At the base of the pyramid, many categories of products and brands can be used as an artifact in the ritual. At Christmas, there is no one specific cate-gory of gift required. Your brand may be selected as an artifact in this ritual, but it is not specified as a requisite artifact.

At the next stage of the pyramid are rituals that call for a specific category of artifacts, but not specifically your brand. For example, it is customary to give a greeting card on Mother's Day. Hallmark may be one brand of card, but it is not the only brand consumers consider or use in the ritual.

The top level of the pyramid contains rituals that require the use of a specific brand within a specific category. To fully participate in the ritual of MacWorld, you need an understanding of a Macintosh.

There are few widespread rituals that call for brand specificity. Most rituals that require brand specificity are designed around the

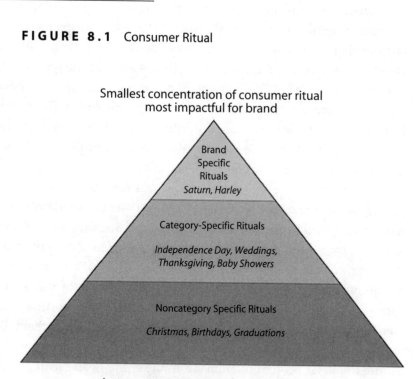

FIGURE 8.1 Consumer Ritual

Smallest concentration of consumer ritual
most impactful for brand

Brand
Specific
Rituals
Saturn, Harley

Category-Specific Rituals

*Independence Day, Weddings,
Thanksgiving, Baby Showers*

Noncategory Specific Rituals

Christmas, Birthdays, Graduations

Largest concentration of consumer ritual
least impactful for brand

brand platform itself. The Saturn Homecoming is a ritual with many participants. The common artifact is a Saturn car. Saturn, the company, orchestrates and organizes this ritual, which is apparently meaningful to the hundreds of consumers who travel many miles to participate.

In addition to artifacts, rituals generally unfold according to a script, which may be very elaborate, like a wedding ceremony, or vaguely constructed, such as a dating ritual. Rituals also have performance roles that demarcate the participant's relationship to the ritual activity. A bride and groom have specific roles in the wedding ceremony.

Finally, rituals have a ritual audience—a group of people who watch the ritual unfold. In some cases, the audience and the participants are one and the same.

When you think of sacred consumer rituals and their relevance to your brand, think broadly. Sacred rituals can take many forms, some less obvious than surface assumptions. In her book, *Ritual: Perspectives and Dimensions,* author Catherine Bell suggests six broad categories[2]: rites of passage; calendrical rites; rites of exchange and communion; rites of affliction; feasting, fasting, and festivals; and political rites. Throughout history, people have participated in rituals connected to one of these six activities. To determine where your brand might play a role, you should first consider which of these six ritual dimensions applies.

For many people, the first purchase of a new car is both a rite of passage and a rite of exchange. It can be a very meaningful experience if unencumbered by the monotony and pain of the sales process. Even when the sales process is onerous, many people feel a rush of energy the first day they drive their new car home. It has taken many years, but automakers are finally learning about the power of this experience—and turning it into a ritual. Saturn is most noteworthy—commemorating the event with a photo calendar and a special chant. But high-end automakers have followed suit, introducing "new owner" feature tours, and congratulations from the entire dealer team.

Playing in ritual space. A powerful and overlooked means of cultivating a brand culture is to play a part in the culture's ritual activities. Following are some suggestions on how to do this.

- If you are fortunate, rituals already exist within your brand space. If this is the case, your job is to determine how your brand can become an indispensable part of the ritual. For example, one-time-use cameras are now frequent artifacts of wedding rituals. They are usually left on the tables at the reception so that guests can capture candid images of the dinner group. If you manage the Kodak brand, your job is to determine how Kodak can better participate in the wedding ritual, moving up the pyramid of specificity, so that only Kodak will do.
- Create your own ritual events. These are very closely related to promotions, the difference being that a ritual event lets all con-

sumers participate in a way that brings the brand narrative to life. The Guggenheim stages a motorcycle ride to Las Vegas every year. This ritual is both promotion and narrative activation point.

- Find ways to sacrilize your brand through its use, transforming what might otherwise be a mundane habit into a sacred ritual. Every time runners put on a pair of Nike shoes, they can potentially participate in a sacred ritual. The onus is on Nike to bring the brand narrative to life. Instead of the obligatory morning jog, the consumer could perform the great rite of self-advancement. It can become a living way to activate the Nike brand narrative.

- The clearest sign that a brand culture has formed is the presence of ritual activities, no matter how trivial. Be on the lookout for these activities. The ones originated by the consumer are the ones with the greatest potential. Sit in a Starbucks for a length of time, and you will begin to see interesting ritual patterns. These are the leverage points for brand building.

Legendary Brands can and do make great use of consumer ritual activities. When consumer ritual is at its best, it is inextricably connected to the brand narrative and provides the consumer an opportunity to live the story. There is no right or wrong way to go about experimenting with consumer ritual, and there is no specific formula to bring it to life for your brand. Leverage the four elements of ritual, work to make your brand a more specific part of consumer ritual, and consider all of the potential ritual domains to make it work for your brand.

NURTURING BRAND CULTURE DEVELOPMENT

This chapter led with two important elements evidenced in many brand cultures: symbol usage and consumer ritual. As a brand manager, however, there are many things you can do to nurture, shape, and protect your culture. Following are some general thoughts.

Support Those Who Support You

Brand cultures have a way of attracting zealots and activists. If you currently manage a Legendary Brand, you know who these people are because you receive a lot of mail from them. These are the customers who speak up when they don't like your latest brand extension, or they don't care for your new spokesperson, or they want you to change your package design. Not only do these people contact you, they are often known to stage protests and events.

When New Coke was introduced, it took a few days before the nation understood what a marketing disaster it was. At Coke headquarters, however, they should have known within minutes, because their most loyal fans spoke up instantly. They hated it. It stood against everything Coke meant to this loyal following.

The problem with zealots and activists is that they appear crazy. We cannot believe that any sane person has that much time to care about the color of our new package design. We assume that this group of people is on the fringe and not representative of our brand culture. There may be some truth to this assumption, except that it is also possible that this fringe group is just an overamplification of your brand culture. While the remaining 95 pecent of our customer base might not write a letter or stage a sit in, they might stop buying the product, or they might consider an alternate brand choice.

Do not abandon the faithful. No matter how crazy they seem, treat them with the same respect as the average customer. In fact, give the zealots and activists the credit they deserve. They are zealots and activists for your brand—not your competitors'. Provide them with resources you don't give to the average customer. Maybe you help them to organize a plant tour and a lunch with someone on the production team. Maybe you create a support group that they can lead. Maybe you ask them to beta test new products and you listen to their feedback (you don't have to use what they say, you just have to listen with honesty).

Conversely, be careful not to overindulge the truly fanatical customers. Dancing with the overzealous consumer is like playing with a Ouija board. It may seem perfectly harmless at first, but it is amazing how an innocent reply to an email on a community chat board can snowball into a battery of flaming message posts. Before you know it, rumor spreads and opinion about your brand takes a turn for the worst.

Stage Cultural Events

One of the easiest ways to promote the development of a brand culture is to stage events and activities that allow your culture to congregate and feel a part of the brand narrative. Each year, Ben & Jerry's invites their shareholders out to their Vermont corporate headquarters to sample the product and relax to the sound of live bands and Grateful Dead recordings. These shareholders are also the strongest participants in the brand culture, so the event delivers double benefits.

Quiksilver sponsors local surfing, skating, and snowboarding shows and competitions. They do everything they can to make the events fun and in the spirit of the brand. They associate themselves with legends in the field and up and coming talent. In the process, they enable their brand culture to touch the brand narrative. They don't stop there, either. They produce "magalogs," hybrid magazines and product catalogs that provide compelling editorial content. This is how the brand culture learns about upcoming trends, achievements, and events.

Amazon.com allows users to create lists of their favorite books, and post these lists directly on the Amazon Web site. They also enable customers to review books, rate them, and post commentaries. And they do not stop there. If you are looking for a recommendation, Amazon compares your purchases with those of others and offers you a chance to see what else might be of interest to you. Besides being a great upsell opportunity, Amazon's investment in collaborative technologies enables the brand culture. Customers feel more a part of the literary experience that is sharing and discussing books.

Following are a few additional guidelines.

- Provide activities and resources to your customers so that they can develop into a culture, but do not overdo it. Work too hard to develop the culture and you look ridiculous. Your motives will be questioned.

- Everything you do is for the customer, not for you. If you serve them well, your culture will reward you with loyalty in the *long run.* But do not expect instant results. Do not force a sale in every staged event. In fact, some of your events may have no direct sales opportunity. If you do your job right, and link the event back to your brand narrative, the culture will walk away with greater brand preference on their next purchase occasion. You will have achieved your goal. Too many staged activities fail in the final act because bottom-line oriented brand managers required the time to make a sale.

- Be consistent. Stick to the themes and story arcs of your brand narrative, especially those that are playing through. The events and activities you plan for your culture are effective when they reinforce an established brand narrative. They are less effective when used as a platform to launch a new brand narrative or a new and unfamiliar story arc. There are always exceptions, but you are better off using your experiential activities to reinforce your current communications platform, rather than lay the groundwork for the platform you plan to launch next month.

- Listen, observe, and participate! Staged events and activities are the best opportunities for you to connect with your consumers for two reasons. First, you capture them in an environment with other consumers. That social effect is important. People do different things when together than when they are alone. They also do different things when they are congregated in a cultural context. You will gather rich observations from your experiential brand activities. Second, you capture a kind of brand rapture when you listen to consumers at brand events. True, you have to filter some of this zeal to make it work in everyday brand management, but it still holds value. It allows you to see the purest and most charged emotional associations with your brand narrative. It allows you to see where rituals may exist. It helps you identify the significance of your brand symbols. Finally, it helps you to be at one with the culture.

BEYOND YOUR CONTROL, BUT WORTH YOUR EFFORT

Brand culture is the one aspect of Legendary Brands that managers cannot control with any form of precision. They cannot even guarantee that such a culture will emerge—all they can do is hope. When a brand culture does emerge, it can generate benefits or costs for the brand. The actions of the brand manager largely determine which course it takes.

Managing a brand culture is like being a good public servant. You must steward it with an invisible hand and interact with it warmly and generously. All the while you must be cognizant of your competitors who will covet your culture and attempt to make it their own. The key to keeping your brand culture is to remain true to your brand narrative.

Larry: What does the Kodak brand stand for?

Carl: The consumer Kodak brand is about warmth, stories, memories, good times, happiness, family, and values. It stands for social currency and ease-of use. You have to remember that when George Eastman created the brand in the late 1800s, he set out to do two things. First, he came up with a name that meant nothing in any country of the world—it would never fail translation. Kodak is a series of letters that means nothing. He wanted to systematically add meaning over time so he started with a clean slate. He also invented the phrase, "You press the button, we do the rest," to stress ease-of-use and to stand by the Kodak brand. Second, he came up with a pair of colors, yellow and red, that would be unmistakable, and again, had no cultural holding. That's visionary in the 1800s—planning to build a *global* brand.

The ingredient you see in the exposition of our brand is strong emotional equity. We purposefully go for a connection that cannot be explained verbally. It creates a welling up effect. "Daddy's Little Girl," a spot in which the father gives away his daughter as a bride to the waiting groom, speaks as emotionally now as it did when it was created 20 years ago. It really tugs at the heartstrings. It makes you think of warm memories, a story that you have as well.

Larry: Your new campaign, "Share Moments. Share Life." feels more aligned with that emotional narrative than its predecessor, "Take Pictures. Further." Why do you think that is?

Carl: You hit on something we consciously did, for a lot of good reasons. We launched "Take Pictures. Further." to put the spotlight on product performance and digital transition. We were fighting price wars. Competition wanted to sell their products on price. We had to show we have properties, we have values, we have benefits that go beyond emotional equities. Our products perform better with better characteristics. Here are the advantages. Here is the reason we are a premium brand. And it worked.

But we also realized about three years ago that if we had a steady diet of product benefit advertising, unique selling proposition advertising, we could lose our emotional equity that took 100 years to build. So we began to swing it back. "Share Moments. Share Life." is more of an experience story. It is more of an emotional Kodak story.

Larry: Looking at the legacy of your advertising, it seems clear that Kodak is really a brand ultimately owned by your consumers, more so than it being owned by its shareholders. Have you found that consumers hold you to account?

Carl: You are absolutely right. No company owns its brand. It is only the steward of it. It is owned and operated by, governed by, the belief dynamics that are part of the end-user. All you can do is make some promises and communicate those. Everything else is owned by the end-user. So he or she will decide: Are you living up to that [promise]? Are you pleasing me? And they will decide what you stand for.

We never for a moment think that we control and own the brand. But we can totally control the fulfillment of the promise of the brand. We lean on our people—hard—inside the company to deliver great products and to innovate. There is a covenant between us and the end-user, and we spend an awful lot of time saying, "Are we doing the right things, here? Are we living up to that covenant?"

Larry: What advice do you have for other brand stewards?

Carl: First of all, you cannot build a brand quickly. You cannot build a great brand by avoiding risk. You cannot maintain a brand based on precedent.

You've always got to be on the edge. You have to have sweaty palms. You have to wake up in the middle of the night and say, "I am the steward of this hugely valuable brand. Have I gone too far?" Unless you feel that way, all the time, you are slipping into "old and the same." You're becoming wallpaper.

On the other hand, if you are in the news every day and are controversial all the time, you're probably slipping too far to the other side. Do not become such a prima donna or egomaniac that you think you are right and no one else appreciates the "art" you are producing. In the one case you are talking to the select few, which do not represent the total brand. In the other case, you're talking to the safe majority. You must know your heritage and legacy, your future, your customers, and their future. You must listen to the market constantly, innovate, meet the market needs, and have very satisfied customers. Happy customers will value your brand forever.

PART THREE

III

Part Three is a field guide for the marketer. Armed with a theory for Legendary Brands, and the basic tools for managing these brands, the chapters herein provide special cases and topics that may be of use to you in your endeavors.

Chapter 9 explores the world of cobranding and marketing partnerships. Many brands align with others to expand their reach, provide complementary consumer benefits, or augment their marketing image. Legendary Brands often derive benefits from well-planned partnerships, but they just as often discover liabilities.

Chapter 10 focuses on brand agents—the people, places, and things that can link the narrative of the brand to the sacred beliefs of consumers. Selecting and managing brand agents is a difficult task. This chapter provides some guidelines and watch-points.

Chapter 11 explores the power of branding in nonlinear environments; that is, marketing channels that do not allow for a linear progression of story development. We study Ian Schrager hotels and the rich, sensory methods they use to tell their stories.

Chapter 12 focuses on brands on the brink of disaster. How does a Legendary Brand recover from a crisis? This chapter follows the resurrection of one such brand, the Jack in the Box chain of restaurants.

Chapter 13 explores the world of politics, because many political campaigns are but a social extension of Legendary Brands. In particular, we examine the dynamic political environment in America from 1992–1994, beginning with the Clinton-Gore campaign and closing with the historic congressional turnover led by House Republicans in 1994. In each case, narrative played a pivotal role.

Chapter 14 flirts with the "dark side" of brand narrative. Narrative is an influential sales agent. It can bring out the worst in consumers as easily as it can the best. One aspect of brand narrative taps into the dominant themes of every story ever told: sex and violence. We discuss the reasonable uses of these themes and the responsibilities marketers must live up to.

CHAPTER 9

COBRANDING, SPONSORSHIP, AND PARTNERSHIP MARKETING

Partnering by and between Legendary Brands is a pervasive movement. More brands are joining forces to reach relevant consumers with targeted offers. At its best, brand partnering delivers effective benefits, generates tremendous consumer appeal, and deploys marketing capital with extreme efficiency. At its worst, it egregiously wastes scarce corporate resources and alienates brand cultures. Before you invest time and money to commune in the Legendary Brand country club, you need to carefully weigh the benefits and risks.

THE BENEFITS OF BRAND PARTNERSHIPS

Brand partnerships are at their best when they offer tangible benefits to all participants. Tangible benefits include measurable sales opportunities or exclusive channel rights and privileges. In each case, the benefits achieved through the partnership are linked to quantifiable metrics. Much more difficult to measure are the intangible benefits that often serve as the sole partnership rationale, such as the emotional equity derived by your association with the brand. These perceived qualitative benefits often overshadow rational judgment. Many brand partnerships fail because the desire to market with the sexier partner is so inebriating that the associated costs are ignored.

The Halo Effect

Nearly every sponsorship pitch includes a discussion about the *halo effect* of the brand partnership. In other words, the property selling partnership rights believes that the buyer will inherit part of its brand equity by association. Olympic sponsors pay handsomely because they believe their brand will be elevated to a higher status merely by adding the Olympic brand marks to their advertising and promotional executions. Empirical evidence exists to support this belief. The companies that sponsor the Olympic Games often witness dramatic increases in sales, awareness, and consumer preference during the season of the games. This increase is arguably due to the halo effect and the benefits of association.

When the opportunity is right and the brand association is relevant, your brand can benefit from the halo effect. You effectively borrow or inherit emotional equity. The assumption you must believe to accept the premise of the halo effect is that consumers make a cognitive association between your brand and the partner brand for which they have the affinity. That is to say that, rationally or irrationally, consumers favor your brand because it appears to support or be endorsed by the partner brand. The halo effect is somewhat controversial because research findings are contradictory and inconclusive. NASCAR provides the most compelling evidence that the halo effect works. Many retailers have witnessed double-digit increases in store traffic and sales on the days that the NASCAR they sponsor appears at the store.

Distribution Benefits

Beyond the halo effect, brand partnerships may deliver distribution and channel benefits. You can often enter new markets or reach your consumers through new channels as a result of a solid brand partnership. Beverage companies are among the brands that most understand the value of distribution partnerships. Through their dealings with leading sports and entertainment attractions, Coca-Cola and Pepsi have secured powerful and often exclusive distribution channels. These new channels increase the sale of product in the context of sponsored events. Through channel marketing, they also allow the opportunity to influence future purchase decisions.

Blocking Rights and the Lure of Exclusivity

Perhaps the most compelling benefit is the promise of exclusivity. Many brand partnerships include restrictions preventing one or both sides from engaging in activities with competitors. Certainly, in the sponsorship field this is true. In fact, the price of sponsorship for very popular consumer properties is often escalated by the bidding between competitive brands seeking to lock each other out of the channel.

Great value can derive from an exclusive brand partnership. For starters, it may assure that your marketing efforts with your partner will not be thwarted by competitors. In carefully controlled marketing environments, exclusive brand partnerships provide a rare opportunity to engage the consumer without resorting to defensive posturing. Instead of saying why the consumer should ignore your competitors, you can focus on developing the brand narrative and leveraging the equities of your brand partner to do so.

Exclusive brand partnerships also offer a viable means to attack the competitor's consumer base. The brand you partner with owns a share of your competitor's customers. These customers have an affinity for your brand partner. By leveraging your new and exclusive relationship with the brand partner, you have an opportunity to convert these customers to your brand because of your association.

Resource Synergies

The best brand partnerships truly create synergy, perhaps the most maligned business buzzword in use today. Most brand partnerships forged by Legendary Brands are sizable. As a result, the marketing resources that both parties add to the equation exceed the resources of either partner. When these resources are combined to exploit the unique strengths of each party, the value is truly greater than the sum of the parts.

For example, American Express partners with a number of leading arts organizations in exclusive arrangements. While these arts organizations may accept competitive cards, they offer exclusive benefits for American Express card members, such as preferred seating, private events, and other "unanticipated rewards." It would cost American Express much more than the price of the partnership to deliver these experiences to their members. Conversely, the arts organizations, leaders in their own right, would be hard pressed to purchase the marketing resources American Express utilizes on their behalf, such as bill stuffers, custom print advertisements, and in some cases, broadcast media.

Similarly, the partnership between McDonald's and Disney creates benefits far in excess of the individual contributions. Disney's entertainment content drives the sale of McDonald's Happy Meals. Conversely, the thousands of McDonald's restaurants worldwide provide a unique venue to market Disney products.

THE RISKS OF BRAND PARTNERSHIP

For all its potential benefits, there are many hidden risks in a brand partnership. The greatest risk of all is that you will gain nothing, no matter how much you spend.

Loitering

Some brand partnerships fail due to lack of relevance. In irrelevant partnerships, one partner loiters within the other's brand space. Consumers do not take kindly to this infringement of "sacred" territory.

Two recent sports examples illustrate this point. San Francisco's Candlestick Park, home of the San Francisco 49ers, was recently renamed 3Com Park after the technology company entered into a multimillion dollar title sponsorship agreement. Fans were not amused. Television coverage of games at 3Com Park frequently includes shots of fans hoisting homemade signs decrying the death of Candlestick. To these fans, 3Com slew a beloved cultural asset.

Worse yet was the naming of Mile High Stadium in Denver, Colorado, home to the Denver Broncos. Local citizens petitioned to stop the renaming of the facility, which is now sponsored by Invesco. The new name: Invesco Field at Mile High Stadium. Two concerns were raised. First, Invesco is a mutual fund and investment services company. Many complained that this seemed a poor fit for a facility that is home to the area's most popular athletic franchise, steeped in western imagery. Second, Mile High Stadium is practically a trademark of the city of Denver. Its famous elevation is as much a signature of the city as the Rocky Mountains. Many locals saw the sponsorship as a dilution of a landmark and part of the city's identity.

Since its inauguration, the community and the media have widely criticized the brand partnership between Invesco and Mile High Stadium, generating cause for alarm within the sponsorship community. In fact, many sports commentators refuse to acknowledge Invesco when discussing games held at the venue. They continue to refer to it simply as Mile High Stadium.

Any time two or more brands partner, they must ensure that their efforts, jointly and severally, are relevant to one another. Otherwise, it will appear that one partner is exploiting consumer affection for the other partner, taxing fans with unnecessary media and incremental brand exposure. Remember, we exist in a consumer culture that is marketing savvy and very suspicious of your motives. If you plan to position your brand within the brand culture of another Legendary Brand, make sure that you have a reason for being there, and that the reason is something other than the desire to make money off of someone else's customers.

Ambush

You found the right brand partner. They have an enthusiastic and highly valuable consumer base. More important, you have identified a great, relevant way to partner with this brand. You intend to deliver true consumer value. So why is your competitor getting more play out of the partnership than you are?

Ambush marketing by competitors is a serious concern in the brand partnership community. Recently, in the 2002 Winter Olympic Games, ambush marketing took center stage. AT&T has been an Olympic sponsor for decades, and they continued their association in the 2002 games. Nevertheless, Sprint PCS received more attention during the games than AT&T. Sprint PCS launched a clever advertising campaign that highlighted winter sports, competition, and Olympic athletes. They referred to themselves as "the official sponsor of all things innovative." The juxtaposition of the imagery, the athletes, and the tag line, along with an aggressive media buy, created consumer perception that Sprint PCS sponsored the Olympic Games. AT&T's nontrivial investment in the games inured to Sprint's benefit.

Clutter

Brand partnerships suffer from clutter, especially in the promotional and sponsorship marketing segment. Brands that are capable of attracting corporate sponsors and promotional partners find it difficult to set limits. Instead, they frequently carve the playing field into exclusive categories. Thus, they might sell you the exclusive rights to be their automobile partner, while retaining the right to sell exclusive rights to other companies in noncompetitive categories.

In theory, this approach protects your interests because it prevents your direct competitors from marketing against you within the domain of your brand partnership. However, it does not account for the clutter factor. If your brand partner sells rights to fifteen different companies, each in exclusive, noncompetitive categories, you become one of fifteen brands competing for consumer attention. Sometimes, a few of these brands are more dominant than the others, creating the potential for your brand to be eclipsed by a larger or more relevant participant. Worse yet, when there are so many messages competing for attention, consumers tend to filter out all of the sponsor messages.

Clutter resulting from too many brand partners can be controlled contractually, but clutter sometimes results when there is only one brand partner—you. When you overbrand within the partner's brand space you effectively clutter the property. After awhile, the multiple exposures and messages become just as problematic as too many brands in the space.

Bait and Switch

It is not uncommon to find brand partnerships contemplated in one fashion but delivered in another. Your brand partner promises to let you use their property to market your goods and services. After the honeymoon, you suddenly find that many of your core equities are problematic for your brand partner, and off limits for copromotion. Perhaps your brand partner allows you to copromote, but its control over the execution serves their interests more than it serves yours. As a result, you are provided the right to leverage the property, but it fails to deliver value.

Most bait and switch scenarios occur because the partners did not perform due diligence in the courtship phase. They failed to ask the right questions and consider the execution and implementation aspects of the partnership. It is rarely the result of misleading promises.

FORGING A BRAND PARTNERSHIP THAT WORKS

The success of brand partnerships is largely a function of the symmetry in brand narratives. The partners you seek are more than likely Legendary Brands in their own right. You seek a partnership with them because they have a deep attachment with a group of consumers. This attachment is so intense that you believe an association with them will benefit your brand. If such an attachment does exist, chances are that it is rooted in a brand narrative. Thus, your first consideration is to evaluate how well your brand narratives align.

Narrative Alignment

Figure 9.1 geometrically illustrates the alignment of good brand partnerships. It considers only two brands in the partnership. If you envision a brand partnership of more than two brands, then you must

FIGURE 9.1   Alignment of Good Brand Partnerships

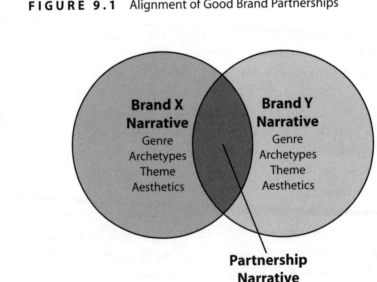

add another circle. As you can imagine, the more circles you add, the more difficult it is to ensure narrative congruence.

When you partner with another brand in a manner that involves copromotion or joint marketing, your task is to make sure that one story fits naturally with the other. If you were to intertwine the stories of Little Red Riding Hood and Rapunzel, no one would be particularly surprised. Both stories inhabit the world of fairy tales, and they have similar themes and characters. A clever writer could weave these two stories together in a fashion that creates a new meaning and an unexpected plot. In fact, that is just what Stephen Sondheim did when he wrote *Into the Woods*.

On the other hand, if we tried to weave the story of the television series *Baywatch* with *Little House on the Prairie*, people would roll their eyes and suspect the involvement of the Fox Network. Yes, perhaps some great writer out there may find a clever way to blend these two stories (David Lynch comes to mind), but the fit is not immediately evident. This is precisely what quells some of the biggest and most advertised brand partnerships. The stories do not mix well.

Following are recent partnerships that had all of us scratching our heads.

- *Taco Bell sponsorship of the Discovery Science Center in Santa Ana, California.* Taco Bell targets teen audiences, which are one of the largest segments of their consumer base. Yet the Discovery Science Center caters to young children. Also, unless Taco Bell is engineering new forms of meat, it is unclear how a sponsorship of the Science Center builds their brand—or vice versa.
- *CMGI Field—The new home of the New England Patriots.* Other than the fact that CMGI is a Boston-based company,

there is no relevant connection between this holding group of Internet companies and football. It is a pure chest-pounding play that does nothing to accentuate the fan affinity for the New England Patriots.

- *The Los Angeles Marathon, presented by Honda.* Aren't you supposed to *run* in a Marathon?
- *The Boston Marathon, presented by Citgo.* Citgo operates gas stations and convenience stores. Apparently marathon runners drive more than they run and they eat more junk food than we assumed.
- *Orkin sponsorship of Smithsonian insect exhibit.* Technically, they both deal with insects. But it is odd that a company that makes money by killing bugs would sponsor an exhibit that studies them. Using the same logic, perhaps PG&E, California's electric company, should sponsor an exhibit on capital punishment.
- *Tri-Con sponsorship/promotions with Star Wars franchise.* Many quickservice brands link to popular motion picture franchises, but this partnership crossed the line when the Taco Bell dog, Colonel Sanders (of Kentucky Fried Chicken fame), and the Pizza Hut delivery girl appeared in commercials brandishing light sabers and battling Imperial forces. There are multiple problems with this idea. First, it is a stretch to imagine the three characters coexisting in the same narrative. The Taco Bell Chihuahua evokes west coast imagery, the Colonel draws upon a turn of the century Southern ethos, and the Pizza Hut delivery girl is too generic to convey any narrative at all. Why are

these three together other than the fact that they share a
parent company (which most consumers do not know
about)? More important, these characters demonstrate
zero relevance to the Star Wars narrative and all its equity.
They truly loiter within it. Contrast this execution with the
very familiar and popular Energizer Bunny tie-in with Star
Wars. It showed Darth Vader about to attack someone
with a light saber only to learn that its batteries were
dead. As he curses the heavens, the Energizer Bunny rolls
through. Though on the edge, this execution combined
narratives in an engaging and appropriate manner.

To partner well with another brand, you must first know the
story of your own brand. If you have not constructed a brand bible, or
at least formed vague opinions about your brand story from the feedback of consumers, you have no business thinking about a brand partnership. You are the candidate most likely to experience the risks
outlined above: brand loitering, ambush, clutter, and bait and switch.

Only knowing your own brand narrative, however, will not be
sufficient to structure a good partnership. You must be able to articulate the brand narrative of your potential partner. Find out what your
customers perceive about that brand narrative. Talk to the customers
of the potential partner. What do they perceive to be the brand narrative? How do they perceive your brand narrative?

For instance, Kodak sponsors the new home of the Academy
Awards, the Kodak Theatre in Hollywood, California. The 3,500 seat,
state-of-the-art theater was constructed in a six-hundred-million-
dollar real estate development shepherded by TrizecHahn Development. This development, situated on the historic corner of Hollywood
Boulevard and Highland Avenue, tells a fascinating story, though totally contrived. It features architecture reminiscent of an earlier time in
motion picture history. It satisfies some of the expectations people

have about Hollywood. For years, this intersection housed seedy souvenir shops, dilapidated office buildings, and garish tourist attractions. In the words of the TrizecHahn Development creative team leader, David Malmuth, it was "the most disappointing corner in America." People came expecting to experience the Hollywood dream, and found only the slums.

With the establishment of the Hollywood & Highland development, the Academy of Motion Picture Arts and Sciences found an opportunity to bring their famous awards show back to Hollywood. Working with TrizecHahn Development, they created a beautiful, broadcast-ready performance venue with lush, nostalgic interiors by architect David Rockwell. There was only one brand that could effectively partner in this narrative experience: Kodak.

George Eastman, Kodak's founder, and Thomas Edison created the motion picture. Even to this day, Kodak earns nearly ten percent of its annual revenue from the motion picture industry. Leading cinematographers insist on Kodak film stock because of its quality and color precision. Even consumers recognize Kodak as a part of motion pictures. The naming of the Kodak Theatre, and Kodak's participation in Hollywood's latest jewel, made perfect sense for all parties. Celebrities and the average consumer alike have little quarrel with the association. In fact, they see it as a natural alignment of brand narrative.

Accentuating the Partnership Narrative

Narrative alignment serves primarily as a preventative measure. It prevents participation with your brand partner from conflicting with the established narratives of both parties. Great brand partnerships go beyond narrative alignment. They accentuate the myth of partnership.

The myth of partnership is favored and timeless. Whether it is the Japanese story of *The Seven Samurai*, the British tale of *The Lord of the Rings*, or America's revolutionary legends, the theme and the narrative are essentially the same. These narratives all speak to the power of teamwork. People enjoy hearing the story of seemingly dissimilar people coming together to solve a common goal. When constructing a brand partnership, the goal of the participants is to activate the myth of partnership in a way that benefits each participating brand.

Imagine for a moment that you are sitting in a coffeehouse somewhere. At a table close by sits a group of people who obviously know one another well. They are catching up over a cup of overbrewed coffee. Though you are not eavesdropping, you cannot help but hear bits of their conversation, which suddenly turns toward your new brand partnership. What would you want to hear them say about it? How would these consumers perceive the association? Would it be diabolical or thoughtfully clever?

Consumers Come First

To preserve your brand narrative and activate the myth of partnership, you must put the consumer first—not just your own consumer, but also the consumer of your brand partner. As self-evident as such a statement may be, many brand partnerships are predicated on the premise that the consumer does not matter. Brand managers often talk about gaining consumers as though they were poker chips, rather than living beings with emotions and free will.

Figure 9.2 depicts a conceptual model called "The Partnership Trinity." The most striking feature of the trinity is the fact that the consumer sits on top.

Great brand partnerships stem from the engagement and inclusion of consumers. The consumer perspective must be as important in the relationship as the business objectives of the contracting parties. In a sense, the consumer is a silent contractor. Though they may not sign the binding agreements, their actions will determine the success of the partnership.

As you develop brand partnerships of your own, consider a worksheet like the one illustrated in Figure 9.3, "The Partnership Brand Audit." For each party, you must articulate the benefits gener-

FIGURE 9.2 The Partnership Trinity

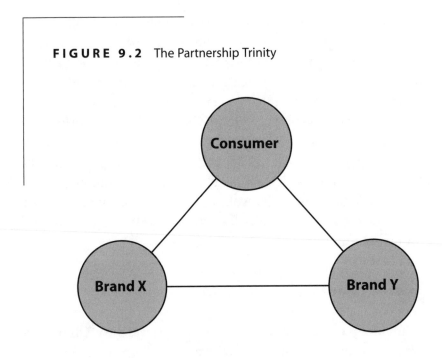

ated by the partnership and delineate the value received by each party, including the consumer. Consider how the value is delivered. Most importantly, identify the value characteristics and the boundaries required, to protect each party's self interests.

Systemic Value

Brand partnerships derive their value from the system that propels them. The fact that Brand X goes to market with Brand Y does not necessarily create any incremental value. In fact, it can destroy value if the brands are not aligned. A Sea World sponsorship by Exxon would probably cause an outrage in the environmental community, possibly hurting the sales of Sea World admission tickets.

Systemic value goes beyond the surface value of cobranding. It looks at all the drivers of business success. When the system underneath a brand partnership is well constructed, it is harder for com-

FIGURE 9.3 The Partnership Brand Audit

	Your Brand	Their Brand	Consumers
What narrative benefits will be generated by the brand partnership?			
How will these benefits be delivered?			
Why are these benefits important?			
How will the delivery of benefits be evidenced? (How do you know the benefits were delivered?)			
What risks are involved?			
What boundaries must the partnership not cross? (What are the "sacred cows"?)			

petitors to copy it or ambush it. Also, the partnership is more likely to stand the test of time—brand partnerships, like modern marriages, have a high divorce rate.

Figure 9.4 provides the consideration points for analyzing the systemic value of brand partnerships. Under each are questions that help to evaluate the relative strength of each consideration point. For example, your brand narratives may be in perfect alignment, and you may have a terrific opportunity to communicate the myth of partnership in traditional media, but your distributions systems could be difficult to synchronize or control. When this is the case, you open yourself up to ambush opportunities. Why? Because it is difficult to make your brand live in the brand culture of your partner. There is a level of abstraction that affords competitors the opportunity to cause doubt, or at least, confusion.

FIGURE 9.4   Planning the Partnership Narrative

Narrative Planning	Communications Planning	Channel Planning
• How does each brand partner activate consumer narrative?	• How do the individual partners communicate their narratives?	• Where do the partners communicate their brand narratives?
• How do the profiles of the partners' consumers overlap or complement one another?	• What are the current and planned story arcs used by the partners to promote or activate their brands?	• Where do the brands activate consumer narratives? (Where used?)
• What archetypes and/or genres are consistent or complementary between the partners?	• How can the existing brand campaigns tie to the communications of the partnership brand narrative?	• How can the partners leverage each other's channel to position their brand narrative?
• What new narrative benefits (if any) can the partnership deliver?	• When are the best times to communicate the partnership brand narrative vs. the individual brand narrative? (What are the windows?)	• How can competitors ambush the partnership brand narrative?
		• Which channels would consumers designate as "out of bounds"?

Michael Porter, perhaps the world's most insightful guru of corporate strategy and competitive economics, argues that it is systems that create true competitive advantage. In other words, companies create a sustainable point of differentiation by managing value delivery systems that are efficient but difficult for competitors to replicate.[1] This concept also applies to brand partnerships. The best brand partnerships create a business system that delivers value to consumers and the brand partners in a manner that is unique and differential. Unfortunately, most brand partnerships are created without any consideration for the system. Champagne is uncorked, the media is alerted, and everyone congratulates each other. The next day, they experience a massive hangover that lasts the entire run of the partnership.

Brand Partnerships Need Brand Management, Too

There's an old saying that a camel is a horse designed by committee. Though an analogy that is wholly unfair to the camel because it is, in fact, a very efficient desert pack animal, brand partnerships managed by committee rarely succeed. Each brand has its own brand manager, held accountable by a different senior executive. Managing the brand partnership is a small fraction of everyone's total responsibility. They have scarce time to steward it, and they have pressing internal brand objectives that take priority. Thus, the brand partnership becomes an unwanted step-child, an orphan really. When this unnurtured entity fails to perform, the parents blame each other and put the child up for adoption.

Brand partnerships require dedicated brand management. They require a strong, empowered leadership that puts the partnership first, and the independent goals of the brand owners second. This concept ties back to the theory that the consumer matters first, and what they really care about is the narrative activated by brands—alone or in partnership.

At the far end of the spectrum, you can treat your brand partnership like a joint venture and employ a full-time, third-party brand

manager. At the other end of the spectrum, you can create a joint governing body, but take care not to make it a giant committee. If the partnership is to have committee management, limit the leadership to two
people, possibly a third as tie breaker. Perhaps hire an agency to give
the partnership dedicated attention. The more people you add to the
equation, the more likely you will end up with a camel.

Brand partnerships should be well managed. Everything that applies to your own brand management should also apply to the partnership. Partnerships should have an independent brand bible. They
should have a tactical calendar and a long-term strategic plan. At a
minimum, they must have clear business objectives that consider the
stakeholders—including the consumer.

Brand partnerships also require ongoing care and investment.
Too often, the partnership is neglected after the deal is inked or the
first execution is complete. Many times, the brand that spends the
most to enter the partnership fails to promote it because they over-
spent to acquire the partnership rights. The result is exactly what you
might expect. A great partnership opportunity was purchased, but no
one knows about it because it has not been given the same promotional attention all of the other brand initiatives receive. Brand partnerships often require more attention than your solo initiatives.

CHAPTER 10

BRAND AGENTS

"You are a funny animal," he said at last. "You
are no thicker than a finger . . ."
"But I am more powerful than the finger of a king,"
said the snake.
The little prince smiled.
"You are not very powerful. You haven't even any
feet. You cannot even travel . . ."
"I can carry you farther than any ship could
take you," said the snake.
He twined himself around the little prince's ankle,
like a golden bracelet.
"Whomever I touch, I send back to the earth from
whence he came," the snake spoke again.

Antoine de Saint-Exupéry, *The Little Prince*

Ask Julia Roberts—the highest paid actress in motion picture history. Ask Tom Clancy—an author who commands million dollar advances not only for his books, but also for the movies and video games that bear his name. Ask Mariah Carey—who earned more than $60 million for the privilege of changing record labels. Ask any celebrity how he or she feels about agents. Arguably, their respective agents made the difference between fame and obscurity, fortune and famine.

Granted, Hollywood's definition of an agent is a far cry from the agents that Legendary Brands employ. Or is it?

Celebrities pay their agents to generate new business. Legendary Brands rely on brand agents to access new customers, create new markets, and introduce new products.

Hollywood insiders rely on talent agents to keep their name abuzz in the industry. Legendary Brands use brand agents to keep the narrative alive.

Talent agents often prove to be a curse, rather than a blessing to entertainment players. Some would call them a necessary evil. So, too, do Legendary Brands struggle with the excessive cost and frequent liability of the agents they marry to their brands.

As we discuss in Chapter 2, Legendary Brands rely on them to convey the brand narrative and offer physical proof for the sacred beliefs espoused by the brand. Effective brand agents are, therefore, as essential to the success of a Legendary Brand as the narrative they convey. While they can assume various forms, each has the power to make or break your brand. Like the snake in *The Little Prince*, brand agents can carry your brand farther than any ship, or return it to the earth from whence it came.

The objective of this chapter is to familiarize you with brand agents, demonstrate their effectiveness, and provide you with tools and concepts to manage them.

IDENTIFYING BRAND AGENTS

Brand agents, like nouns, can take the form of a person, place, or thing. Michael Jordan is a brand agent. So is Walt Disney World. A Kate Spade handbag is also a brand agent. In each case, the agent is tangible and an object that can be named, categorized, and acted upon. More importantly, each of the above examples speaks uniquely to the narrative of the brand it represents.

Each form of brand agent is accompanied by its own set of virtues and flaws. People provide a human and personable dimension, but the brand will outlive them. Places can provide an immersive, scalable narrative experience, but they require frequent upkeep and investment. Things, usually products, can be touched by a massive consumer audience, but they possess a limited ability to emote and stay fresh. They are also subject to fads.

There is no rule that states a brand must choose one and only one form of brand agent. In fact, many Legendary Brands employ several. The only rule to follow is this: Understand the capabilities and limitations of each form, and manage their relationship with your brand accordingly.

Economists often discuss the agency costs of management. Agency costs are costs corporations face when the objectives of the company's management are not aligned with the company's investors. Legendary Brand managers must also consider agency costs, which often exceed the fees paid to celebrity spokespeople, innovative product designers, and publicity-generating architecture firms.

Human Brand Agents

Founders and CEOs.

- *Advantages.* Aligned with brand business objectives; generates authenticity.
- *Disadvantages.* Not all are capable of being agents; brand story may change while they do not.

Sometimes a Legendary Brand is born with a brand agent in tow— its founder. Playboy (Hugh Hefner), Martha Stewart, Apple Computer (Steve Jobs), Kentucky Fried Chicken (Colonel Sanders), and Microsoft (Bill Gates) are all brands with legendary agents. In each case, the individual and the brand were inextricably linked. In each case, the narrative of the founder is at least one of the brand narratives.

Founders and CEOs are probably the most powerful human agents a brand can possess. Unlike celebrities and other third parties, these individuals' objectives are most aligned with the objectives of the brand. The brand's success *is* their fortune. They also provide the brand with an authenticity that resonates with consumers. For example, consumers purchase Dell computers for their quality, low cost, and ease of purchase. But many Dell customers also remain loyal because they believe in the vision of Michael Dell. As a brand agent, he lends credible authenticity to the brand and its narrative of entrepreneurial gumption. Despite the fact that Mr. Dell is one of the wealthiest men in America, many of his customers see him as an affable, industrious guy that built a business from a garage. That authentic association is part of Dell's brand equity.

Of course, CEOs can ruin that which they create. It is an interesting fact that many entrepreneurs are forced to exit the companies they created once those companies truly realize success. Sometimes the legend of the brand eclipses the legend of the founder. In other instances, the very human qualities that make legendary founders such strong brand agents are also the qualities that bring about their downfall. To err is human, but to punish the errors of legendary founders is the business of the media. When scandal erupts, the founder becomes a liability that can inadvertently destroy the brand.

Celebrities and spokespeople.

- *Advantages.* Star power; instant recognition; ability to "rent a narrative."
- *Disadvantages.* Celebrity objectives rarely align with brand's business objectives; success comes with incremental costs.

A profitable cottage industry exists within the ranks of major talent agencies and public relations firms. It is the business of securing endorsement and representation deals for celebrities. The industry exists because Legendary Brands are often built on the backs of celebrity brand agents.

Tiger Woods is a celebrity agent. So are William Shatner, Michael Jordan, Bob Dole, and the latest music act to tickle the fancy of popular culture. Celebrity agents are usually a means to an end, and that end is establishing or sustaining a brand narrative for a product or brand that is otherwise undifferentiated. For example, pop star Britney Spears is the current celebrity agent-de-jour for Pepsi-Cola. She joins a long list of pop culture personalities, including Michael Jackson and Shania Twain, who have sustained the Pepsi brand narrative for years. Pepsi's chosen niche in the cola market is to tell the story of popular culture, whereas Coke often speaks to American heritage, lifestyle, and tradition. Without this narrative infusion, Pepsi would have a difficult time sustaining itself as a Legendary Brand. In a sense, it uses celebrity agents to borrow narrative.

For all their power, celebrity narratives come with big liabilities. First, they are expensive, and the more their star power proves a return on investment for the brand, the higher their price tag. Second, celebrities are not known for living humble, quiet lives. They live in the constant glow of the spotlight and paparazzi—that is, after all, why you pay them. However, sometimes the spotlight turns onto less than desirable activities. The covers of grocery counter tabloids are populated with the very same celebrities that some Legendary Brands attach to their brand narrative.

Fictional characters.

- *Advantages.* Can be created to suit your needs; owned by the brand.
- *Disadvantages.* Easy to wear out, lack authenticity.

If you cannot afford a celebrity, and your CEO is not photogenic, you can always create a character to act as your brand agent. Mickey Mouse, the trench-coated Sprint PCS agent, the Nestlé Quick bunny, the Taco Bell chihuahua, and the Maytag repairman are all examples of characters that personified the brand narrative.

The trouble with characters is that they aren't real. While that fact has certain advantages, such as lower costs with higher control, it is riddled with its own set of challenges. Characters require nurturing, else they wear on audiences. On the other hand, they are sometimes the victim of their own success. Many brand managers are reticent to retire characters that have lived a natural and profitable life, even when the signs are clear that the narrative they convey is out of step with the brand. Even worse, sometimes the success of a character agent leads to a loss of meaning.

For example, Mickey Mouse is clearly the brand agent for The Walt Disney Company. He has been so for more than 75 years. When he debuted, in 1928, he gained instant fame as a whimsical, unassuming Everyman drawn as a mouse. Like Chaplin's loveable tramp, Mickey innocently skipped into adventures while pursuing simple goals: flying an airplane upside down to steal a kiss from the flirtatious but coy Minnie Mouse (*Plane Crazy*), or piloting a steamboat down a river while being pursued by a brutish cat (*Steamboat Willie*). Adventures such as these made Mickey a character recognized instantly throughout the world. He was a charismatic and crafty agent for the Disney brand narrative and the animated personification of Walt Disney. Thankfully, audiences were spared the pain of seeing Walt Disney's health deteriorate or his mental faculties wane. Fate has not been so kind to Mickey.

Mickey today is more a logo than he is a character that conveys Disney's narrative. He is relegated to the role of corporate spokesperson, muted or dubbed at public events and brandished ubiquitously on business cards, signage, and other corporate identity paraphernalia. Contrast Mickey with Bugs Bunny. Bugs is as mischievous today as he was in the 1930s. We expect him to pull a fast one, get into trouble, and outsmart his onscreen counterparts. His value to Warner Brothers as a brand agent persists because he has not lost the essence of his character.

Location-Based Brand Agents

Owned and operated places.

- *Advantages.* Complete narrative control; authentic representation of the brand.
- *Disadvantages.* Expensive.

While we are on the subject of Disney, it is only fair to address what they do best. A Disney theme park is the *sine quo non* of location-based brand agenting. Stepping inside a Disney theme park is to literally step within the Disney brand narrative. Excepting only when they try too hard to sell guests incremental goods and services, Disney engulfs the guest in imagination, wonder, and fantasy. None of it is by accident. Every inch of the park is designed with story in mind. Credit two groups of people with its phenomenal effect: the park operators, who are the unsung heroes that tenaciously attend to every detail 365 days a year; and the creative geniuses ensconced at Walt Disney Imagineering, who relentlessly focus on story to make even the mundane seem magical.

You do not have to build a theme park to bring your brand to life in a place. Many Legendary Brands communicate their story through their retail facilities. Done right, these locations afford the brand the opportunity to create a physical environment that speaks the brand narrative. Visit a Gap, an Apple Store, The Body Shop, or an Armani, and you will connect with the brand narrative instantly. Prada recently launched a plush, stylish retail store in the heart of New York's SoHo district. The 24,500 square foot store designed by famed architect Rem Koolhaus features a 200-seat auditorium, dressing rooms that include touch-screen displays, and mirrors that allow customers to see an outfit from any angle. The sleek flagship is a fitting demonstration of Prada's brand narrative, which combines old world attention to quality with stylish, modern designs.

Cohabitated places.

- *Advantages*. Allows the brand to narrate where others are merely making noise.
- *Disadvantages*. Lots of noise.

Another choice for many Legendary Brands is to create a place to tell the brand story within a larger unbranded, or multibranded environment. For example, Calvin Klein rarely allows its product to rest on the same shelves with competitive products. Each year, Calvin Klein creates branded environments in major department stores. These environments stand out from the rest of the store and provide a tangent for the consumer to touch the brand and receive the narrative via specially designed display units. All of the merchandise associated with the brand is featured in the branded environment, which is clearly demarcated to differentiate between Calvin Klein's sacred space, and the mundane world that occupies the rest of the store.

Sponsored places.

- *Advantages*. Opportunity to leverage other's narrative; sales activation possibilities.
- *Disadvantages*. Can be cluttered; may not say anything about your brand.

Sponsoring a venue is a viable way to create a brand agent for many Legendary Brands. The benefits of sponsoring a place like a ballpark, stadium, theater, theme park, or other place is the ability to leverage its narrative and associated consumer affinity. Such opportunities are particularly valuable when the place is pristine and uncluttered by competing marketing messages. Unfortunately, many places that can be sponsored, already are. The challenge is for the Legendary Brand to find an activity that links the narrative of the venue with the narrative of the brand in a way that makes them inseparable in the mind of the consumer.

For example, baseball stadiums are notoriously oversponsored. They frequently showcase so many brands that consumers filter them all out of the picture. Nestlé adopted a different approach for its sponsorship of Edison Field in Anaheim, California, home to the American League's Anaheim Angels. Nestlé sponsored the outfield seating area and named it the "Nestlé Family Zone." This area is designed for baseball fans with small children, who often grow restless during the first inning. The Nestlé Family Zone offers special concessions geared specifically toward children (predominantly Nestlé products, of course). It features colorful murals and interactive features that appeal to children. It is also the designated area in which all family programming occurs during the season.

Artificial places.

- *Advantages.* Inexpensive; able to utilize linear branding elements.
- *Disadvantages.* Two-dimensional.

It is now possible to create an artificial place for brand narrative—specifically through the Internet and other digital environments. A Web site, if well designed, can create an environment that conveys the brand narrative. For instance, a few years ago Mercedes Benz created a themed online environment to showcase the M class sport utility vehicle. The environment was media rich and linked to an international spy theme. Information on the car arrived in "briefings" via "suitcases" and "dockets." Navigational elements appeared as gadgets. The richness of the environment provided a narrative that well matched the sophisticated styling of Mercedes Benz and its variation on the sport utility vehicle. Rather than collect data from potential customers in an unimaginative fashion, Mercedes exploited the narrative of the environment to capture this information. Users were asked to provide their "alias." To learn which product features were important, users were asked to assess what kind of mission they would pursue. At each point of contact, Mercedes stayed true to the narrative, rather than break the suspension of disbelief.

Things as Brand Agents

Product.

- *Advantages.* Direct relationship—it is the object of the brand.
- *Disadvantages.* Can be boring and a poor narrator.

A Kate Spade handbag is the best agent the brand will ever own. Its design speaks volumes about the brand. The styling between Kate Spade handbags is artful, inspired, and consistent. This consistency, or repetition with variation, creates the story. The same is true for a Macintosh, Palm (particularly the Palm V), Nokia, Restoration Hardware, and Coach. Each of these Legendary Brands speaks the brand narrative through the agent of its product.

The challenge with product-oriented agenting is that it requires constant work. Some products achieve the goal through consistency (e.g., Kate Spade, Mont Blanc, Rolex) others do it through artful variation (e.g., Apple, Restoration Hardware, The Body Shop). The challenge is to know which is right for your brand.

Promotional items and other objects.

- *Advantages.* Very flexible—can be developed and implemented on an as-needed basis.
- *Disadvantages.* Tendency to be driven by impulse, rather than strategy; many fail to deliver any narrative at all.

Sometimes, a Legendary Brand finds an object other than its product to tell its brand story. It is no easy feat, and the examples are few. One example is the regional, but legendary, Jack in the Box food chain brand. We discuss the success of Jack in the Box in the next chapter, yet one of its brand agents is worth examining now: a miniature plastic ball featuring a painted Jack in the Box face and matching conical hat. This self-liquidating promotional item affixes to the antenna of your car. The origins of the antenna ball actually go back many years, before the rebranding effort that truly made Jack in the Box legendary.

When the item was rediscovered, it proved to be an effective method for sustaining the brand narrative of the fictional, no-nonsense executive with the ridiculously large, ball-shaped head.

The McDonald's Happy Meal, in some ways, achieves the same purpose. McDonald's is a family brand that appeals most to young children. The Happy Meal is one way of sustaining the brand narrative of McDonald's, although in recent years it has become more of an entertainment promotional vehicle than a meaningful connection point between consumer and brand.

The problem with promotional items and nonproduct objects is that they easily become fads, the marketing world's version of the one hit wonder. Over time, these items may be nostalgically locked in our minds, but they lose their power to activate the brand narrative.

MANAGING BRAND AGENTS

Managing brand agents is no easy matter. It is an endeavor that often launches and ends the careers of Legendary Brand managers. Essentially, you must focus on three sets of activities: promoting growth of equities tied to the agent, mitigating risks associated with the agent, and sustaining agent-narrative alignment.

To determine which set of activities should earn your attention, consider the grid in Figure 10.1. The horizontal axis concerns the strength of your brand narrative, independent of the agent. To determine this, you need to consider the overall strength of the underlying brand myth.

The vertical axis concerns the strength of the brand agent(s). There are a variety of ways to measure agent strength, including straightforward aided and unaided quantitative analysis.

Managing Symbiotic Agent-Narrative Relationships

The dream of most brand managers is a ranking in Quadrant I. Brands that rank there have both a strong set of brand agents and a strong brand narrative, and they are presumably working in concert.

FIGURE 10.1   Strength of Brand Agents

Brand Narrative

		Strong	Weak
Brand Agent(s)	**Strong**	**Quadrant I** • Symbiotic relationships • Diversification • Frequent rejuvenation	**Quadrant II** • Agents possess reasonable market power • Brand narrative drafts off of agent narrative
	Weak	**Quadrant III** • Brand narrative sensed more than demonstrated • Clues to brand agents probably rest in culture	**Quadrant IV** • Brand narrative may have aged or outlived usefulness • Agents may no longer resonate with culture

In this ideal scenario, brand agents are reinforcing the sacred beliefs of the brand (and the consumer), and the connection between the two is articulated perfectly by the narrative activities of the brand.

If you are fortunate enough to rank in this quadrant, your job is deceptively easy. It is deceptive because you have every indication to believe that you are doing everything right. What could be easier, right? Wrong. Your brand has the most to lose and it is the most vulnerable to the pressures of direct competitive strikes, agent extortion, and consumer apathy. Like an aircraft in level flight, the smallest turbulence can cause these brand systems to take a nosedive.

Promoting growth of a symbiotic system. Take care not to oversaturate the market with the agent. Consumers grow weary of brand agents that just won't go away. This problem is compounded when your brand agent is not wholly owned by you. For instance, if you have secured a major celebrity or professional athlete to agent your brand, you need to control the level of agenting that individual performs for other brands. Some celebrity agents have a habit of making themselves into human NASCAR vehicles, endorsing a dozen or more brands and products. With each additional brand they represent, they become less valuable to your brand. Below are some precautionary tips to prevent this from happening to your brand.

- Review all of the existing—and immediately contemplated—endorsement agreements held by the agent.
- Ensure that your agreement with the agent provides safety mechanisms that protect you from the agent's oversubscription to other brands. Such mechanisms may include early termination clauses to your benefit, or penalties for oversubscription.
- If you are sure the agent works well for your brand, secure a longer-term agreement with that agent, provided you have ample safeguards regarding oversubscription. Longer-term agreements protect you from competitive encroachment and agent extortion, a concept we discuss in greater length shortly.

Sometimes, oversaturation has little to do with the actions of the agent. Instead, it is caused by the brand manager. Remember, there can always be too much of a good thing. Often, when a brand establishes a powerful agent for the brand narrative, the temptation is to "go big." After awhile, the consumer cannot get away from the agent and the brand. On every turn, it faces them again. This frequent consumer response is either annoyance or apathy—neither benefits the brand.

When you strike on the magic formula of brand agent and brand narrative, the onus is on you to innovate. Do not rest on your laurels. Find new ways to present the agent within the narrative. Craft new story arcs that govern new campaigns. Surprise the brand audience by creating unexpected twists in the narrative.

Although largely advertising-driven, a good example of a campaign that maintained alignment through innovations is a McDonald's campaign that featured Michael Jordan and Larry Byrd in a game of HORSE. Neither Jordan nor Byrd came cheap. Each had sundry other endorsement deals. McDonald's managed this noise with the sheer power of its media buy. The creativity, however, kept the investment alive. The first spot aired during the Super Bowl in multiple segments. In each segment, Jordan or Byrd challenged the other to a seemingly impossible shot. The winner earned a Big Mac.

McDonald's agency, DDB Needham, could have stopped there. They could have run the same spot over and over again. They could have propped life size stand-ups of Byrd and Jordan in every McDonald's. In short, they could have bled this campaign until it prematurely wore itself out. Instead, McDonald's kept it alive with twists. The grand finale coincided with the release of the Warner Brothers feature-length animated movie, *Space Jam*. McDonald's signed on as a promotional partner. The payoff: Jordan recreated the original spot, but this time against Bugs Bunny. In the film, he actually plays a league of animated contenders. The campaign eventually expired, but it generated a significant return for McDonald's because it innovated and found new ways to use the brand agent within the brand narrative.

In addition to variation in your story arcs, also consider variation in your communications channels. This is not an invitation to blast your brand communications through every available channel. That leads to oversaturation just as quickly as repetition, perhaps faster. Varying your communications channels means that you select the appropriate channel for the message and surprise consumers by the form, and not the content, with which you choose to engage them.

Ironically, this is an area in which McDonald's often fails. The Happy Meal may be the greatest promotional invention in marketing history. Yet, McDonald's has driven the Happy Meal to a tiresome youth-marketing formula.

Mitigating Risk in a Symbiotic System

External risk factors are your biggest concern. External risks have nothing to do with the actions of the brand manager. They are imposed by things beyond their control. Short of a crystal ball or a date with Shirley Maclaine, there's really no way to anticipate an external risk factor. There are, however, some preventive measures you can take.

- Diversify the agent portfolio; don't allow your narrative to rest on one agent source alone. The likelihood of an external risk factor affecting all three forms of brand agent (person, place, thing) is slim.
- Prepare a contingency plan. Seriously. The White House and the Pentagon make it standard operating procedure to run through drills of random situations, from an alien invasion to a catastrophic drop in currencies. Your brand should determine, for example, how it will respond if your supposedly whole-some, family-oriented celebrity brand agent is surreptitiously photographed in a Nevada brothel, dining with Hustler CEO Larry Flynt.
- Develop a secondary or spin-off brand narrative, and have it ready to go. This plan is a close cousin to the one above, with exception that it allows you to switch the entire focus of your brand communications. Having a secondary narrative primed and ready to go can allow you to switch gears effortlessly with-out looking too reactive. Remember: level flight, subtle course corrections.

Managing Brands with Weak Narratives and Strong Agents

From a risk perspective, one of the most untenable positions for your brand rests in Quadrant II, when you possess a strong brand agent but a weak overall narrative. First, it is likely that you are borrowing a narrative from your agent, which is fine if you are also taking steps to graft that narrative and make it an inseparable part of your brand platform. Regretfully, agents often have finite lives, while brands do not. If you do not develop a brand narrative that stands on its own, you risk losing your consumer base should something hap-pen to your brand agent.

Consider the case of Palm and the Palm V handheld device. The Palm V was revolutionary. Its styling alone made a bold statement about the future of technology. With a graphite shell and curved lines, this handheld looked nothing like the first generation, which was bulky, plastic, and dull. Overnight, the Palm V was a must have. Retailers could not stock them fast enough. It was then that Palm, the company, should have seized the moment and established a brand narrative that would govern all its products and marketing. Instead, it got caught up in IPO mania. Its competitors, including Microsoft, imitated the design and added new features. To add insult to injury, Palm's next generation handheld, the Palm VII, lacked the design integrity of its forebear. In no time at all, Palm's fate was to be just another handheld offered in bland display cases in a lineup of imitators. It has no dominant brand story to tell, and for the moment, no brand agent from which to draft.

Contrast Palm's fate with that of Nokia. When Nokia debuted, it was a third-tier player. Motorola owned the market for wireless phones, with its slim and sexy StarTac, a black-winged flip phone that was a sign of distinction in corporate circles. Through a series of brilliant incentive initiatives, Nokia convinced cellular providers to offer its phones at a low price. They essentially bought share; however, they did it with a phone that, although bigger and bulkier than the StarTac, featured customizable items. You could change the faceplate on a Nokia cell phone. You could play games. Eventually, you could also send text messages to your friends. One Nokia advertisement depicted a young man and woman sitting on a sofa at a loud party. The young man tries to tell the woman something, but she cannot hear him. He then sends her a text message commenting on the quality of the cheese served. It was an irreverent portrait of how the brand fit within a younger, more casual lifestyle. While business users did not initially care about these features, the younger audience did. Nokia established a brand narrative in a critical audience segment. Whereas Motorola was about the StarTac, and nothing else, Nokia became the brand of choice for a younger, pop culture segment of the market. Using styling and design that has remained remarkably consistent, Nokia is, as of this writing, the dominant player. Its narrative has spread to a number of wireless providers, who actually use Nokia as an agent for their brand.

If your brand rests in quadrant two, you need to take some immediate actions, even if the current business climate seems rosy.

- Diversify your portfolio. You have no narrative to fall back on, so work quickly to establish new brand agents, especially in different forms. If your brand agent is a celebrity like Michael Jordan, focus your efforts on making your product or your locations a valid brand agent.
- Of course, to add those new brand agents, you need to define and establish your brand narrative. Fortunately, you have a clue about what resonates with your consumers. Deconstruct the strong agent you already possess, and reverse engineer your way to the sacred beliefs and hidden narrative it represents.

The above actions are intended to cure your addiction to a strong brand agent. Working to establish a stronger brand narrative does not mean that you must abandon the agent that is working so well for you. Quite the contrary. If a stock in your investment portfolio continued to rise, you probably would not sell it off until you believed it had peaked. You may have many years of productive life ahead with this agent, but you should be prepared to continue without it tomorrow.

Managing Brands with Strong Narratives but Weak Agents

Congratulations. You are in a quadrant that provides you wide latitude to grow and develop your brand. Quadrant III brands are on the cusp of greatness. They possess a narrative that is felt by consumers; however, a strong agent is the missing link between good and great. Provided they have adequate resources, these brands have nowhere to go but up.

Well, perhaps the picture is not so rosy. Unless they are the CEO or an influential member of the senior management team, most brand managers have limited influence over two of the three categories of brand agents (product and location). Some have only partial influence in the third.

Textbooks often claim that an ideal business environment leads, rather than follows, with marketing. In this idealistic business construct, the market team "defines the value" that engineers and sales teams ultimately deliver to the consumer. Such a business system is nirvana, and it does exist when the CEO, founder, or some other influential leader has the power to command resources greater than the advertising budget. Steve Jobs, for instance, has the luxury of defining the value. He happens to be a gifted marketer and the CEO simultaneously.

Most brand managers control a limited budget that is primarily earmarked for traditional advertising and promotion expenditures. Few of them find a welcome mat in the engineering or product development department, a fact that limits their ability to influence product design in favor of brand narrative. The same is true for operations, which generally manages the locations owned by the brand. That makes it difficult for the keeper of the brand narrative to influence locations as a brand agent.

About the only thing most brand managers can control is the people dimension. They may be the custodian of the founder or senior executive that serves as agent for the brand. They may have a budget to secure third party people, places, and things as surrogate brand agents. Corporate sponsorship budgets are generally managed from the marketing department. Even here, however, many brand managers face an uphill battle. Celebrities attract attention, and event sponsorships cry boondoggle more than they do marketing mechanism. These influences often attract interference from high-ranking executives with ulterior motives.

What is a brand manager to do? To start with, have hope. You have solved the biggest challenge—establishing a strong brand narrative. Agents are ultimately necessary, but the brand momentum will not stop overnight because an appropriate agent is lacking. Here are some suggestions.

- Find a senior-level champion in the company, preferably the CEO. If they believe in the virtues of the brand narrative, such champions can move mountains to bring the rest of the company in line, or empower you to do so.

- Share what you know with design, manufacturing, and operations groups. Share it openly and often. Do not keep the brand narrative hidden in the marketing department. Give it credibility by backing it with solid consumer research. (You'll have to do your homework.) Engineers and operations managers will be reluctant to take a gamble on your thinking if there isn't credible evidence you are right, as they should be.

- If you are fortunate, and have a crack product design team or retail group, take their lead. Too often, the problem is not that these divisions will not cooperate. The problem is they're right and the marketer is wrong. Be willing to draft off of their work. Remember, your brand narrative should be based on a timeless myth. There are many ways to tell it. It is very possible that your design teams are telling the narrative, but they are focusing on different scenes, characters, or story arcs than you are. Make your job easy, follow their lead.

- Focus your attention on the 80 percent of the equation you *can* control—the marketing budget. Use the resources you have to secure rentable brand agents. You don't have to command a $100 million annual sponsorship budget to secure quality celebrities, cultural organizations, entertainment properties, or athletes. Most brand managers make the mistake of chasing the same properties everybody else wants. This leads to a bidding war and the placement of your brand in an overpriced, cluttered environment. You basically reduce your effectiveness. Like so many other activities in this book, go beyond surface value. Do you really need to sponsor a major league baseball team, where you will share the outfield with 25 other brands? Why not pursue the minor leagues? It may work for your brand. Better yet, why not consider a property outside the sports domain?

- Finally, consider building your own brand agents. For example, if you decide that your brand narrative needs an edgy, youth agent, you might establish a national skateboard tour. You could partner with an organization that develops and manages such matters, but retain sole ownership. The downside is that it will cost you. The upside is that you own and control it. The skateboard example is merely an illustration, but the concept has true merit though it is rarely utilized.

Managing Brands with Weak Narratives and Brand Agents

New or emerging brands lack established brand narratives and corresponding brand agents. Consumers are not familiar with these brands, which hinders their ability to have shared meaning and narrative, although not completely. Generally speaking, you will have more success if you focus on the narrative of the emerging brand. Brand agents can be easily added at a later time. In fact, during the narrative crafting process, most brand managers simultaneously uncover agents. It's intuitive and organic.

There is another scenario in which a brand may find itself without a strong narrative or a strong brand agent. Occasionally, a venerable brand wakes up to find itself devoid of meaning. For whatever reason, its brand agents have atrophied or fled. Its brand narrative may have lost relevance slowly, over time, or it may have been weak to begin with. The brand manager has two options: if the brand is a candidate for a second lease on life, start over; or harvest the brand. Few brand managers choose the latter; the former is easier said than done because of the baggage the brand continues to carry from its past.

If your brand is new, has lost its narrative, or requires narrative rejuvenation, one alternative is to find brand agents that can quickly lend a narrative. Fidelity Investments executed on this strategy a few years ago when it signed various comedians to appear in its television advertisements. Fidelity's own brand agent, Peter Lynch, was depicted running into these famous faces and giving them investment advice. In each instance, Lynch delivered very dry analysis of the stock market, while the comedians gave color commentary or showed their lack of interest. The message was simple: Fidelity has done the thinking for you, because you only care about how your money performs—not why. But the narrative received a larger boost. Fidelity became more than an institution, it became the narrative of Peter Lynch and his relationship to exaggerations of the average consumer.

If you decide to use brand agents to shore up your brand narrative, follow these guidelines:

- Unless you anticipate that you will need to use the agent for a long span of time, bind yourself to them in reasonably short-term deals. You risk needing them later and being held hostage when their success leads to a pay raise, but you buy yourself the flexibility to go elsewhere and eliminate a brand narrative that is too linked to the borrowed brand agent
- Select multiple agents. The Fidelity campaign did not rely solely on one comedian. It used several. A famous Discover campaign invited a number of celebrities to showcase what they bought with their Discover card. The Got Milk campaign has featured hundreds of celebrities donning the milk mustache. If you wish to generate a narrative by leveraging brand agents, cast the net wide. This will also help you to identify the archetype of the brand and the appropriate genre to flesh out the underlying brand narrative.

CHAPTER 11

NONLINEAR BRANDING

The Myth of the Place

Throughout history, a select group of cities have served as a font for narrative inspiration. London, Paris, Rome, New York, Jerusalem, Beijing—these are all great cities of the modern world that are linked to storied history. Thinking of these places instantly conjures a narrative, real or imagined. They often convey mystical themes and they nearly always serve as the backdrop for grand narrative events. Some cities are blessed/cursed with archetypical powers. People are referred to as New Yorkers, Angelinos, from the Bay Area, or a Bostonian. In each instance, the reference serves to paint an instant picture of the individual personality. To tell someone that the man you just met was thoroughly Texan says more about him than describing him as "assertive," "independent," and "proud."

"The chronicles of urban life are divided between the real and the fantastic, as men and women have dreamed of golden cities, hidden cities, invisible cities, ruined enchantments such as Pompeii, mystical realms like Shambhala, and labyrinthine worlds like Jorge Borges' Tlön. . . ," says mythologist Phil Cousineau. In his book, *Once and*

Future Myths, he describes the remarkable power great cities possess—keeping their narrative alive for centuries.[1]

The great mythic cities are Legendary Brands. The brand narrative is delivered by the sensory events they house, and the way those events roll up into collective consumer experience. A Yankee game, a Broadway show, a trip to the observation deck of the Empire State Building, the Statue of Liberty, and shopping on Fifth Avenue are all events and places within and around Manhattan that activate the New York experience. So does the smell of hot dogs from the carts of street vendors, the feel of warm steam from the vents of the subway, and the taste of great deli food. It is the sights, sounds, tastes, smells, and feeling of each event or place that triggers the narrative and delivers the experience. Places like New York perpetuate a long-standing practice of mythologizing a city.

In the Middle East, Jerusalem is a land so steeped in myth and narrative that people continue to lose their lives in pursuit of it. It is one of the rare places in the world where the centers of three powerful world religions intersect, each claiming historical and spiritual significance. Jerusalem is a place that inspires devotion, pilgrimages, and holy wars. Those that have visited the holy city often pepper their accounts of the journey with deeply moving images linked to the narrative of their faith.

Paris is the secular equivalent. As it has for centuries, the City of Light attracts artists, philosophers, and bohemians. It is a city with great mythic power. People lose themselves in Paris, filled with romance and idealism. It is probably well that the French fight vehemently to preserve French tradition. Without it, Paris might lose its mythic qualities and its power to inspire the artist and lover within each of us.

MYTHOLOGIZING CONSUMER SPACES

Visit a Disney theme park. You will not have to look hard to find narrative and myth. Disney theme parks are constructed according to story—it is the basis of every attraction, every restaurant, every guest service facility. Nothing exists in a Disney park that is not crafted around story. When designing the environment of a Disney park, "the obvious function of a building is secondary to its primary purpose: to help tell the story. Each building's foundation not only supports a physical structure, but it also supports a story structure.[2] The "magic" of a Disney theme park or resort emanates from the narrative touch points engineered into the architecture and environmental design.

Recall the last time you visited a Victoria's Secret, or a Gap, or a Restoration Hardware store, or a Starbucks. These are not conventional retail environments. Each one maintains a consistency of design and an attention to detail that triggers the brand narrative on impact. Victoria's Secret meticulously plans their retail environments. Remnants of the Victorian styling can be seen from the street as an enticing clue that something intimate waits within.

Restoration Hardware is a small retail chain and catalog business. According to its management, around every corner of a Restoration Hardware store "you discover something unexpected, yet pleasantly familiar, be it a rich leather chair, that satin-nickel fitting for the bath, or 464 thread-count bed linens. It's a hardware store unlike any other, filled with products linked by classic design, affordable pricing and an abundance of product information."[3]

The description is more than hype. Walking into a Restoration Hardware store is akin to walking back in time. It is as if you turned a corner and found yourself smack in the middle of Main Street, USA. The company encourages this narrative thought progression by interspersing items of nostalgia between modern products with classic styling. Many of these nostalgic items are available for sale, for example, a Crosley Record Player. (Remember records? Those were the big black vinyl discs we used to play to hear recorded music.) The Crosley Record Player was a staple item, recalled by many with warm memories. It closed like a suitcase and featured an imitation leather exterior. By resurrecting and offering the Crosley Record Player, Restoration Hardware placed a clue that triggers emotional memories for many consumers and uses these memories to sustain its brand narrative.

Clues are an important part of nonlinear branding. Recall that we all share a collective unconscious. If the narrative you tell has local, regional, or cultural significance, the narrative can be activated with subtle effort. There is no sign on the wall of a Restoration Hardware store that details the story of the brand. They don't hand out brochures that paint a fictional story to support their brand narrative. Rather, they provide sensory clues. The artisan craftsmanship of the solid wood goods, the smell of the genuine leather furniture, the classic colors and styling of the interior and the interspersion of cherished products from our collective pasts—these are all clues charged with the essence of the narrative. They are more than enough to leave consumers with a clear understanding of the story beneath the brand.

Creating sensory clues is not an easy task, but when executed well, these clues coax the narrative out of consumer experience at a deeper level than any other form of branding. The guidelines for generating such experiences are culled from the study of sacred places and places of deep cultural meaning. To study their application to consumer brands, we need a model case study.

CASE STUDY: Ian Schrager Hotels

Ian Schrager is a legend in his own time, and his unique sense of style now permeates the hotel chain that bears his name. Schrager was a cofounder of Studio 54, the 1970s disco nightclub that inspired thousands and became part of the mythology of the wild disco era. Studio 54 was a place so charged with narrative that it could stand alone as an independent case study. Alas, it no longer operates. Fortunately, Schrager's latest project is equally rich in its use of nonlinear branding devices. Ian Schrager Hotels have become such a sensation that they are now heavily copied, most notably by the W hotel chain owned by Starwood Hotels and Resorts.

Though there are only a handful of Schrager hotels, each enjoys certain fame. Schrager Hotels is a Legendary Brand small in physical and geographic constitution, but great in narrative reputation.

Demarcating Sacred and Profane Space

The first step in any nonlinear branding exercise is to differentiate between the space the brand will occupy (sacred space) and the perimeter of the outside world (profane space). The word *profane* is actually derived from Latin to mean "outside the temple"—*pro* meaning "before" and *fanum* meaning "temple." Ancient peoples defined sacred space in ways as rudimentary as a circle of rocks or stones.[4] Your perimeter may simply be the walls of your retail environment, or the panels of your hospitality tent, or the confines of your Web site. Disney theme parks are defined by the park *berm*, a term used to describe the walls and gates that encircle the park. Restoration Hardware typically separates its sacred from profane space by classically styled, wainscoted walls.

Schrager Hotels, our case model, make their perimeter very clear. Walking down West 44th street in midtown Manhattan, you cannot miss the entrance to the Royalton, one of four Schrager Hotels in the city. Nestled between ordinary office buildings and street cafes, the Royalton is lit with a warm glow, mahogany doors, and a stately fa-çade supported by Doric columns. Its perimeter creates a strong contrast to this typical Manhattan street scene, clearly demarcating the brand's narrative perimeter.

Thresholds: Entry into Brand Space

People enter sacred spaces through a threshold that physically signifies a change in space and time. The profane, or at least the mundane, is left behind once the person passes through a threshold. In houses of worship associated with most of the world's religious traditions, thresholds are an integral part of the architectural design. Sometimes, thresholds stand mysteriously alone, marking the entry to mystical or metaphysical dimensions. The Japanese countryside is populated with freestanding, doorless gateways that honor various deities. Travelers customarily pause at each threshold and perform a ritual or meditate. Many believe passing through the threshold sanctifies their souls and protects them from harm on their journey.

Thresholds are often so critical to the narrative of the place that many include threshold guardians—an entity designed to protect sacred space from potential defilers. The gargoyles poised on the rooftops of Notre Dame are intended to ward off those who are unwelcome within the cathedral. Joseph Campbell noted that the idea of threshold and guardian has consistent narrative significance. In great stories, the hero is often forced to cross a threshold guarded by a fearsome creature. The noble hero proves his honor by his ability to pass despite the obstacles posed by ominous guardians.[5]

Every Schrager hotel includes a threshold. Perhaps the most stunning is the Delano Hotel located in the Art Deco District of Miami Beach. It is a luxurious oceanfront hotel ornately appointed with décor from an era past. Yet for all its elegant 1930s style, it is thoroughly modern, eccentric, and stylish—the work of famed designer, Phillipe Starke.

To enter the Delano Hotel, visitors pass through a fenced garden path that leads to a slight set of stairs and a curtained patio. White translucent panels of sheer fabric stream from the rafters to the floor. The progression of secluded pathways and luxurious gateways forms a clear dividing line between the outside world and the oasis within— a threshold. And like every Schrager Hotel, a doorman, stylishly attired in Armaniesque clothing and quietly judging the appropriateness of each passerby, serves as threshold guardian.

When you enter a Schrager Hotel, there is no room to doubt that you have passed into a new environment and that a narrative envelopes you. Each hotel offers its own transformation from the outside world to the world of Ian Schrager. In New York, at the Hudson Hotel, visitors pass through yellow neon electric sliding doors to face an escalator that transports them to the lobby level. They literally take a threshold journey up to a new world.

Sensory Clues: Narrative Residue

Once in the environment, the marketer's job is to disperse clues throughout that trigger the intended narrative. Because you have the luxury of using all five senses, those clues can take on myriad forms. Godiva and Starbucks frequently set out product samples, allowing consumers to taste the narrative.

Schrager Hotels excel at the dissemination of sensory clues, across the board. A visit to a Schrager hotel promises to be a visual experience. At the Mondrian Hotel in Los Angeles, guests are confronted by giant potted trees on the outdoor patio adjacent to the understated pool. These trees have an Alice-in-Wonderland quality sparked by their absurd size and close proximity to one another. They dwarf the dining customers that sit next to them.

The Mondrian is also home to SkyBar, one of L.A.'s most trendy watering holes. SkyBar rests within a small cottage adjacent to the pool, and it features a breathtaking view of the Los Angeles skyline, seen through large panels of clear plate glass. It is as if the visitor peers upon Los Angeles "through the looking glass." On a Friday night, the entire outdoor area creates a striking and complementary visual impact, with people scattered about on mattresses and chase lounges. A voyeuristic quality permeates the scene, and through it the brand narrative effuses on to the consumers. For that moment, they are either living or watching the glamorous Hollywood lifestyle.

The Mondrian does not stop at visual stimulation. In the lobby, house music arrests your ears. All Schrager hotels have a unique soundtrack of eclectic, rhythmic house music that sets the tone for the environment. Though subtle, and sometimes faint due to the conversational and ambient noise, this house music has a dramatic effect on people. The rhythmic pulse of house music is similar to the rhythmic musical styles that accompany many religious traditions. It has a trancelike effect that has been documented by neuroscientists. It actually reorients people's sense of place and time.

Action in a Schrager hotel unfolds in its lobbies and bars—sometimes unadulterated action. These public spaces are very much alive. They are also close to Schrager's signature restaurants and bars. Thus, taste and smell are as pervasive as the house music, and the tastes are not ordinary. The Mondrian is home to Asia de Cuba, a unique restaurant that first opened in Schrager's New York hotel, Morgan's. Asia de

Cuba serves up a blend of Cuban inspired cuisine with a decidedly Asian twist. Diners can nibble on pot stickers stuffed with black beans or feast on grilled shrimp served with Asian pesto. These disoriented offerings hint at the hotel's dual narrative, which combines the elegance of L.A. chic with its absurdity. To all of these tastebud clues, add the liberal circulation of cocktails and wine.

Finally, Schrager hotels like the Mondrian are tantalizing to the touch. The environment provides a feeling of the brand. While it is true that a Schrager hotel room lacks spaciousness, it more than makes up for it with the extra expense it takes to deliver linens with high thread count, real goose down comforters, velvet and satin throw pillows, and high quality mattresses. You can touch a Schrager hotel, and when you do, its narrative permeates your senses. It is a narrative of style, luxury, and indulgence.

Narrative Pathways

Nonlinear branding environments are open to interpretation, and the consumer maintains great control. When a consumer enters a baseball park, her first stop might be the concession stand. Then again, she might head first to the restroom. She may choose to go directly to her seat, or she may amble down near homeplate to watch the players warm up. You cannot say with certainty where the consumer will go or to which story elements she will be exposed. If story requires a linear three-act structure, the nonlinear environment threatens to deliver act three before act one.

Though consumer choice is high in a nonlinear branding environment, marketers still have some control over the delivery of narrative. The solution is to deliver distinct but complete segments of the narrative through a series of narrative pathways. Think of it as a novel composed of several short stories. Each chapter is a story unto itself with complete beginning, middle, and end. The sum of all chapters creates a bigger narrative with its own three-act structure. In this fashion, each sensory event you introduce in your environment should have its own three-act structure, but contribute to a bigger narrative.

Theme parks often do this by segmenting their entire environment into smaller chunks of story. Disneyland has at least six major story segments: Adventureland, Fantasyland, Frontierland, Main Street, Tomorrowland, and Toontown. Within each of these segments are still smaller storied areas. For instance, within Frontierland is New Orleans Square. Within this area you find attractions with their own stories, such as Pirates of the Caribbean. Thus, no matter where the park guest travels, they encounter a narrative. It is atomized down to the attraction level, but molecularly it is part of something bigger.

Ian Schrager Hotels do the same. The hotel property may revolve around one narrative theme, but each component part tells its own complete story which is additive to the larger myth. At the Delano, the pool area tells its own story. It is a lush, surrealistic environment—art deco gone to extreme, Salvador Dali meets Phillipe Starke. The pool literally spills out onto the lawn in a gradual meeting reminiscent of the ocean meeting the shore. In the shallowest depths of the pool, a usable table and chairs rest in a couple of inches of water. Meanwhile, private cabanas flank the elegant absurdity of the pool, offering artistic intimacy in period styling. The hotel's opulent narrative is present here, but the pool area reveals its own story.

The long lobby bar offers another distinct story, with its plush shabby chic sofas and corridors fashioned from floor-to-ceiling panels of white fabric (continuing the theme from the porch). Atomizing further, within the lobby bar is a smaller bar area adjacent to a pool table. This area tells a different but complementary story. Adding all of these environments together, a narrative unfolds that is filled with elegance, intrigue, and sensuality.

Find the Center of the World

"Our world is always situated at the center," wrote Mircea Eliade in his book *The Sacred and Profane*. He was referring to the fact that in nearly every cultural tradition, sacred places contain a clearly defined center in which people can orient themselves in sacred time and space. "A universe comes to birth from its center; it spreads out from a central point that is, as it were, its navel."[6]

As you contemplate a nonlinear environment, and this includes the design of digital environments such as Internet Web sites, focus your attention on the center. Centers provide a meaningful way for people to navigate sacred space. It provides a compass and a guarantee that order exists.

Disney theme parks are famous for their hub-and-spokes design. That is, when you enter a park like Disneyland, you always journey down Main Street to a central wheel. From that wheel stretch the paths to the various themed lands. It is a concept that is as old as civilization. Ancient cities were often designed in much the same way. Generally, the temple or holy shrine sat at the center of the city with everything else building around it. Americans stretched the idea to the town square, where city hall usually resided. This makes perfect sense for a country founded on the ideal of democracy.

Every hotel lobby represents the center of the Ian Schrager universe. It is here that you find the most artful design elements and the richest attention to sensory details. True, most hotels start with a lobby. Guests must traverse through some space to access their rooms. Schrager hotels, however, elevate the lobby to sacred space of grand proportions. The scale alone often generates the impact. The ceilings of the lobby at the Delano are greater than 20 feet in height. At the Clift hotel in San Francisco, the lobby leads to the infamous Red Room, which is paneled in opulent redwood all cut from the same tree. Flatscreen displays rotate digitized artwork while rhythmic music and subdued lighting create atmosphere. The lobbies of Schrager hotels connect to a labyrinth of semi-private spaces waiting to activate the living narrative of the consumer. But all of these spaces lead back to the lobby, which is itself a stage for dramatic action. It is in the lobby that Ian Schrager's universe springs to life. It is the center of the Schrager narrative and the defining point of the entire venue.

Consistency Is Key

To create environments such as these, consistency is essential. Too often, marketers deliver mixed messages in their retail and branded environments. A certain styling and design is used in one part of the environment to create a narrative theme, which is then counteracted by conflicting styling design in another environment. Often, the conflicting styling is in areas that are deemed unimportant, like restrooms and guest service areas.

Walk into the restroom of a Schrager hotel and you might be surprised. At the Mondrian in Los Angeles, chalkboards fill one wall so that the "beautiful people" can leave their mark. Many guests at the Royalton are surprised to find the lack of urinals in its lobby men's room. Actually, one of the walls is the urinal, it is just so artfully designed with marble and a constant stream of water cascading down it that many mistake it for art.

Consistency cannot be emphasized enough. To create a truly narrative environment, you must carry the story throughout. If a consumer will see it, touch it, taste it, smell it, or hear it, it must be related to your narrative. Seemingly minor touches often have dramatic effects.

NONLINEAR, NOT NONNARRATIVE

More than a lengthy brochure waxing over the oasis that is a Schrager hotel, this chapter aimed to instill the value of nonlinear branding. It is a rich and personal way to bond with your consumer. Unfortunately, it is not utilized as often as it should be, and when it is, it is often inconsistent or halfhearted. If you decide to bring your brand narrative to life in a nonlinear fashion, do it with gusto. Seek to activate all five senses. Take your designs to the extreme.

In the theater, the sets that you see on stage usually extend well beyond the audience sightlines. Money could be saved by trimming these sets a few feet to save on material costs, but no smart producer or designer would ever make such a cost-cutting decision. If the set were just an inch too short, one member of the audience might see backstage, ruining their suspension of disbelief and intruding upon the narrative presented on stage. As you develop a nonlinear environment, think in this same way. Go the extra inch to ensure that your narrative is never interrupted.

12

RESCUING THE
TROUBLED BRAND

The thick air weighed heavily on his back, while the smell of sulfur stung his sinuses. The sounds of those in agony rang out from the darkness as tiny currents pierced his skin like the fangs of vipers. It was pure hell—Hades to be exact—but Orpheus, the mythic hero of the Greeks, was determined not to let anything stop him from his quest to rescue his bride Eurydice from the clutches of death. His heroic efforts form one of the greatest stories of the ancient world, joining a litany of similar sagas from every culture in the world. Few story genres satisfy audiences more than the resurrection plot.

What do you do when your brand meets hard times? We're not talking about minor downturns in market share, but true catastrophic events that cast the shadow of doubt on your brand's longevity. The brand in crisis is the greatest challenge for the marketer. The stakes are high, the pressure intense, and the margin for error miniscule. Meanwhile, every move is scrutinized and observed by consumers and the media.

The brands that survive such crises are often the stronger for it. Their stories are truly heroic and often inspiring. When their recovery is complete, they experience a ground swell of public support. These are the stories that gain the glorious glow of national media attention, sudden shifts in market share, and honorable mention as Legendary Brands. It should be no surprise that narrative plays an important role in their elevation.

The resurrection plot depicts people at their best: conquering demons (internal or external), utilizing remarkable wit, and persevering when ordinary mortals would otherwise submit. Whether it is the tale of Orpheus, the labors of Hercules, St. George and the Dragon, or *Ferris Bueller's Day Off*, audiences relish the return of the fallen hero.

In this chapter we explore the hero's journey and its application to brands that have fallen from grace. Like the Phoenix, these brands emerge from the ashes and are reborn from narrative roots. We will follow the resurrection of one brand in particular—Jack in the Box, a brand that journeyed about as far as a brand can go into the netherworld, but returned triumphant.

WHEN BAD THINGS HAPPEN TO GOOD BRANDS: The Case of Jack in the Box

In 1993, four children died and hundreds of people became ill from an outbreak of E. Coli bacteria linked to undercooked meat served from Jack in the Box restaurants in Seattle, Washington. The outbreak was one of the worst in United States history and caused widespread panic and outrage. It was the most daunting product crisis since the Tylenol tamperings ten years earlier, and it threatened the future of the Jack in the Box brand.

Jack in the Box is a nationwide chain of quick-service restaurants. The franchise operated predominantly on the West Coast since 1951, and was best known for its original drive-through service windows, where customers gave their orders to a menu board featuring a large, talking clown head. The whimsical clown imagery disappeared in 1980, when the company opted to focus on food quality and variety— prompting its management to summarily and publicly destroy the lovable icon in a shock-style television advertisement that showed the literal explosion of the clown menu board.

For the next decade, the Jack in the Box brand eroded in comparison to other fast food competitors. Though its food quality frequently ranked higher than burgers served at McDonald's, Burger King, and Carl's, Jr., the increasing variety of menu items, and the lack of a brand narrative relegated the Jack in the Box brand to vague, regional obscurity. In a sense, though the company continued to grow, the brand stood for nothing. The people who frequented Jack in the Box restaurants did so because they liked the "flavor of the month," they were enticed by a price promotion, or they were interested in something other than a burger.

Disaster Strikes

Truth be told, the E. Coli crisis could have unfolded at any one of Jack in the Box's competitors. In 1993, safety standards in the quick-service food industry were lackadaisical. It was not until the 1993 outbreak that regulatory attention became a priority and the industry leadership capitulated that changes were needed to ensure public health. Prior to the crisis, consumers and industry insiders both took it for granted that the food served in major quick-service restaurant franchises was safe. The notion that a hamburger sold from a major chain could be dangerous seemed so unrealistic that the initial reaction of Jack in the Box management was to vehemently deny the charges, despite the rising toll of seriously ill customers.

Nothing fuels media fascination more than the harming of children. When those children died at the hands of a major corporation, a media circus formed. Jack in the Box was thrust into the spotlight, and its executives blinked under heavy perspiration. What was already a tragedy became a serious crisis. According to CEO Robert Nugent, who took the post after the fact, the company's management made a major mistake when they listened to the company's lawyers rather than their consumers.

Though Jack in the Box may have responded poorly to the media, internally it made immediate and dramatic steps to change the way it conducted business. It not only improved its food safety standards, but also pressed for industrywide reform. Later that year, it became the first restaurant in the industry to implement a comprehensive Hazard Analysis and Critical Control Points (HACCP) food-safety system, which was originally developed by NASA to ensure safe food for astronauts. By 1997, Jack in the Box helped pass legislation in the state of California that mandated minimum cooking temperatures.

In addition to reforms in its operations, Jack in the Box addressed the victims of the outbreak. They covered medical costs and made amends with families as best they could. Despite these proactive efforts, it remained the brand that killed kids. If Jack in the Box were to survive as a brand (which seemed doubtful), it needed to be reborn. It needed to stand for something more than better food variety and taste.

Resurrecting the Ghost of a Brand

"Metaphorically, at least, we needed to hang an Under New Management sign on the door of every Jack in the Box," said Steve Le Neveu, the account planner at Chiat\Day, the advertising agency Jack in the Box tasked with rescuing the brand. It was anything but easy. In field research, Le Neveu found that most consumers had no specific attachment to the brand, and if they had any feelings toward the brand at all, it was negative as a result of the E. Coli outbreak.

Bob Kuperman, the head of Chiat\Day's Los Angeles office at the time, had previously worked on the Jack in the Box account when it was at the Wells, Rich, Green agency, the agency that ritually destroyed the clown menu board in television advertisements. Kuperman suggested that bringing Jack back might provide a basis for a brand platform. Armed with this notion, Le Neveu went back into the field and found that, though it registered faintly, there was some lingering consumer attachment to Jack.

"We had three thoughts on the wall: under new management, bring back Jack, and people's former emotional connections with the clown. We fused them into one thought, which was to bring back Jack and make him the new CEO."

That kernel of inspiration, championed by creative director Dick Sittig, inspired the narrative that would ultimately breathe life into the Jack in the Box brand. Suddenly Jack was not an icon, but a character. Sittig, who also voiced Jack's dialogue, thrust Jack onto the scene as the one man who could bring the company back—the mythic hero who returned to save the company.

Every Narrative Needs a Hero

The beauty of the Jack in the Box advertising was its wit. Jack didn't return as an animated character. Jack was as human as you and me, except that he had the head of a toy clown. Dressed in no-nonsense business suits, surrounded by a conservative office suite, and speaking with Sittig's dry, rational voice, Jack was as polished a corporate executive as Michael Eisner, Jack Welch, and Herb Kelleher all rolled into one. The juxtaposition of the ridiculous clown head with the matter-of-fact business persona made the "Jack Is Back" campaign an instant success.

In the first advertisement, Jack addressed the audience directly. He reminded them of his unfortunate accident (the menu board explosion). Through the miracles of plastic surgery, Jack had bounced back and was on the scene to change the way things were done at Jack in the Box. Though he did not directly reference the E. Coli disaster, he made it clear to audiences that he thought the company was in trouble—and he was going to do something about it. In fact, Jack exacted the ultimate revenge. He blew up the Jack in the Box boardroom.

Subsequent spots featured Jack shaking things up around corporate headquarters. He streamlined menus and returned the focus to the classic items that established the company, such as the Jumbo Jack hamburger. More than that, Jack appeared to make the company customer friendly. In a later spot, a wise-cracking customer at the drive through squawk box joked that he wanted to talk to Jack. The congenial employee complied and within seconds the customer heard the familiar voice of Jack through the speaker.

Jack as Strategy Wonk

The story of Jack was more than just an advertising campaign. It permeated the entire corporate culture. Le Neveu hinted at the power of the narrative, "I think that arguably the most important thing we put on the table—that we made happen for Jack in the Box—was not just a great advertising campaign, but actually the ability for others, or the clients themselves, to ask, 'what would Jack do?'" Jack's narrative became a galvanizing force that served as role model, morale boost, and management strategy.

Le Neveu compares Jack to Lee Iacoca—a no-nonsense hardliner who puts the customer first and executes business activities to suit that purpose. This mentality filtered down to front-line employees. In fact, when the campaign launched, a postcard from Jack was sent to every employee. In the postcard, Jack announced his return and asked employees to consider what they could do to improve the company; a motivating message reminiscent of John F. Kennedy's famous, "Ask not what your country can do for you, but what you can do for your country." Many employees enthusiastically responded to the cards. Employees were evidently inspired by Jack's narrative.

But it takes more than inspired employees to produce profits. It was inspired consumers that ultimately proved the value of the strategy. The new campaign generated quick results. Sales went up and research showed that consumers were prepared to give the company a second chance. In fact, the advertising spots were so powerful that they allowed Jack in the Box to break free of a media planning tradition that constrained its competitive ability.

The team at Chiat\Day pleaded with Jack in the Box to reduce the practice of churning the menu. Each month a new menu item was introduced or rotated because the company's management believed that it was variety that sustained their competitive advantage. The folks at Chiat\Day were concerned that the endless rotation created a fickle consumer base, who visited only when the special of the day appealed to their appetite. The reliance on menu-driven advertising created the need for an extremely heavy media budget to make any kind of impression. Every advertisement that featured a new product needed to run several times to impact the consumer—it was like launching a new product every month. If the company mixed in Jack-focused signature spots, Chiat argued, the media could be put to more efficient use.

Jack promoted his "back to basics" menu, drawing attention to menu classics. When Jack promoted a menu item, sales increased. This led to another interesting revelation. The new advertisements generated very powerful consumer recall. Chiat soon found that they didn't need to repeat the messages that featured Jack as frequently as had been the practice. In fact, they feared that overplaying the same spot might tire Jack's popularity. Soon, the media budget was reallocated, with advertisements running at strategic times. With the media investment optimized, a greater variety of Jack advertisements were created, extending the narrative and the team's opportunity to flesh it out.

When Narrative Becomes Reality

Though Jack was a fictional character, consumers felt a true attachment to him. Deep down in their hearts he stood for something special. The Chiat team learned a lot from what consumers said about Jack. They used this material to explore his character and sustain the suspension of disbelief. Occasionally, reality and fiction intersected in such a way that the brand delivered a "Wow!"

For example, after the E. Coli crisis, Jack in the Box cooking standards exceeded those of any competitor, but it came at the cost of taste. The company overcooked its burgers. Beef derives its flavor from fat content. Fat is lost from meat when cooked. If overcooked, the fat is entirely removed, which means you end up with a burger devoid of flavor. With all the attention placed on the staple item of the menu (burgers), the company was set up for failure. Its brand would be sabotaged by its commitment to safety and quality.

After much research, someone finally hit on the idea that increasing the fat content would preserve the flavor in the burger. Jack in the Box made a systemwide change, at no small expense. Simultaneously, Jack went on the air telling consumers that he had improved the taste of Jack in the Box burgers. Consumers gave the burgers another try with resounding approval. They also believed that Jack truly had something to do with the change. Life imitated art, which in turn imitated life.

Brand Symbols Put into Action

Though he was a fictional character, Jack served as a powerful brand agent. He personified a set of beliefs that resonated with consumers. Every new commercial sanctified Jack and kept the narrative alive. Over time, a brand culture developed inside and outside the company. That became quite clear with the introduction of the antenna ball.

During focus group research, a respondent commented that Jack's head would make an attractive addition to her car antenna. Le Neveu took the concept back to the team, and a new product was born. Sittig developed a fitting story arc to suit the launch. A series of new television spots was created characterizing the antenna balls as a league of missionaries for Jack. In one advertisement, Jack organizes an offsite retreat attended by hundreds of his faithful antenna ball team members.

The campaign worked and consumers welcomed the brand symbol back into their lives and onto their cars. Jack in the Box was reluctant to produce very many, at first. According to Le Neveu, the Chiat\Day team recommended that the company order a quantity of one million. Unconvinced that the balls would be that popular, the company ordered about 100,000 instead. They sold out within 48 hours. Not only did the antenna balls enjoy rapid adoption, they turned a small profit as well.

Narrative Meets Investor

Jack's role in the brand narrative did not stop with consumers. In the most recent company annual report, Jack's art collection is featured in "The Art of the Meal." Within the pages of the glossy yearbook, Jack addresses shareholders directly, arguing that legendary casino developer Steve Wynn urged him to share his collection of famous artwork. Reproductions of his "private stock" are then featured within the pages of the 2001 annual report. Of course, the paintings featured are witty turns on the masters. Matisse's Icarus features the Jack in the Box logo instead of a blood red heart. An impressionist painting shows two French ladies relaxing in the park next to an unwrapped burger. Keith Harring's famous figures hold burger, fries, and drink.

The annual report extension of the campaign is an interesting use of the narrative because it addresses an audience often overlooked by brand marketers—investors. Jack in the Box fully developed their brand narrative by finding a story arc that worked well for each audience, including the one that holds shares of the company's stock.

LESSONS FROM JACK IN THE BOX

The Jack in the Box story is an excellent case to demonstrate the power of narrative to resuscitate a brand in crisis. There are others with equal merit: Apple Computer and "Think Different" or Volkswagen and the new Beetle. The Jack in the Box story deserves special attention, however, because of its sweeping effect throughout the system. Following are some lessons learned that may help you should your brand fall on harder times.

Demonstrate Hope for the Future

Jack succeeded because it didn't dwell on the past. Instead, it focused on the future and did so with great optimism. The new brand narrative depicted a company that was dramatically different from the past, helmed by a charismatic, no-nonsense personality. Thematically, the idea that a new CEO entered the scene to shake things up had a very motivating effect on employees and consumers. Jack's attitude provided hope and a sense that change was underway.

Make Your Narrative about Dramatic Polarities

Jack didn't just fade into the Jack in the Box narrative, he blew up the boardroom. The initial thrust of the Jack Is Back campaign was that things were about to change. The old way of doing business was no longer tolerated. On the surface level, this polar change in attitude was funny and motivating, but deeper down it demonstrated the company's commitment to make good for the tragedy of 1993.

If your brand must come back from the brink, your narrative must portray a brand committed to change. Thrust your brand agents into conflict—the toughest conflict imaginable. Jack did not have an easy job. The commercials poked fun at the idea of turning a company around, but the audience knew that such an endeavor was anything but easy. Each time Jack made an improvement, he faced an even bigger challenge. In 1996, Jack even made a presidential bid—giving rise to the idea that what worked for the company might work for the country.

Audiences love to see sweeping change. The more that your narrative can polarize the change, the more powerful your narrative will resonate with audiences.

Brand Turnarounds Need Several Audiences

The Jack in the Box story is all the more powerful because it did not address a single audience—it addressed many. Each audience it touched affected the rejuvenation of the brand. Consumers were the core focus, but so were employees and shareholders.

If your brand needs to stage a comeback, include all of the stakeholders. Craft a narrative that extends to each audience. If you don't, you risk sending out conflicting messages. You also risk looking un-committed to change. Jack's personality permeated every piece of com-munication the company issued. That singular narrative, culled for each specific audience, had just the galvanizing effect the company needed to demonstrate that the crisis was in the past.

Listen to Consumers and Let Them Guide Your Actions

The great triumph of this story is that the consumer mattered. Careful listening led to the foundation of the brand narrative. It also prompted character development and the use of powerful brand sym-bols. While great planning and great creative development played an important role, it was the participation of consumers that generated the spark.

AN INTERVIEW WITH STEVE LE NEVEU

Steve Le Neveu is Planning Director of Publicis West, and was the Planning Director at Chiat\Day responsible for the Jack in the Box campaign.

Larry: What advice would you give to marketers working on a brand that must come back from the brink?

Steve: It is not easy advice to follow, but I would advise brand managers facing a crisis to think like a CEO. I think that brand managers do not normally get paid to think like CEOs, they get paid to "manage" the "brand." It's quite hard. It is easy to say, "Have some balls" and ask yourself questions like "What would I do if this were my company?" But they don't get paid to think like that. They get paid to not rock the boat. However, in times of crisis they have a license to think like the CEO. When things are going well, brand managers are faced with the mentality of "it ain't broke so don't fix it." When things get desperate, they must entertain much more creative options, potentially.

Larry: Anything else?

Steve: Frame questions in the future tense. One thing that holds us back as marketers is that so much of what we do is in the present tense, which means it's really in the past because you're looking in the rear-view mirror. Instead of asking, "What is this brand?" you could ask, "What could this brand *be*?" Instead of, "Who is the target audience?" you could say, "Who would we like the target audience to *be*?" Think about the kind of future that you want to create.

13

BRAND NARRATIVE
AND THE BODY POLITIC

Our democracy must be not only the envy of the
world but the engine of our own renewal. There is
nothing wrong with America that cannot be cured
by what is right with America.
And so today we pledge an end to the era of
deadlock and drift, and a new season of American
renewal has begun.

President William Jefferson Clinton
Inaugural Address, January 20, 1993

The American political landscape between 1992 and 1994 may endure as one of the most intriguing in our nation's recent history. It was intriguing because it focused on change, renewal, and public interest in government. Beginning in 1992, with Bill Clinton's legendary presidential campaign, and peaking in 1994 with the congressional turnover fueled by the House Republicans and their *Contract with America,* the two-year saga presented on Capitol Hill provided ample material for the evening news and the history books.

It was a drama of conflicting ideologies, dueling hypocrisies, and opposing legislative platforms. Yet, this American retelling of the battle between Montague and Capulet contained narrative devices that favored neither side. Each political party used a common thread of a narrative in its own way to command public attention and fuel the brand.

Branding is not isolated to the realm of capitalism. *Republican* and *Democrat* are Legendary Brands. Candidates are brand agents. And political parties are brand cultures of conflicting, organized social philosophies—or sacred beliefs. Campaigns are story arcs and thematic devices that execute on the narrative foundation.

American history offers abundant examples of brand mythology and the use of narrative to sway public opinion. All the great presidencies and the most influential political movements operated within the brand mythology cycle defined in this book. Teddy Roosevelt, FDR, Kennedy, or Reagan would have made fine case studies, but the Clinton presidential campaign and the first two years of the Clinton presidency are worthy of attention for two reasons: it is still fresh in our minds, and it contained a defining victory for each party, although at different times.

It is a tale of two parties engaged in a grand conflict. It is the drama of William Jefferson Clinton, a charismatic tragic hero if ever there was one, with strong archetypal character traits. His narrative begins the day he accepts the call to adventure and pursues a rendezvous with destiny. As in every good story, his actions initiate a series of opposite reactions—namely from the grand old party. Though the final act would not be complete until several significant characters were defeated and the President impeached, the first and second acts of this operatic narrative are terrific examples of Legendary Brands and their role in politics. We shall explore both sides of the conflict, for each drew upon a distinct and galvanizing mythology to rally public support.

MR. CLINTON GOES TO WASHINGTON

On July 17, 1992, Governor Bill Clinton and Senator Al Gore boarded a bus in Little Rock, Arkansas, and literally started down the road to the Executive Office. Having just recently won the nomination from the Democratic Party, these unlikely partners set off to tour the nation by bus with their wives, their staff, and 130 journalists. Their mission: win the people's vote.

The seeds of this story began months earlier with a surprise coming of age. Bill Clinton was not the candidate most people expected to go the distance. The front runners before the New Hampshire primary were Governor Mario Cuomo of New York and Senator Bob Kerry, of Nebraska, a respected member of Congress and a Vietnam veteran. Most people outside of Arkansas had never heard of Bill Clinton. His obscurity evaporated when he finished second in the New Hampshire primary, despite negative media attention only weeks earlier surrounding an alleged romantic affair with Gennifer Flowers.

If sacred beliefs are the foundation of Legendary Brands, then it is no surprise that Bill Clinton won the Presidency and navigated two terms in the White House with some of the highest approval ratings in American history. The beliefs he stood for were well constructed before he boarded the bus that day in Arkansas. They burned within him and resonated in his words and deeds well before New Hampshire. Paul Begala was one of Clinton's lead campaign strategists in 1992. Recalling his decision to serve Clinton, he remarked:

> Most politicians, when they meet with a guy like me, or a guy like [James] Carville, tell you about how they can win. . . . They would give you the strategy. Clinton gave us the policy. . . . And then he went through the policy specifics, and he focused on these two things. He said, "Economically we're sliding down, and socially we're coming apart." I used to tease him that he had three solutions for every problem, but he went on like this for hours, and we were completely bowled over.[1]

Fundamentally, the Clinton campaign was such a success because of the same factors that make Legendary Brands a success: a set of sacred beliefs that resonate strongly with consumers, linked inextricably to an inspirational brand agent. Bill Clinton did not just stand for a world-view. He *was* the worldview. This quality gave him considerable dura-bility. At the end of the day, he could weather the many scandals because they predominantly concerned issues that were apart from his worldview. Tawdry sexual affairs had little to do with improved access to health care, welfare reform, and family leave. As George Stephan-opoulos would later recall:

> . . . in January 1992 a lot of people around the country were worried about the economy. People were hurting. And the very basic message—that the campaign should be about everybody else's future, not my past—was very powerful to a lot of people watching, especially in New Hampshire."[2]

The Clinton campaign's weaknesses were the ghosts and skeletons of the candidate's past. These weaknesses did not keep Clinton from his objective any more than the flaws of other tragic heroes. In their book, *The Hero and the Outlaw*, Margaret Mark and Carol S. Pearson attrib-uted Clinton's resiliency to his archetypical similarity to Zeus in the ancient Greek myths. It was widely known that Zeus was sexually pro-miscuous, yet he maintained his power and control over Olympus.[3] Even in the great works of Shakespeare, the heroes we adore err fa-mously. Hamlet, after all, avenged his father's death despite his bouts with rage (summarily murdering Polonious), cruelty (emotional bat-tering of Ophelia), and general depression.

Another brand agent played a pivotal role, smoothing out Bill Clinton's tragic flaws, which threatened his ability to win the White House. As a human being, Al Gore was in some ways a polar opposite to Bill Clinton. Many were surprised that Gore agreed to share billing because of his own flirtation with the Oval Office, long before he was pared with Clinton on the Democratic ticket. The polished son of a widely respected Tennessee senator, and an influential senator in his own right, Gore was coldly analytical where Clinton was passionately inspired. Gore reveled in ideals, theory, and erudite policy, whereas Clinton enjoyed the pursuit of hard and measurable objectives, practical but elegant solutions, and the occasional compromise. As politicians, however, the two men held remarkable common ground. When it came to the platform—the worldview associated with the campaign—they complemented each other's strengths and weaknesses perfectly.

Al Gore was an indispensable brand agent for the Clinton brand. As political consultant, Dick Morris elaborated:

> I think that the reason Clinton chose Gore was that he was an example of what Clinton was like. He was kind of almost like the yellow Magic Marker that you use to highlight the text so that you can really remember what are the most salient features of it. He wanted to choose someone who was a metaphor for himself: who was his age, who was from a nearby state, who was also a moderate Democrat, concerned about the environment. And he wanted to choose someone next to whom his own virtues would be highlighted, almost the way you choose the backdrop on a set. If you have blue eyes, you want a blue backdrop so your eyes stand out. He was kind of using Gore almost as sort of the backdrop for his candidacy.[4]

Completing the brand mythology cycle, the bus tour provided the narrative that linked agents and worldview. The bus tour had such an impact on the Clinton-Gore campaign, that it is now the stuff of legend. *Newsweek* editor Eleanor Clift remarked, "They got more positive coverage on this bus tour than the Beatles got on their first tour of America. More reporters were oohing and aahing. It was almost embarrassing."

New Hampshire was but a preamble to the story that would unfold as Clinton and Gore visited the "real America." Their travels generated a story that caught national media attention. Those who could not meet Bill, Hillary, Al and Tipper first hand could meet them virtually every night on their television.

Bill Clinton's warm, energetic presence, youthful appearance, and articulate command of salient issues contrasted the stiff, status quo identity of incumbent George Bush. Like mythic heroes, Bill Clinton's character was revealed through his actions. He played the saxophone on MTV's "Rock the Vote." He bolted into crowds and met with everyday citizens—not as a stiff politician, but as a man of the people—and in every case, the people found him to be sincere, warm, credible. He resurrected the concept of "town meeting" and made it a national television event. Most important, he appeared to listen. Rather than spout sound bites and policy rhetoric, Bill Clinton engaged people personally. He asked their opinion. He made it clear that he heard and understood what they said, and what mattered.

Said Begala, "He's the smartest guy I ever met, but his most compelling attribute is that interpersonal empathy. When he is connecting with someone, the whole world melts away." This empathetic nature played out for all the world to see, as he swung voter opinion state by state.

The Clinton brand narrative worked because it relied on a practically literal representation of the hero's journey. The nation came to know a man raised from very humble upbringings in the rural South. He was inspired at an early age to reach for the presidency when, as a 16 year-old member of Boys for America, he met John F. Kennedy on the White House lawn. That photograph circulated with the campaign and helped to build the story of the hero called to adventure. After attending Georgetown, Yale, Oxford, and becoming a Rhode's Scholar, Clinton entered public service, eventually becoming Governor of Arkansas for five terms.

The Clinton campaign drew on three brand narratives that intertwined in a resourceful way. First was the narrative of the American Everyman—the native son raised from depression and obscurity to deliver hope to a nation. Second was the narrative of the baby-boom presidency. It is fitting that the most famous biography on Clinton is David Maraniss' *First in His Class*. It is an apt title for the narrative that generated the aura around the first Baby Boomer to occupy the White House. In some ways, the Clinton presidency was the final act of a social narrative that began in the 1960s. Finally, the campaign drew upon the narrative of the partnership between Clinton and Gore, also including Hilary Clinton. The nation was to have a team of equals—a team of smart people who represented their interests. All three of these narratives were set against the engaging backdrop of the American political process. They gave birth to dozens of story arcs that fascinated the American people and they generated a brand culture. At a time when the country was lost, ambling for direction after the "Go-Go" 1980s, Bill Clinton appeared to many Americans as the candidate that was one of "us." His connection to this culture was so strong that even a congressional impeachment could not dilute their dedication to him. Based on polling data and expert opinion, it was widely speculated that if Bill Clinton could have run for a third term, he may well have kept his seat in the Oval Office.

If the Clinton campaign was a true consumer brand, it would indeed be legendary. Sacred beliefs, brand agent, brand narrative were all there, supported by the patriotic symbols and cultural attributes that accompany a presidential campaign. We could construct the road to the White House in three-act form, or according to the hero's journey. It was a campaign filled with dramatic conflict, each one more challenging to the hero, and each one propelling him forward. It communicated a narrative that supported the personal identity of millions of Americans. Finally, it contained themes that were not only inspirational, but highly relevant.

On November 3, 1993, the nation elevated the brand to legendary status when it elected William Jefferson Clinton to be its 42nd President. He won only 43 percent of the popular vote, hardly a mandate, but he was the first Democrat to occupy the Oval Office in twelve years, and he was backed by a Democratic-controlled Congress—for a time.

GOVERNMENT OF THE PEOPLE, FOR THE PEOPLE

In the grand scheme of things, Bill Clinton's White House victory may have marked the end of Act I in the Clinton brand narrative, but it only initiated the first act for the Republican party and the narrative they were about to tell. Clinton's election was *the* inciting incident.

It was not long after Clinton's victory that the story changed for his administration. The nation waited perhaps too long to learn who would fill all of the administration posts. Tremendous expectations generated during the waning days of the campaign applied daily pressure to a new President and a political party that had not truly dealt with the Executive Office in more than a decade. When the cabinet was finally assembled, the inspirational style that favored the campaign created temporary chaos.

Meanwhile, the Democratic majority in both houses of Congress provided Clinton with air cover, but such protection came at a price. Clinton's fear of repeating the failed presidency of Jimmy Carter led him to bow to seasoned Democratic leaders—leaders with a more liberal legislative agenda. The President began to stray from the sacred beliefs that gave his campaign its brand foundation. Though there were many minor victories, the major initiatives launched by the Clinton administration in its first two years failed.

Republicans watched the shenanigans at the White House with utter contempt. This was a party that still basked in the limelight of Ronald Reagan, who like Clinton, was a popular public figure who sustained a powerful brand narrative despite scandal and negative media attention. Though Clinton's true agenda was decidedly moderate, the course he initially pursued was the glaring antithesis of the Republican platform. It was not just partisan politicians who were upset. Many of the same citizens who voted for Clinton in 1992 were getting restless. The healthcare initiative spearheaded by Hilary Clinton was one of many public fiascos that tried these people's patience, causing a shift in public opinion. That shift fueled an opportunity for the Republican Party.

"It was clear to us that after a year in the White House, President Bill Clinton did not intend to govern on the agenda which people elected him to lead the country." So said Representatives Newt Gingrich and Dick Armey on behalf of the House Republicans in their book, *Contract with America*. "*Contract with America* was an instrument to help repair a fundamental disconnection between citizens and their elected officials."

1994 was an election year, and though the Republicans could not storm the White House, they believed they could control Congress. The idea seemed ridiculous to most inside the beltway, but the Republicans saw an opportunity to "get back to basics." They witnessed the way many people in the country awakened to the song of change during the 1992 Clinton campaign. Thus, an unlikely effort began in an unlikely place—*Contract with America* in the House of Representatives.

Like the Clinton campaign, the Contract with America began with a set of sacred beliefs: individual liberty, economic opportunity, limited government, personal responsibility, and security at home and abroad. These five philosophies became the outline for a portfolio of ten legislative bills to be passed in the first 100 days of the new Congress if Republicans were awarded control.

The Contract with America was a brilliant brand initiative. Republicans needed a powerful agent to stand for their set of sacred beliefs. Without the aid of a Presidential "front man," they came up with a document. The Constitution and Declaration of Independence are the enduring brand agents of the American brand narrative, and the Contract with America was the brand agent for the new Republican Party. It was backed by more than 300 incumbent and hopeful Republican Congressional leaders, who assembled on the West Front Steps of the U.S. Capitol on September 27, 1994. Simultaneously, it was published in book form and on the Internet, and it ushered in a new face, Representative Newt Gingrich.

Gingrich was an apt hero for the Republican brand narrative, and an equally apt opponent to Clinton. He held a Ph.D. in History, and was a popular professor at West Georgia College. Like Clinton, he heard the call of public service at a young age, reportedly during his experience visiting the sites of former World War II battles during a period when his family lived in France. He could be very articulate and charismatic, and he particularly enjoyed the scholarly and political realms of conversation. He would become a popular face for the brand narrative. In 1995, like Clinton in 1992, Gingrich would be named Time Magazine's "Man of the Year."

The Contract with America and the election of 1994 was not about Newt Gingrich, however. Gingrich was merely a brand agent to a much bigger narrative. He was one of its authors, its frequent voice, and part of its leadership, but the Contract with America resonated with Americans because of what it promised them, not because they liked or disliked Newt Gingrich.

True, part of Republican success in 1994 was owed to fortune. The Clinton administration faltered and lost its guard. That played into Republican hands. But it is foolhardy to believe that a few missteps were responsible for the dramatic change in leadership that occurred in the election. The Democrats lost control of both houses of Congress. Republicans had not previously controlled the House of Representatives since 1952. If Clinton's election was not a mandate, the change in congressional leadership certainly was.

Republicans achieved their victory by tapping into a decidedly American myth. The brand narrative of 1994 was about the people, opportunity, and the right of the people to make change. Government (and by default, the Clinton administration) was the enemy. The Contract with America held promises, real promises, written down to hold Congress accountable. These promises were not open-ended; they were linked to a strict timeline of 100 days. Like the Magna Carta and the Constitution, the Contract with America was more than a campaign promise—it was a living document, and the blueprint of a story. Even more profound, it was a franchise.

If you are unfamiliar with the mechanics of franchise, here is a quick summary. The brand and certain standards of operation and quality are managed centrally (McDonald's brand marketing originates in Oak Brook, Illinois). Daily operations and interaction with consumer, however, are licensed to third parties, who are only required to adhere to minimum brand standards.

Every Republican running for Congress leveraged the power of the Contract with America. The brand narrative was controlled and managed from Washington, D.C., with superb skill, but the narrative itself came alive at the franchisee level, in the local districts and states that were about to cast their ballots. Former Democratic Speaker of the

House, Tip O'Neil, famously quoted, "All politics is local." The Contract with America proved him right. Instead of launching a one-dimensional, whining brand narrative that aimed with partisan flavor at the President, Republicans crafted a narrative that addressed big national issues but remained relevant at the local level. In a sense, you had one major story, supported by hundreds of smaller, deeply personal stories.

LESSONS FROM GOVERNMENT

- Political campaigns are stories. They are specifically stories about a Legendary Brand—the candidate. The same rules applied to brands elsewhere in this book must govern the political campaign, particularly when the prize is the White House. Your candidate needs a brand bible. You need to listen to your brand audience through consumer research. Most importantly, you must nurture the culture around your narrative.
- In the United States, the best campaigns retell the myth of America. Because so many politicians draw upon this narrative, it is the candidate who can articulate it in a new way that earns our attention. Clinton's idealistic retelling with the voice of the baby-boom generation set his campaign apart. Conversely, the Republican Party's no-nonsense commitment told through *Contract with America* awoke a sleeping giant.
- The narrative structure of the campaign is just as important as the quality of the candidate. When planning a political campaign, you must marry the brand agents to strong genres, archetypes, themes, and aesthetic triggers.

AN INTERVIEW WITH MICHAEL KAYE

I close this chapter by going straight to the source. Michael Kaye is a seasoned political consultant who served as campaign advisor to

Senator Bill Bradley for more than ten years. Prior to his work in politics he was an art director at Doyle Dane Bernbach. His insights and experience draw from many years managing Legendary Brands.

Larry: How do you win a political campaign?

Michael: That is a million-dollar question. I think you must approach a political campaign, particularly a presidential or congressional campaign, as though it were like any other product or brand. It is exactly the same paradigm. In many cases, the candidates are like identical products. It is very hard for the public to differentiate between them. So your job is to create a difference. You want the candidate to mean something to voters. The easiest way to accomplish this is to focus on your opponent, rather than your candidate.

I always approached the campaign by thinking about how to separate my brand from the other brand. It always comes down to the story the opponent is telling versus your candidate's story. The way to win is to decide what story your opponent is going to tell, and then box him in.

Larry: How do you anticipate the story your opponent will tell?

Michael: Research. Research. Research. Discipline is also important, because you have to know when to shut up and hear what the other guy is saying. But research and the interpretation of your findings is the greatest weapon in your arsenal. It is the only way to find your opponent's Achilles' heel. Once you have a feel for where he's going, you use research to determine how well your candidate is reaching the population.

Larry: What do you look for?

Michael: How do they perceive the candidate? Do they really know him? What are his positive and negative attributes? Really, 98 percent of what they tell you should already be known to you. So what you are really looking for are little "nuggets" that give great insight into the associations and themes that can make your candidate great. It takes practice and requires a great deal of patience, because candidates notoriously hate the cost of polls, but they learn to love the information produced from them.

CHAPTER 14

THE DARK SIDE OF
BRAND MYTHOLOGY

Most enduring narratives, even those with unhappy endings, forge a bond with audiences through protagonists that are basically good, conscientious people. We find the good in our souls living vicariously through the actions of George Bailey, Atticus Finch, and Indiana Jones. Occasionally, geniuses like Billy Wilder introduce us to protagonists with a shady side, but deep down we empathize with these characters because they are not evil, just merely human and flawed.

However, there exists a segment of narratives that revolve around patently bad characters. They exist in Shakespeare (*Macbeth, Richard III, Julius Caesar*), the Greek tragedies (*Medea*), and modern motion pictures (*Taxi Driver, Seven, Interview with a Vampire*). Even in stories where the central narrative is wholesome and positive, certain antagonist characters stand out that gain enthusiastic audience empathy (Susan Lucci's Erica on television's "All My Children," Iago in *Othello*, Stanley Kowalksi in *Streetcar Named Desire*, and Darth Vader in *Star Wars*).

Why do people so enjoy rooting for the bad guy? What makes consumers gravitate to things they know are not good for them? Why does emotional attachment develop to products that purposefully rub against the grain of cultural standards?

In this chapter we explore the "dark side" of brand mythology. We seek to understand why narratives with cruel intentions resonate with consumers, and we learn how to utilize antiheroic narratives in brand marketing. We also discuss the responsibilities of the marketer and the line in the sand that separates wicked fun from socially irresponsible business activities.

The dark side of brand narrative is an intriguing field because it deals with all the prurient themes our mothers warned us to avoid. Writers have an old saying about plots, your story is either about sex, violence, or sex and violence. I would reframe this assertion slightly to guide you through the dark side of brand narrative. The themes we will explore are either about indulgence, rebellion, or both.

THE CONTINUUM OF DARK NARRATIVES

Figure 14.1 depicts a theoretical scale measuring the magnitude of a dark narrative, or a narrative containing antiheroic elements. On the milder side, the far left, are the narratives that focus on provocation. The narratives that fall on this end of the scale are not generally violent, but they contain characters and incidents that purposefully agitate mainstream culture.

In the middle of the spectrum are narratives that are indulgent. Indulgent narratives are also provocative, but they do more to provoke our appetites than they do to provoke cultural feedback. Sex, gambling, substance abuse, and overeating are common activities of the indulgent narrative. Another name for this narrative is the so-called sin products and services, or "guilty pleasures."

On the far right reside the stronger, more controversial themes. This end of the spectrum is for mature audiences only. Actually, what distinguishes it from the rest is that it combines indulgence with provocation and ventures into activities that cause harm, destruction,

FIGURE 14.1   Continuum of Dark Narratives

Mild		Strong
Provocative	**Indulgent**	**Harmful**
insubordinance	envy	criminal intent
minor destruction	gluttony	harm to others
pranksterism	greed	inciting riot/
rebellion	lust	danger
	sloth	self-infliction

or serious consequences. These consequences can be to the self, to others, or to both. Of the legal brands that occupy this space, tobacco brands are the "poster children" for strong, "harmful" brand narratives. Like tobacco products, many brands that occupy this space are subject to governmental oversight, regulation, or serious public scrutiny.

To understand how each of these dimensions works for Legendary Brands, we must revisit the concept of personal narrative. Recall that postmodern theory suggests that each of us shapes our experience and our identity around a narrative. Our story is constructed in our subconscious and is constantly revised and augmented.

Most of us believe that we are good people. We believe that our actions are aligned with morally appropriate principles. Writers know that in order to write a good villain, you must assume that the villain believes what he or she is doing is right. Villains are the heroes of their own stories. Few of us set out to do what is wrong for the sake of doing so. This is the definition of pure evil—participating in activities that cause harm or suffering to others for no other purpose.

Our dominant personal narrative strives to do what is right. It is generally grounded in "true north" principles—or those principles that have stood the test of time in moral thought. Yet, if you subscribe to the postmodern school, you believe that we have multiple narratives that script our various identities. Often, one of those identities compensates for our tendency to "do good" in the others.

Freud and Jung referred to this as the alter ego—the mirror of our consciousness. Jung elaborated on this concept, referring to *shadow* and *anima* in an essay:

> The darkness which clings to every personality is the door into the unconscious and the gateway to dreams, from which those two twilight figures, the shadow and the anima, step into our nightly visions or, remaining invisible, take possession of our ego-consciousness.[1]

For each of us, there is narrative identity that opposes our dominant narrative and occasionally emerges, motivating antiheroic behavior. The health-conscious marathon runner might suddenly binge on a chocolate milkshake, or the conservative banker, normally accustomed to saving and bargain hunting, ventures to Las Vegas to bet on "red."

There is nothing wrong with our darker side. In many ways, our sanity relies on our "inferior" narrative identity. It serves as a pressure valve, keeping the psyche in balance.

Narratives of Provocation

Adam Granger (not his real name) attends a prestigious private high school in the San Fernando suburbs of Los Angeles. His parents are both senior professionals and well-to-do members of the local community. Adam attends school with scores of teenagers that come from money.

All students who attend Adam's school are required to wear a uniform. Violations of this rule are serious offenses, which result in detentions, parental conferences, and suspension. The school dictates precisely what students can add to their uniforms and details how the uniform should be worn—except for guidelines on socks. Adam exploits this loophole. He enjoys wearing loud socks of alarming contrasting colors and patterns. The practice so upset school officials that Adam's parents were contacted and the dress code guidelines revised.

When socks were no longer an option for Adam, he found a new annoyance—wearing bright-colored print T-shirts beneath his white button-down uniform shirt. The result: the prints of the T-shirt show through.

Adam is basically a good kid. He has never been in serious trouble. He receives high marks in his classes and he is active in athletics and student government. So why would a model student like Adam wish to "push the envelope" with school officials?

Adam, like many of us, enjoys a personal narrative of provocation. It is a way for him to establish his own identity and his authenticity. Adam desires to be the black sheep to orient himself in a disorienting world. Besides, it is fun. He takes great pride in finding the one "legal" thing he can do that goes completely outside the boundaries the establishment hoped to achieve. Like R. P. McMurphy in *One Flew over the Cuckoo's Nest*, Adam enjoys disrupting the system.

I choose Adam as an example because the narrative of provocation is most often found in Legendary Brands that cater to youth. Our youth is a defining time in our lives, when we challenge the abstract to find ourselves. Part of that challenge is to test boundaries for their validity. Legendary Brands that offer the provocative narrative encourage youth to define their own boundaries or to define boundaries that differ from those asserted by authoritative powers.

Mountain Dew has long appealed to youth segments through its edgy marketing approach. By associating itself with skateboarders and urban music, and communicating with irreverent commercials that often contain shock reversals, Mountain Dew aligns well with consumers that like to agitate others through extreme behavior. The product itself gained fame because it contains an elevated level of caffeine for no other purpose than "jolting" the adrenaline of its consumer.

Mountain Dew's advertising today is a diluted version of its former self and a victim of its own success. The problem is that Dew's advertising and communication efforts are more mainstream. In an attempt to stay edgy while growing aggressively, the provocative narrative is less effusive. It is still a favored brand of young people, but it is gradually becoming legitimate, accepted, and part of the cultural norm. As a result, it is forging its attachment through narrative channel different from the provocative.

Sustaining a provocative narrative over time is a difficult task. Consumers gravitate toward this narrative because of its rebellious quality and its ability to assert uniqueness through minority opinion. When these brands become Legendary Brands, the provocative roots frequently wane. This results in a shift in sacred beliefs and the loss of the original brand audience.

When this narrative is at its best, it presents characters and situations that will offend some audiences. The offenses are generally mild. Most of us would claim the material is merely distasteful. Carl's Jr., a quick-service food chain, employed such a strategy with its "Don't Bother Me. I'm Eating." campaign. Carl's decided to target young males at the expense of females. Carl's changed their food preparation to add more condiments to its burgers. To promote this, it created advertising that featured people eating burgers and dripping ketchup, mustard, and special sauce all over themselves. They also created advertisements that showed men engaged in decidedly male behavior: eating like gluttons, living like slobs, and gaping at good looking women.

Female viewers typically find these advertisements disgusting, gross, or just "stupid." Male viewers responded. The campaign was so successful it has provided Carl's with a sustainable position in the competitive burger market.

JOE ISUZU

In 1986, Isuzu Motors introduced a character named Joe Isuzu in their television advertisements. Joe, played by actor David Leisure, was a perpetual liar. He made grand, false claims about Isuzu automobiles in an effort to close the sale. The humor in the campaign was twofold. First, Joe's lies were so grandiose that you knew he was lying. Second, while Joe lied on screen, subtitles countered his claims and pointed out that he was indeed lying.

The Isuzu campaign was very successful and ran for four years, boosting Leisure's career and leading to his supporting role in the television series, "Empty Nest," in which he appeared as a similar shifty character. Part of the campaign's success was its play within the destructive side of brand narrative. The Joe Isuzu campaign emphasized something familiar to every car buyer— the obnoxious car salesman. People despise car salespersons. Rather than claim to have a different kind of car salesperson (the tactic of Saturn), Isuzu made fun of theirs. Joe blatantly lied, and we laughed at each exaggerated claim. Isuzu acknowledged the fact that even their dealerships are prone to despicable characters, but they made that fact fun. In fact, audiences rather liked Joe. He was a man you loved to hate.

Recently, Isuzu resurrected the Joe Isuzu campaign. Leisure is back, but his role has changed. Instead of being a slimy sales guy, he is now the silver-tongued spokesperson for the brand. Instead of making ridiculous claims and openly lying to the consumer audience, he is seen as a hero for the brand, and in some ways, the consumer. The new line of ads is not testing as well, which may stem from the fact that Joe is no longer associated with the dark side of brand narrative. He's lost his wickedness and joined the ranks of respectable auto pitchmen.

Narratives of Indulgence

Marketing research abounds with discussion on the use of sex in advertising. So much of what we see and hear relies on sexual imagery.

Sex sells. It is perhaps the ultimate indulgent activity. Man is one of the only species on the planet known to engage in sexual activity for purposes other than reproduction. We are also the only species on the planet known to enjoy referring to, watching, and fantasizing about sex.

Indulgent narratives connect Legendary Brands with pleasure centers. Erotic narratives appeal to those of us with a voracious interest in carnal desire, or a twisted sense of sexual fun. But sex is not the only indulgence of brand narratives. Food is a frequent arbiter of indulgence. Godiva is a Legendary Brand that openly appeals to our indulgent desires. For some people, chocolate is as much a sensual pleasure as sex. Godiva uses sexual imagery (Lady Godiva rode through town in the nude) to make its product even more indulgent. Its product is packaged in gold. It is sold primarily through exclusive, branded stores with ornate detail and attentive customer service. Even the price is an example of indulgence, as Godiva chocolates cost two to three times as much as those of comparable competitors. Yet, for the Godiva brand, paying more is part of the pleasure. It activates the sense of committing a pleasurable sin.

Las Vegas is a Legendary Brand built on the back of pure indulgence. No one goes to Vegas to hold back. Las Vegas is synonymous with excess, promiscuity, and play. It is also inextricably linked to sex, gambling, and alcohol—all indulgent pastimes. Though it has become somewhat gentrified in recent years, Las Vegas is ostensibly known as the "city of sin."

While some go to Vegas to let loose and indulge their whims, others stay at home and gain pleasure from a taboo industry that is launching its own variety of Legendary Brands. Sales of pornographic videocassettes, DVDs, and on-demand programming now outpace those of the domestic motion picture box office, an estimated $12 billion in 2001. As one industry executive put it, with numbers that big, pornographic movies are clearly being bought by a wider audience than seedy guys in trench coats.

Vivid Video is the dominant industry player. In its more than 20-year history, the company has established itself along multiple criteria, including the quality of its talent, content, and management savvy. As a brand, however, Vivid is gradually achieving legendary status by sticking to indulgent narratives, even by pornographic standards. It developed a highly successful line of pornographic video features targeted specifically at women. It also leveraged its ability to house the most popular actresses in the industry as a brand narrative for male consumers. Vivid is an instantly recognizable brand, and it is beginning to convey a narrative that speaks to a certain set of sacred beliefs about erotic pleasure.

The most effective indulgent narratives are those that appeal to the prurient appetite in each of us. They tap the secret yearnings we conceal from the rest of the world. They do this in very subtle, subtextual ways, much like the devilish snake in the Garden of Eden. Alfred Hitchcock once remarked that it was far scarier to provide hints of a murder and let the audience fill in the blanks, rather than show every graphic detail. The same is true for indulgences. We are far more engaged when our imagination is activated.

Narratives of Destruction

There was a time in America when consumer awareness of the dangers of tobacco was low. For the last fifteen years, however, you would have to have lived in a cave not to have been exposed to anti-smoking information. In-school educational programs, public service announcements, and grass-roots efforts in the medical community have clearly articulated that smoking is linked to cancer, lung disease, heart disease, and various other maladies. Yet people still smoke—and not just the people who smoked well before the public relations push. The American Lung Association estimates that 4.5 million adolescents (people under the age of 18) take up smoking each year. Experts estimate that of the smoking population, 80 percent began smoking before the age of 21. Further, while cigarette smoking is showing small signs of decline, health advocates quickly add that the decline is due in large part to people who quit smoking, not a decrease in people who start smoking.

With all the information disseminated about the ill-effects of cigarette smoking, why do people start? The answer ties back to the dark side of narrative. When provocative and indulgent narratives mix, the result is what can best be called a destructive narrative. Here, the consumer wishes to indulge an appetite and cause harm at the same time—either to themselves or to someone or something else.

Many people possess a compelling desire to mix with life-threatening activities. Bungee jumping, sky diving, and untethered rock climbing are a few examples of activities that exhilarate because of their danger quotient. Actually, such behavior is more pervasive than surface observations would indicate. Flirting with mortality is a powerful way to assert your place among the living.

In Japan, Fugu is a delicacy served at the finest sushi bars. It is an extremely poisonous blowfish, but if prepared properly, it is harmless. Most people like the fish not for its taste, but because of their taste for danger. The best sushi chefs realize this fact and are careful to leave just enough poisonous residue to tingle the taste buds, thereby delivering a death defying culinary experience.

When indulgence and provocation merge, consumers provoke a response from others through their indulgences. Many smokers appreciate the fact that the world appears out to get them. They enjoy the fact that many people hate smokers. The fact that smoking is potentially harmful to them provides an even greater provocative experience. This is not to say that these smokers smoke because they want to upset those around them and make a statement. Far from it. They also enjoy the soothing pleasure of a drag. They say that smoking is calming. Their pleasure is delivered from the fact that what they do is not sanctioned behavior, yet it is a remarkably indulgent experience.

Though not yet a bona fide Legendary Brand, Grim Reapers is a noteworthy case example. Grim Reapers is manufactured by Poison, Inc., a discount tobacco company based in North Carolina. Its packaging is all black and features the profile of a human skull. It brands itself as a "full flavor" cigarette, and it has enjoyed ardent interest from a segment of smokers.

"Wait until a couple of years when the government requires cigarette companies to put pictures of diseased lungs on the pack," quoted one of the company's founders, Chuck Peters, in a recent *BrandWeek* article.[2] He refers to a recent lawsuit against tobacco companies arguing for just such a graphic inclusion on cigarette packaging. But Peters believes this addition will appeal to the consumers of Grim Reapers and possibly boost sales. They are loyal to a product that makes no "bones" about its brand promise.

DARK BRANDING AND MARKETING RESPONSIBILITY

Marketing to indulgence and provocation is a controversial activity. You appeal to the devil within the consumer. You tempt the consumer with behavioral impulses they ordinarily suppress. You conjure restless emotions and hidden character desires.

Reality: A majority of the advertising viewed in prime time runs this course. Advertisers routinely appeal to the wicked instincts in all of us. But there is a borderline between routine salesmanship and irresponsible marketing.

Many of us were counseled by our mothers or other mentors to "listen to our conscience." For many marketers, however, this advice is bothersome. If a tobacco company hired you to manage a cigarette brand, you cannot tell your shareholders that you feel guilty tempting consumers to take up smoking. That is your job. You need a more resilient guideline to navigate the space between socially acceptable brand marketing and recklessness.

Do not deceive the consumer. Believe it or not, even when you manage a brand that causes harm to consumers, the same consumer-focused reverence applies. You must put the consumer first. You must tap into their worldview, espouse their sacred beliefs, and convey a narrative that supports these. You must not, however, use any of these elements to deceive or mislead the consumer. The controversy that culminated in the landmark settlement between tobacco companies and the government revolved around deception. Tobacco companies knew smoking was harmful long before the average consumer did, but the tobacco companies continued to promote it as a coveted lifestyle. This was wrong. The tobacco companies misled consumers and endangered their health.

The situation today is different. Marlboro is a venerable Legendary Brand. Marlboro's brand narrative depicts a rugged life. The Marlboro Man appeals to those who believe life is filled with grit, hard work, and pain. It is a cowboy narrative that claims what doesn't kill you, makes you stronger. These men know the dangers of smoking, but smoking is unlikely to fade from their lives. It is a symbol and a symbolic activity of their worldview. They are well aware that smoking may claim their lives, but they maintain a fatalist attitude. It is as if to say, "I'm going to go anyway. I might as well go doing something I enjoy. It is who I am."

Certainly, there is an argument to be made that the Marlboro Man and the brand narrative he conveys perpetuate this attitude. Yet, in my experience, most people identify with the Marlboro brand because it conveys beliefs they already embrace, not the other way around.

Camel, on the other hand, is an example of a brand narrative that crosses the line. The Joe Camel campaign used animated characters to create a fantasy. It downplays the side effects of smoking and equates it with being "cool." Though its brand managers claim the campaign is not targeted at children, young people are certainly aware of it and often fancy the tobacco-smoking pack animal. Camel misleads the consumer. It paints an exaggerated view of reality to lure consumers in. It irreverently says that smoking will make you cool. Smoking will aid your sexual pursuits. Smoking will convey an image of style, fashion, and success. Camel advertising never hints at the downside of smoking, whereas Marlboro nearly glorifies it the same way it might glorify the consumption of liver-damaging hard liquor and arteriosclerosis-causing cowboy dinners.

Marlboro doesn't claim that its lifestyle is healthy, it claims it is rugged. It depicts a stoic, self-destructive, tragic hero like Ethan Edwards, John Wayne's vengeful cowboy in John Ford's *The Searchers*, or

Jim Stark, James Dean's angst-ridden character in *Rebel without a Cause*. These characters appear to welcome death, and their lifestyle contains no regard for longevity. Smoking provides trusted solace to their mournful pursuits. It will exact a toll, but unlike other things in life, it can be relied on to deliver what it promises. This is a far cry from the message Camel conveys, which links smoking with hedonism. Camel promises excessive pleasure and benefit from the smoking lifestyle.

Marlboro is not exempt from criticism. Outside the United States, the Marlboro brand is one of many that deceives consumers with an affinity for the American brand narrative. Japan struggles with a health epidemic caused by the rapid adoption of cigarette smoking in the post war years. The Japanese coveted all things American. The Marlboro Man epitomized their view of true America. Many Japanese men took up smoking because they idealized the abstraction of the Marlboro Man, and Marlboro actively encouraged this fallacy.

The fast food industry and the soft drink industry are going under the microscope. As of this writing, two major class action lawsuits are pending. The same public interest groups that challenged the tobacco industry now assert that the makers of fast food and soda pop have knowingly deceived the American people at the expense of the People's health.

More than 60 percent of the American population is overweight. In the 1970s, the medical obesity rate in the United States was estimated at 12 to 13 percent. By the year 2000, that rate increased to more than 25 percent. Compounding the problem, national health authorities are gravely concerned with the significant rise of Type 2 diabetes, particularly in adolescents. Despite these concerns, the major soft drink brands persist with misleading marketing. They engage near-anorexic pop stars to promote products with very high sugar content. In musically charged, overproduced television advertisements, these celebrities endorse the product exuberantly in choreography that is squarely aimed at youth. The misleading message seems to say that these beautiful people look and act the way they do because of the cola they endorse.

Similarly, many fast food brands engage professional and Olympic athletes to promote their products. A recent commercial during the

Winter Olympic Games showed various high-performance athletes buying Big Mac's and munching on French fries. When these same athletes and celebrities appear in local Los Angeles or New York establishments, however, their lean, often muscular figures are rarely seen drinking Pepsi or Coke. Mineral water is more often consumed. Given that their career depends on their looks and physical abilities, it is doubtful that many of them regularly consume fast food either, with its high fat content and general lack of certain essential nutrients. Yet, to the American public, this is the message that is communicated.

Anytime you manage a brand whose narrative rests on the far right of the spectrum depicted in Figure 14.1, you are likely to encounter absurd discussions and analyses that ultimately leave everyone unsatisfied. In this realm of marketing, where temptation and arousal can lead to real harm, significant moral and social issues exist that are not easily resolved. If you plan to tap the dark side of brand narrative, do so with due regard and diligence for your consumers.

NARRATIVE STRATEGY AND THE DARK SIDE

Dark side brand narratives utilize the same techniques and principles as other brand narratives. There are a few unique considerations.

Tap the Pressure Valve

The best of the darker brand narratives tap the suppressed urges of the consumer. Generally, these are harmless indulgences. The success of these brand narratives stems from their ability to allow the consumer to live their shadow, or their inferior, narrative identity. Las Vegas is a Legendary Brand that activates this narrative. So does Porsche. Most people who have the resources to own a Porsche live fairly risk-averse lives. For some of those consumers, Porsche opens a pressure valve and allows them to indulge in a bit of recklessness or conspicuous consumption.

Remain Empathetic

"The protagonist must be empathetic; he may or may not be sympathetic."[3] These words of wisdom from Robert McKee apply to your brand narrative, as well. When you employ the dark side, take care to construct a thread in your narrative to which your consumer audience can easily relate. They may not like some of the things about your brand, but they can connect with something it stands for. You create empathy, usually because your brand is built upon the same worldview as your consumer.

As we saw in the Joe Isuzu campaign, audiences can be less than sympathetic toward some of your brand agents, but continue to develop an attachment to your brand. I've often thought that Microsoft is held back from being a true Legendary Brand because of its unwillingness to accept the fact that many people hate the company and hate its founder, Bill Gates. They willingly accept that Microsoft has the best products (empathy), but they find it hard to cheer for the company or Mr. Gates (sympathy). Instead of advertising that paints the world blue with hope thanks to Microsoft, consumers might enjoy a campaign that acknowledged and poked fun at the Imperialism of the company. Instead of a sweatered Bill Gates telling us the "future is looking good," how much more would we enjoy Gates, or a fictional surrogate, portrayed like the Simpson's Mr. Burns.

Sanction, but Do Not Deceive

More often than not, what consumers seek in the dark narrative is a sanctioning of their occasional indiscretions. They seek approval. Legendary Brands assert a powerful effect on consumer behavior. If the brand empathizes with the consumer, and sanctions their occasional indulgences or bouts with provocative behavior, the consumer gains a sense of relief, authorization, or vindication.

Often, when you select a dark side strategy to expand or develop your brand narrative, your objective is to provide this sanctioning effect. Though it is not always a vindication for behavior directly associated with your product or service, it usually does have some less than altruistic connection. Because of this, you have a responsibility to your consumer and to the public. It is one thing to vindicate your consumer for occasionally indulging in activities that cause no great harm. It is quite another to profit from the ill effects of behavior you incited.

For many brands, this is not a problem. Godiva chocolate certainly sanctions the joy of chocolate. Yet few consumers are in danger of overdosing on Godiva or eating it to such excess that they suffer severe health problems. Some consumers who frequently purchase Godiva may have other eating disorders or indulge too frequently in sweets or overeating, but you would be hard pressed to blame Godiva for this condition.

Other brands have a greater responsibility. There is no clear guideline, because each brand and each product contains its own spectrum of goodwill. Your job, as brand manager, is to ensure that you plot a course for your brand that provides the sanctions sought by consumers, without misleading them or abusing their trust in you.

END NOTES

CHAPTER 1

1. *Webster's Collegiate Dictionary.*

2. Strinati, Dominic. *An Introduction to Theories of Popular Culture.* London: Routledge, 1995.

3. Strinati, *Theories of Popular Culture.*

4. Gitlin, Todd. *Media Unlimited.* New York: Metropolitan Books, 2001.

CHAPTER 2

1. Eliade, Mircea. *The Sacred and the Profane: The Nature of Religion.* New York: Harcourt, 1959.

2. Pinker, Steven. *How the Mind Works.* New York: W.W. Norton & Company, 1997.

3. Ibid, 525.

4. McKee, Robert. *Story: Substance, Structure, and the Principles of Screenwriting.* New York: HarperCollins, 1997.

5. Spence, Gerry. *How to Argue and Win Every Time.* New York: St. Martin's Press, 1995, 126.

6. Newberg, Andrew, M.D., Eugene D'Aquili, M.D., Ph.D., and Vince Rause. *Why God Won't Go Away*. New York: Ballantine Books, 2001.

7. Appadurai, Arjun, ed. *The Social Life of Things*. Cambridge: Cambridge University Press, 1986, 67.

8. Campbell, Joseph. *Primitive Mythology: The Masks of God*. New York: Penguin Group, 1959.

9. Newberg, *Why God*, 80–81.

10. Kawasaki, Guy. *Selling the Dream*. New York: HarperCollins, 1991.

CHAPTER 3

1. Brunvand, Jan Harold. *The Vanishing Hitchhiker*. New York: W.W. Norton & Company, 1981.

2. Campbell, Joseph. *The Hero with a Thousand Faces*. Princeton: Princeton University Press, 1968.

3. Cousineau, Phil. *Once and Future Myths: The Power of Ancient Myths in Modern Times*. Berkeley: Conari Press, 2000.

CHAPTER 4

1. Vranica, Suzanne, "Ad Giant Interpublic Shops for Literary, Talent Agencies," *The Wall Street Journal* (June 14, 2002).

2. Gabler, Neal. *Life the Movie: How Entertainment Conquered Reality*. New York: Vintage Books, 1998.

3. Riesman, David, Nathan Glazer, and Reuel Denney. *The Lonely Crowd*. New Haven: Yale University Press, 1969.

4. Holt, Douglas B., "Why Do Brands Cause Trouble? A Dialectical Theory of Consumer Culture and Branding," *Journal of Consumer Research*, 29 no. 1 (June 2002).

5. Tzu, Lao. *Tao Te Ching: A Book about the Way and the Power of the Way*. Translated by Ursula Le Guin. Boston: Shambhala Publications, 1997.

CHAPTER 5

1. Pinker, Steven. *The Language Instinct: How the Mind Creates Language*. New York: HarperCollins, 1995.

2. McCracken, Grant. *The Long Interview*. Newbury Park: Sage Publications, 1988.

3. Ochs, Elinor, and Lisa Capps. *Living Narrative: Creating Lives in Everyday Storytelling.* Cambridge: Harvard University Press, 2001.

4. Zaltman, Gerald, "Rethinking Market Research: Putting People Back In," *Journal of Marketing Research* (November 1997).

CHAPTER 6

1. Jung, Carl. *The Archetypes and the Collective Unconscious.* Princeton: Princeton University Press, 1969.

2. Mark, Margaret, and Carol S. Pearson. *The Hero and the Outlaw: Building Extraordinary Brands through the Power of Archetypes.* New York: McGraw-Hill, 2001.

3. Forster, E. M. *Aspects of the Novel.* Orlando: Harcourt Books, 1927.

4. Howard, David, and Edward Malbey. *The Tools of Screenwriting: A Writer's Guide to the Craft and Elements of a Screenplay.* New York: St. Martin's Press, 1993.

5. McKee. *Story.*

6. Ibid.

7. Ibid.

CHAPTER 7

1. Steel, Jon. *Truth, Lies, & Advertising.* New York: John Wiley & Sons, 1998.

2. Schmitt, Bernd, and Alex Simonson. *Marketing Aesthetics: The Strategic Management of Brands, Identity, and Image.* New York: Free Press, 1997.

CHAPTER 8

1. Rook, Dennis, "The Ritual Dimension of Consumer Behavior," *The Journal of Consumer Research* (1985).

2. Bell, Catherine. *Ritual: Perspectives and Dimensions.* New York: Oxford University Press, 1997.

CHAPTER 9

1. Porter, Michael. *Competitive Advantage.* New York: Free Press, 1986.

CHAPTER 11

1. Cousineau, Phil. *Once and Future Myths*. Berkeley: Conari Press, 2001.
2. The Imagineers. *Walt Disney Imagineering*. New York: Hyperion Books, 1996.
3. Restoration Hardware [Internet]. <www.restorationhardware.com>.
4. Stevens, Anthony. *Ariadne's Clue*. Princeton: Princeton University Press, 1998.
5. Campbell, *Hero with a Thousand Faces*.
6. Eliade, *The Sacred and Profane*.

CHAPTER 13

1. "The Clinton Years" [television], PBS/Nightline (2001).
2. Ibid.
3. Mark, Pearson. *The Hero and the Outlaw*. New York: McGraw Hill, 2001.
4. Ibid.

CHAPTER 14

1. Jung, C. G. "Concerning Rebirth." In *The Archetypes and the Collective Unconscious*. Princeton: Princeton University Press, 1959.
2. Beirne, Mike, "Fuse Is Burning for Little Tobacco: What Spells 'Healthier' Smoke? FDA?" *BrandWeek* XLIII, no. 14 (April 8, 2002).
3. McKee, *Story*.

INDEX

Abercrombie & Fitch, 95
Absolut, 54
Abstractions, 169–71
Abstract thinking, 20–21
Activism, 10
Adaptation motive, 118
Advertising
    account planning, 166
    campaign, 166
    change in, 13–14
    content integration, 14
    cult brands, 6
    episodic, 171–73
    extensions, 174–75
    fragment arcs, 173–74
    inspiration, 178
    media, 178–82
    narrative development and, 65
    participative communication model,
        183–85
    product placement, 14, 167, 181
    purpose of, 1
    story arcs and, 171
    story-driven, 13–14
    strategy, 175–78
    three-act formula, 139–41
Aesthetics
    activation, 92–94
    image library, 146–47
    narrative construction, 123, 145–46
    sensory exercises, 148
    soundtrack, 147
    war room, 147–48
Agency costs, 235
Agent
    artificial places, 241
    belief system connection, 25–36
    celebrities, 135, 236–37
    CEOs, 235–36
    character activation, 91–92
    cohabitated places, 240
    external risk factors, 246–47
    fictional characters, 237–38
    founders, 235–36
    identification, 234–43
    location-based, 239
    management, 213, 243–53
    market saturation, 244–45

Agent, *continued*
  multiples, 253
  narrative and, 142, 247–53
  political movement, 280, 281–83, 289
  portfolio diversification, 247, 249
  profiles, 132, 134–35
  promotional items as, 242–43
  spokespeople, 236–37
  sponsored places, 240–41
  strength of, 244
  tobacco industry, 304
  things as, 242
Alsop, Stewart, 4–5
Alter ego, 296
Amazon.com, 207
Ambush marketing, 220
American Express, 40–41, 218
Anima, 296
Antihero, 138
Apple Computer
  advertising campaign, 14, 179
  agent, 46, 48–49, 235
  belief system, 45, 49
  case study, 43–50
  culture, 3
  narrative, 87, 126–27
  symbol, 196, 198
Archetypes, 127–30
Armey, Dick, 286
Armstrong, C. Michael, 89
Artifacts, 202–3
Artificial places, 241
AT&T, 220
Atheists, 23–25
Atomization, 10–11
Audience
  brand turnaround, 276–77
  response, 94–95, 101
  ritual, 203
Authenticity, 93–94
Automobile, 41–43

Baby boomers, 10
Bait and switch, 221
Band communities, 22
Beat, 52–57, 140
Begala, Paul, 281
Behavior, 34–36

Behavioral objective, 175–78
Belief system
  atheists and, 23–25
  agent connection, 25–36
  band communities, 22
  forms, 24–25
  narrative, 28–36, 142
  purpose of, 20–21
  social culture link, 29–30
  symbiotic relationship, 25–28
  validation of, 21–22
Bell, Catherine, 204
Ben & Jerry's Ice Cream, 85–86, 207
Body Shoppe, 138–39
Boston Marathon, 224
Brand agent. *See* Agent
Brand association, 216
Brand bible
  aesthetics, 145–48
  agent profiles, 132, 134–35
  annotated narrative history, 149
  archetype, 129–30
  bottom-up approach, 150–51
  consumer biographies, 130–32
  content, 124
  creation of, 122
  form, 124
  genre, 138
  glossary, 149
  governing theme, 143–44
  image library, 146–47
  narrative plot, 135–43
  purpose of, 124–25
  subordinate themes, 144–45
  top-down approach, 150
  translation, 151–52
Brand communities, 36–38, 47–48
Brand culture
  assessment, 194
  brand ownership and, 191–92
  consumer profiles, 194
  control efforts, 190–91
  immersion, 195
  knowledge of, 193–95
  management of, 209–12
  myths, 188–93
  narratives, 195–205
  nurturing, 98, 205–9

observation, 194
political movement, 280
rituals, 38–40, 201–5
social understanding, 36–38
symbols, 40–43, 196–201
Brand management, 231–32
Brand marketing, 100
Brand mythology
agents, 25–28
consumer bond, 20–22
narrative, 28–36
overview, 19–20
system, 22, 23
worldview, 25–28
Brand narrative. *See* Narrative
Brand police, 189–90
Brand responsibility, 12–13
Brokaw, Tom, 10
Brunvand, Jan Harold, 60
Bugs Bunny, 238
Byrd, Larry, 245–46

Calvin Klein, 128, 240
Camel, 304–5
Campbell, Joseph, 68, 128, 141, 260
Candlestick Park, 219
Capps, Lisa, 116
Carey, Mariah, 233
Carl's Jr., 298
Cause, 144, 145
Cause-and-effect relationship, 52–57, 78
Celebrities, 135, 233–34, 236–37
Celebrity status, 7
Center, 263–64
Channel marketing, 217
Character, 90–92
Chiat, Jay, 166
Citgo, 224
Clancy, Tom, 233
Cliché, 72–75
Clift, Eleanor, 283
Climax, 55, 140
Clinton, Hilary, 284
Clinton, William Jefferson, 280–89
Clutter, 220–21
CMGI Field, 223–24
Coach, 95
Cobranding, 213

Coca-Cola, 93
advertising campaign, 175
brand culture, 206
distribution partnerships, 217
narrative, 149
product samples, 148
sponsorship, 167
symbols, 197
Cohabitated places, 240
Communication, 98
channels, 246
collaborative, 183–84
objectives, 175–78
planning process, 176
Complication, 55, 139
Consistency, 208, 265
Consumer
antibrand segment, 85
biographies, 130–32, 133–34
bond, 8, 20–21
brand behavior, 132
brand selection, 87–88
burn out, 199–200
buying habits, 17
control of, 12–13
day in the life, 131–32
deception, 303–6
enthusiasm, 3–6
identity, 8–9
insights, 166
life movie, 80
loyalty, 3–4
narrative, 81–82
participation, 277
perception, 7, 132
pressure valve, 306
priority of, 227–28
profile, 113, 194
ritual, 201–5
self-image, 132
space, 256–58
voice of, 166
Consumerism, 11–13
Consumer research
accuracy of, 104
brand development and, 105
communication barriers, 103–4
data analysis, 112–14

Consumer research, *continued*
    environment, 106–7
    first-hand, 102
    focus group, 110–11
    importance of, 101
    limitations, 102–6
    logic tree, 107–8
    long interview, 111–14
    narrative inquiry, 114–16
    nonverbal response techniques, 116–17
    observational techniques, 114–16
    participation, 107
    presence studies, 109–10
    respondent proficiency, 109–10
    rightbrain methodology, 118–20
    surveys, 110–11
Consumption habits, 11
Contingency plan, 247
Contract with America, 287–89
Controlling idea, 144
Converse, 5
Core motives, 118
Co-tellership, 116
Cousineau, Phil, 70–71, 255–56
Covey, Steven, 72
Creative brief, 166
Crisis management, 214
Cult brands, 3–6
Cultural events, 207–9
Cultural order, 8–9
Cuomo, Mario, 281

D'Aquili, Eugene, 30–31
Data analysis, 112–14
Deception, 303–6
Delano Hotel, 260, 263, 264
Dell, Michael, 236
Dell Computer, 236
Design, 6
Destructive narrative, 301–3
Diction, 123
Direct communication advertising, 1, 2
Direct response, 95
Discover, 253
Disney theme parks, 256–57
    agent, 239
    brand culture, 190–91

hub-and-spokes design, 264
marketing approach, 151–52
narrative pathways, 263
partnerships, 218
perimeter, 259
Dodge, 93
Dogma, 9–11
Dole, Bob, 237

Eastman, George, 226
Edison Field, 241
Eisen, Rich, 172–73
Eliade, Mircea, 20, 263–64
Emotional objective, 175–78
Emotional response, 30–34, 38–40
Enablement, 88–90
Entertainment era, 79–82
Entertainment media, 179–82
Episodes, 171–73
Erotic narrative, 300
ESPN, 73–75, 172–73, 195
Ethics, 99
Expectation motive, 118
Experience, 110
Expressive themes, 170–71
Extensions, 174–75

Fad, 199–200
Fashion, 41
Fictional characters, 237–38
Fidelity Investments, 252–53
Film noir genre, 138
Flowers, Gennifer, 281
Focus group, 102, 110–11
Forster, E.M., 130
FoxSports, 74–75
Fragments, 173–74
Franchise, 288
Franklin Covey, 71–72

Gabler, Neal, 8, 80
Gallo, 6, 93
Gap, 140, 175–78, 257
Gates, Bill, 307
GE, 142, 149
General Motors, 4
Generational effect, 193–94

Generation X, 10
Generation Y, 10
Genre, 135–39
Geography, 6
Gillette Mach III, 201
Gingrich, Newt, 286–88
Gitlin, Todd, 13
Godiva, 300, 308
God particle, 96
Goldwater, Barry, 32–33
Gore, Al, 280, 282–84
Governing theme, 143–44
Grim Reapers, 302–3
Group interview, 106
Guerilla marketing techniques, 60
Guggenheim Museum, 39–40, 205

Hallmark, 35
Halo effect, 216
Harley-Davidson
    archetype, 128
    brand culture, 192–93
    legends, 60
    narrative, 89, 90
    rituals, 202
    worldview, 27
Harper, Jr., Marion, 188
Harvard University, 28
Hawk, Tony, 197
Hays, Seth, 172
Heroic framework, 68–69
Hero's journey, 141–42, 271, 283–84
Hewlett-Packard, 142
Hilfiger, Tommy, 61–62
Honda, 93, 224
Hopper, Dennis, 177
Howard, David, 135
Human persona, 7
Hunter-gatherer behavior, 30–31
Hypotheses, 113–14

Ian Schrager Hotels, case study, 258–65
IBM, 45–47
Identity, 7, 8–9, 80–81
Image library, 146–47
Inciting incident, 140
Individualism, 11

Indulgent narrative, 294, 299–301, 306
Invesco Field, 219
Investors, 275
Isuzu, Joe, 298–99

Jack in the Box
    agent, 271–74
    crisis, 268–70
    investor, 275
    lessons, 275–77
    narrative, 271–74
    reforms, 270
    rescue of, 270–71
    promotional item, 242
    symbols, 274
Jackson, Michael, 237
J. Crew, 90–91
Jobs, Steve, 3, 45–46, 48–50, 250
Johnson, Lyndon, 32–33
Jordan, Michael, 28, 69, 234, 237, 245–46
Jung, Carl, 128, 129, 296

Kate Spade handbag, 95, 234, 242
Kawasaki, Guy, 46
Kaye, Michael, 289–91
Keith, Jack, 172
Kelleher, Herb, 170
Kentucky Fried Chicken, 61, 235
Kerry, Bob, 281
Kinkade, Thomas, 86–87
Kistler Vineyards, 6, 93
Kodak
    brand culture, 209–12
    narrative use, 33–34, 149
    ritual participation, 204
    sponsorship, 225–26
Krens, Thomas, 39
Krispy Kreme, 3, 36–37
Kuperman, Bob, 270

Las Vegas, 300, 306
Lauren, Ralph, 29–30
Lear, Norman, 122
Legacy brands, 3–4
Legend
    distortion of, 59–60
    guerilla marketing techniques, 60

Legend, *continued*
    as key, 7–8
    orientation, 63–64
    survival of, 60
Leisure, David, 298
Leisure activity, 13
Le Neveu, Steve, 270, 272, 274, 277–78
Leverage, 217–18
Lexus, 180–81
Ley, Bob, 172
Life experience, 78
Life movie, 80, 193
Lifestyle advertising, 175
Liminality, 38, 88
Linux, 38
Listening, 98, 208
Location-based brand agent, 239
Logic tree, 107–8
Loitering, 219–20
Long interview, 111–14
Los Angeles Marathon, 224
Lynch, Peter, 252–53

Mabley, Edward, 135
McCracken, Grant, 112, 114
McDonald's
    agent, 245–46
    partnerships, 218
    promotional item, 243
Macintosh, 46–47, 198, 202
McKee, Robert, 28, 136, 140, 144, 307
MacMaster, Lin, 118–20
Maddock, Richard, 118
Magalogs, 207
Malboro, 304–5
Malmuth, David, 226
Maraniss, David, 284
Mark, Margaret, 128, 282
Market capitalization, 4–5
Market research, 98
MasterCard
    governing theme, 144
    narrative use, 35–36
    subordinate theme, 145
Mazda Miata, 3
Media, 13–14, 178–82
Mercedes Benz, 41, 241

Metanarratives, 9–11
Mickey Mouse, 237–38
Microsoft, 235, 307
Mile High Stadium, 219
Mondrian Hotel, 261–62, 265
Monologue, 14
Montague, Ty, 14, 183–85
Morals, 70
Morris, Dick, 283
Motorola, 248
Mountain Dew, 92, 297–98
MTV, 128–29, 194
Mundane ritual, 201
Murdoch, Rupert, 74, 75
Myth
    cliché versus, 72–75
    definition of, 25
    formula, 68
    meaning, 70–72
    narrative and, 135–39
    once and future, 70–71
    orientation, 63–64
    power of, 51–52, 65
    role of, 62–64
    of sports, 69
    of time, 71–72

Narrative, 8, 14
    abstractions, 169–71
    advertising campaign and, 166
    aesthetics, 145–48
    agent, 142
    behavioral instruction, 34–36
    belief system and, 28–36, 142
    box, 125–27, 136
    case study, 152–62
    change, 276
    characters, 127–35
    cities, 255–56
    crafting, 105
    cueing, 65–68
    dark side, 214, 294–303
    defined, 114, 249
    destruction, 301–3
    development, 65, 98
    elements of, 123–24
    emotional response, 30–34

empathy, 307
entertainment integration, 179–82
equation, 58
genre and, 135–39
hero's journey, 141–42
hope, 275–76
identity, 112
indulgence, 299–301, 306
inquiry, 114–16
investigation, 101–20
marketing responsibility, 303–6
multiple, 143
myth and, 139
orientation, 63–64
pathways, 262–63
placement, 181
political movement, 281, 283–85, 287–88
power of, 29
presence studies, 109–10
print advertisement, 59
provocation, 296–99
purpose, 15–16, 34, 58–59
questions, 125
research, 107–10
respondent proficiency, 109–10
sanction, 307–8
spin-off, 247
strategy, 306–8
strong, 249–52
television advertisement, 59
theme, 143–45
three-act formula, 139–41
weak, 247–49, 252–53
Narrator, 98
NASCAR, 216
National Rifle Association, 188
Nestlé, 241
Neutrogena, 126
Newberg, Andrew, 30–31
Nike, 5, 12
    agents, 26
    fragment arcs, 173–74
    narrative theme, 87
    narrative use, 35
    ritual participation, 205
    sports myth, 69
    symbol, 141–42, 196

Nissan Xterra, 41
Nokia, 248
Nonlinear branding, 255–66
Nonverbal response techniques, 116–17
Nostalgia, 4
Nugent, Robert, 269

Objective world, 140
Observation, 112–16, 208
Ochs, Elinor, 116
Olympic Games, 216
O'Neil, Tip, 289
One-on-one interview, 111–14
Orientation motives, 118
Orkin, 224
Outdoor advertisements, 54

Palm, 247–48
Participation, 208
Participative communication, 183–85
Partnership, 213
    ambush, 220
    bait and switch, 221
    brand audit, 229
    brand management, 231–32
    clutter, 220–21
    consumer priority, 227–28
    distribution benefits, 217
    exclusivity, 217–18
    halo effect, 216
    intangible benefits, 216
    loitering, 219–20
    myth, 226–27
    narrative, 230
    narrative alignment, 222–226
    political movement, 284–85
    resource synergies, 218
    risk, 218
    systemic value, 228
    tangible benefits, 215
    trinity, 227–28
Past experience, 78
Patriotism, 10
Patterns, 114
Pearson, Carol S., 128, 282
Pepsi-Cola, 217, 237
Performance authenticity, 93–94

Perimeter, 259
Perrier, 93
Personal narrative
    aesthetics, 92–94
    brand culture and, 195–205
    character, 90–92
    enablement, 88–90
    identity, 81–84, 87–88
    performance, 88–94
    plot, 88–89
    principles, 295–96
    rebellion, 89–90
    significance of, 96
    theme, 84–87
Peters, Chuck, 303
Piaf, Edith, 93
Pinker, Steven, 103
Playboy, 235
Play motive, 118
Plot, 88–89, 135–43
Political movement
    agent, 280, 281–83, 289
    brand culture, 280
    brand mythology and, 279–80
    environment, 214
    narrative, 281, 283–85, 287–88
    partnership, 284–85
    story arcs, 280
    storytelling and, 32–33
Polo, 29–30
Porsche, 306
Porter, Michael, 231
Postmodernism theory, 9
Prada, 239
Prefontaine, Steve, 28
Presence studies, 109–10
Press release, 59
Priceline.com, 135
Price wars, 210–11
Print advertisement, 59
Problem-solve, 21
Proctor & Gamble
    advertising, 6
    brand portfolio, 17
    legends, 61
Product placement, 14, 167, 181
Profane space, 259

Promotional items, 242–43
Provocative narrative, 296–99

Quality, 5
Quantitative surveys 110–11
Quiksilver, 197, 207

Rapid adoption, 199–200
Rasmussen, Bill, 73
Reflections, 78
Resolution, 55–56, 139
Resource synergies, 218
Response, 94–95
Restoration Hardware, 257, 259
Ricci, Christina, 177
Riesman, David, 80
Ritual, 38–40, 47–48, 201–5
Roberts, Julia, 233
Rockwell, David, 226
Rook, Dennis, 202
Royalton, 259, 265

Sacred beliefs. *See* Belief system
Sacred space, 259
Saturn, 11, 38–39, 203, 204
Schmitt, Bernd, 170–71
Screaming Eagle, 3, 93
Script, 203
Sculley, John, 48
Self-worth, 80–81
Semiotics, 196–201
Sensory clues, 148, 258, 260–62
Sensory touch points, 92–93
Shadow, 296
Shatner, William, 135, 237
Simonson, Alex, 170–71
Sittig, Dick, 271, 274
Situation, 55, 139
Size, 4
Smell, 145, 261–62
Social behavior, 80–81
Social culture, 29–30
Social order, 9
Social understanding, 36–38
Sondheim, Stephen, 223
Song, 123
Sound cues, 146

Soundtrack, 147, 261
Southwest Airlines, 170
Spears, Britney, 237
Spectacle, 123
Spence, Gerry, 29
Spielberg, Steven, 180
Spokespeople, 236–37
Sponsored places, 240–41
Sponsorship, 217, 223–26
SportsCenter, 172–73
Sports myth, 69
Springsteen, Bruce, 93
Sprint PCS, 220
Stand-alone beat, 53–54, 56
Starbucks
    aesthetics, 145–46, 147
    brand enthusiasm, 5
    community, 37–38
    entertainment integration, 181–82
    narrative, 257
    ritual participation, 205
Steel, Jon, 166
Stephanopoulos, George, 282
Stewart, Martha, 26, 91, 235
Stewart, Potter, 19
Stickers, 198
Story
    arcs, 171, 246, 280
    beat, 55–57
    definition of, 55
    influence of, 79–82
    as mechanism for understanding,
      78–79
    orientation, 63–64
    plot, 135–43
    point of view, 58–59
    political campaigns, 289
    strategy and, 121
    structure, 55
    three-act structure, 139–41
Strategic Partners Group, 118–20
Strinati, Dominic, 10
Subjective reality, 140
Subordinate themes, 144–45
Survey, 102, 110–11
Survival motives, 118
Swatch, 93

Symbol, 38–40
    brand culture and, 196–201
    fads and, 199–200
    placement of, 196–97

Taco Bell, 223
Tangibility test, 26
Target, 170
Taste, 123, 146, 261–62
Television advertisement, 59
Tenure, 5
Theme, 143–45, 150
Three-act formula, 139–41
3Com Park, 219
Threshold, 38, 259–60
Time management, 71–72
Timex, 93
Touch aesthetics, 123, 148
Tri-Con, 224
Turner, Victor, 38
Twain, Shania, 237
Tzu, Lao, 86

Universal Studios, 190

Value, 144, 145
Vespa, 39
Victoria's Secret, 257
Visual imagery, 138, 145, 261
Visual metaphor, 117
Vivid Video, 300–301

Wal-Mart, 194
Walt Disney World, 234
War room, 147–48
Warner Brothers, 134–35, 238
Welch, Jack, 142
Williams, Christopher, 198
Wolfe, David, 120
Woods, Tiger, 237
Worldview, 26–30
World War II generation, 9–10
Wozniak, Steve, 45

Zaltman, Gerald, 117
ZMET (Zaltman Metaphor Elicitation
    Technique), 117

Bulk Pricing Information

For special discounts on
20 or more copies of
Legendary Brands,
call Dearborn Trade Special Sales
at 800-621-9621, extension 4307
or e-mail tjoseph@dearborn.com.
You'll receive great service
and top discounts.

For added visibility, please
consider our custom cover service,
which highlights your firm's name
and logo on the cover.
We are also an excellent resource
for dynamic and
knowledgeable speakers.

Dearborn™
Trade Publishing
A **Kaplan Professional** Company